LIFE ⊕F A NURSE

An Insider's View of What Really Happens
in a Hospital, through the Eyes of an RN

Alice Marlett

ARCHWAY
PUBLISHING

Archway Publishing books may be ordered through booksellers or by contacting:

Archway Publishing
1663 Liberty Drive
Bloomington, IN 47403
www.archwaypublishing.com
844-669-3957

ISBN: 978-1-6657-0153-2 (sc)
ISBN: 978-1-6657-0154-9 (e)

Library of Congress Control Number: 2021900602

Print information available on the last page.

Archway Publishing rev. date: 08/19/2021

INTRODUCTION

I had never considered becoming a nurse until, at the age of thirty-six, I was going through a divorce. I had two children: Alex, eight years old, and Susie, six years old. I had recently discovered that the woman my husband said he hired as part of his painting crew (we had a small painting business) was doing more than just painting for him. He said he had painting jobs out-of-town more and more frequently until he was rarely coming home. When I confronted him about it and told him to leave, he moved in with her.

I was a little upset, but I was also happy he was gone. There had been no love between us since Susie was born. While in the hospital, after giving birth to Susie, I was told that I and my baby both had an STD. I only stayed married to him because I wanted to provide a stable home for our kids, and I did not think I could do it alone.

I was working as a furniture salesperson at Montgomery Ward's, but I did not earn enough to pay the mortgage and bills. I thought about my options and decided I should get a college degree. I heard there was a nursing shortage, and the pay was good. I applied for federal loans and grants. I was eligible for them, and I was accepted at a university with a good nursing program.

I continued to work at Montgomery Ward's part-time while in college. I received federal grants to pay for my tuition and used my student loans to pay my mortgage and bills. It took about two years before my divorce was final. I had custody of Alex and Susie.

We were doing okay, and I met a man, Allen, while selling him a sofa. Our first date was on the night of Susie's eighth birthday. He was divorced and had four children. His oldest, Tina, had graduated from college and was married. His daughter Sarah was away at college. His oldest boy, Brent, was going to high school and his youngest, Rick, was in junior high school. We dated over the next few years and eventually became engaged.

About two years after my divorce was final, my ex-husband filed for custody of Alex and Susie. He was still living with the woman he had moved in with when we separated, and they had a baby. He thought that because she was staying home with the baby, she could take care of Alex and Susie too. That way he would not have to pay child support.

Alex had been hanging around with older boys in our neighborhood. They smoked marijuana and were not a good influence. He was getting harder to control and I was afraid he would get into trouble. When we went to court for custody, I offered that Alex could live with his father and Susie would live with me. I thought it would be best for Alex to get away from our neighborhood. It was agreed and there was no child support ordered.

After completing my prerequisite classes, I was able to apply for the nursing program. At first, I was not accepted but put on a waiting list. I was upset, but I spoke with someone in the registration department who said I was at the top of the list and should be accepted soon.

I was accepted and started the nursing program in the fall of 1997. The first semester of nursing school was the hardest one. I heard it is that way so students who are not going to make it through the program will drop out early. But the entire program was intense and included going to local hospitals and facilities for clinical training. Allen was a huge help to me and Susie. He would pick her up from school and take her to soft-ball practice and games when I could not.

Somehow, I made it through and graduated with a BSN (Bachelor of Science in Nursing) in May,1999. My mother and father came for my graduation and stayed for a few days. Allen and I decided to get married while they were still here. We went to the courthouse and got a marriage license. Two days later we were married in the church Allen's mother attends. It was a small ceremony with only immediate family. I spent the next few weeks getting Susie and I settled into Allen's house and applying for nursing positions.

ONE

SKILLED NURSING UNIT

My first nursing position was on a skilled nursing unit known as SNU. It was a sub-acute care unit. This kind of unit is for patients who are not sick enough to stay on an acute-care floor, but too sick to send home. The unit had nursing and physical therapy staff. There were nine rooms with eighteen beds. The day shift had three nurses and two nurses' aides, known as PCAs (patient care assistants). They worked 7 AM to 3:30 PM, Monday through Friday. The second shift had two nurses and two PCAs. They worked 3 PM to 11:30 PM, Monday through Friday. Third shift had two nurses and one PCA. They worked 11 PM to 7:30 AM, Monday through Friday. On the weekend there were nurses who worked twelve-hour shifts Saturday and Sunday. They also had PCTs working with them. Physical Therapy staff was there from 9 AM to 5 PM, Monday through Friday. There was also a secretary on the day shift. I trained on the day shift for two weeks and then started on the second shift.

My second week at the hospital, while still in training, I experienced my first patient death. It was Monday, and I was starting to pass out the morning medications. I did not know all my patients yet, because some had been admitted over the weekend. I was told in shift report (patient information given from one shift to the next) that the patient in my first room did not swallow well, so I crushed his medication and mixed it with applesauce. The patient was sitting in a chair outside of his room, in the hall. He was a large man, about 250 pounds, with pale skin and gray hair.

When I walked up to him with his medication he said: "What's wrong? Something is wrong!" I thought he was confused because the patients in SNU often have dementia. I said: "Try to take your medicine and you will feel better." I gave him about half a teaspoon at a time with small sips of water. He barely finished it when he slumped over in his chair. Another nurse was watching, and she ran to us. She yelled for Rose, our unit manager. A "code blue" (cardiac arrest or respiratory distress) was called.

Within minutes the room was full of staff and a doctor. They were unable to revive him. I was worried that I had done something wrong to cause his death. But Rose talked to me and said what happened was not my fault, and it was probably for the best. The patient was scheduled to go to a nursing home that afternoon. He did not want to go, but his wife was not able to take care of him at home. Rose said the man's wife had told her she prayed he would die before he had to go to the nursing home. He was suffering and being sent to the nursing home because there was no other choice. He would have been miserable there.

That was my only patient death while I was in training. I was not an RN when I started at the hospital, but a GN (graduated nurse). That meant I had a few months to pass the state Board of Nursing test. I had to pass it the first time I took it, or I would lose my GN status. Then I would not be able to work as a nurse until I passed it and got my RN license.

I studied as often as I could and even brought flash cards with possible test questions with me to work. I was nervous about taking the test, as most nurses are, but I passed and got my license. Soon after that I started on the second shift. I also took a part-time job working weekends at a rehab hospital. Two of the day-shift nurses worked there part-time and told me about it.

The charge-nurse on our shift was Mae. She was an experienced nurse from Canada, about sixty years old. She was always finished with her work on time, even though she was never in a hurry. No matter how hectic things seemed, she was always calm.

Our two PCAs were Cindy and Bonnie. They were both in their late forties, and what I would call professional caregivers. They had worked together at the hospital for years and were best friends. They each had private care patients they would visit during the day before their shift started. They took good care of the patients and did not need to be told what to do.

The unit was busy with only the four of us for staff. The patients needed a lot of care. Most of them needed help to the bathroom. Some could not get out of bed, wore diapers and had to be cleaned frequently.

Some of the patients who were admitted to the unit really should not have been there. They were patients who were dying but had used-up all the days insurance or Medicare would pay for on an acute care unit. The hospital was paid less for sub-acute care, but if no other facility would take them, the hospital had to care for them until they died.

I was fortunate to have an experienced nurse working with me. It seemed like I learned something new every day. I also learned a lot about patient care from Cindy and Bonnie.

I was working in SNU on a Thursday evening when Allen called at about 9:30 PM. He had just come in from mowing the yard and was heating up some left-over beef stew. He called to see how I was doing and said everything was fine at home.

About fifteen minutes later he called back and said his son, Brent was having an asthma attack. Brent's fiancé, Maria had called Allen. They lived in an apartment about an hour drive from us. The hospital where I worked was about half-way between our house and their apartment.

Brent had asthma all his life, but it was under control, and he seemed to be growing out of it. He was not taking any asthma medications, except for an albuterol inhaler when he needed it. He was physically fit and a handsome young man. He was going to college to become a respiratory therapist. Brent was twenty-four years old, and the kind of son anyone would hope to have.

Maria told Allen she had come home from work and was getting ready to go to a movie with Brent. He had a cold and had just heated some lentil soup when he started to have trouble breathing. He told her he thought she would have to drive him to the hospital.

Brent was standing in front of a fan trying to breathe, and then fell over and was unconscious. Maria called 911 and then called Allen. She told Allen that Brent was not breathing. Allen asked if he had a pulse and she said: "I think so." She did not know how to do CPR.

Allen thought Brent would be admitted to a hospital like he had been several times before, and then would be alright. I had a sick feeling in my stomach after Allen told me that Maria said Brent was not breathing.

I told Allen I would try to get off work early and he said he would pick me up so we could go to the emergency room together. Mae said she would cover my patients for the rest of the shift. I was trying hard not to cry, and Bonnie asked me if there was anything she could do. I asked her to get directions to the hospital we were driving to.

The drive there from my hospital was only about thirty minutes, but it seemed like hours. When we got there Maria was alone in a small private waiting room. I knew it was bad when I saw her crying, and no one would tell us anything except the doctor would talk to us. The doctor came in and told us they had been unable to resuscitate Brent.

I went over to Maria and tried to comfort her. I think she already suspected the worst. Allen was in shock. I went over to him and held him. He could not speak; he was just shaking. After a few minutes I went to the nurses' desk because I knew someone would have to sign the hospital forms. I did not think Allen was up to it and I had Brent covered as a dependent on my health insurance. They asked me about an autopsy, because the normal procedure in a case of sudden death was to have one done. I told them Brent had asthma all his life and I was sure he had died of an asthma attack. I told them he was studying to be a respiratory therapist and was a good kid. I said I did not think the family would want an autopsy. A call was made to the coroner, and he agreed it was not necessary. I asked where Brent was and if I could see him. I still had my nursing uniform on, so the staff probably thought I would be able to handle the situation.

Brent was in a private room. He looked like he was sleeping. I touched his face, and it was still warm. The nurse asked if I wanted to take his things. There was only his clothes and shoes. They were soiled from what he had been through. I took his wallet out of his jeans and told them they could throw the rest away. I took the wallet to the desk so they could copy Brent's ID and insurance card. Then I went back to the room where Allen and Maria were and gave him the wallet.

A chaplain was called, and Brent's mother came with her husband. We were taken to a chapel, and everyone prayed and cried. A funeral home was called and we agreed to meet there the next day.

I went back to work the day after the funeral, but the grief Allen and I felt was just too much, so I took a week off work. As sad as I was, I could not imagine how sad Allen must have been. It felt like a heavy, dark cloud was all around us.

I realized how precious the time spent with our children is, and I decided that I should spend more time with Susie. I tried to get a day shift, or a weekend option position at the hospital, but nothing was available.

September 5, 2000

I applied at the hospital I had worked at part-time as a nurses' aide while I was in nursing school. It is close to home, and they offered me a position working on the day shift. I can work three 12-hour shifts each week and I will be charge-nurse on the skilled nursing unit. I accepted it. I quit my full-time position but stayed on staff there part-time and will work once every week or two if they need me.

September 26, 2000

I have started working at my new job. The hospital is old and small compared to most hospitals. I really like working here. I have fewer patients and I can give each patient more attention. The other charge-nurse on our unit, who works on the days I am off, has been here about fifteen years. She insists the unit is kept spotless and the patients get the best quality of nursing care. Most of the patients on our unit are older and have had recent surgery. Many of them need IV antibiotics and are too weak to get out of bed.

October 31, 2000

Today when I went to work, I was told the hospital is closing. It had been announced yesterday when I was off. The hospital is in bankruptcy. Patients will have to be transferred to other hospitals in the area.

Our health insurance was canceled, effective yesterday. I had Alex, Susie, Allen and Rick all covered by my policy. Many employees had worked there for years, and some had been saving part of their vacation days to cash in when they retired. All their vacation and sick pay was gone. There was no severance pay. The hospital only offered a bonus of seventy-five dollars per day to employees who would help clean out everything that needed to be shredded, put things away that needed to be stored, or throw away unneeded items. This was expected to take about four days and then the hospital would be closed and locked.

There are two patients I will never forget. One was a large black woman in her sixties. The first time I went in her room, I was shocked by the smell. It was the strongest and most revolting smell imaginable. It was worse than skunk. I tried to hold my breath while I got her tube-feeding ready. Her eyes were open wide, like someone very afraid. She made whimpering and moaning sounds. I asked her if she was in pain, but she just looked at me. She reminded me of a frightened animal caught in a trap. Her legs had been amputated and her arms were weak.

She could not turn or move by herself. I told her I would bring her some morphine.

I left the room to get the morphine and catch my breath. I found an aide and asked her to help me clean the women. I was sure by the smell that she had a BM. After I gave the morphine, we turned her over and what I found was worse than just BM. The patient had a large bed-sore on her sacral area. It was deep and packed with a very foul-smelling dressing that was a dark red, almost black and brown. It was sutured in place and covered with stool. We cleaned her as well as we could.

When I left the room, I asked the other nurse on duty what the dressing was. She told me the patient had gone to surgery about a week earlier. The doctors thought she was going to die and had packed her wound and sutured the dressing in place. But she did not die, and the dressing was forgotten. The terrible smell in the room was due to necrotic tissue, drainage from the wound and stool that had saturated the dressing. I could not remove the dressing without a doctor's order. I was on a unit I had been floated to (sent to work the shift on). I told the charge-nurse about the situation. A few days later the packing was removed because staff were complaining about the smell.

Another patient, on our unit, was a young Hispanic woman. She was only in her twenties and married with children. She was pretty and sweet. She did not speak English and she never complained.

I remember the day she was admitted. She came to the ER because she had a fever. When she was sent to our unit, I noticed a brown fluid dripping down her thigh. At first, I thought it was stool, but it was not. Then I thought it must be coming from a wound. I cleaned her leg and looked for a wound but did not find anything. As I continued to look for where the fluid had been coming from, I saw more of the brown fluid oozing out from a crack in the skin. It was not coming from a wound; it was just oozing out. She was started on antibiotics.

I do not think the doctors took her condition as seriously as they should have. Probably because she was young and looked healthy. Her only obvious symptom was fever. She stayed in the hospital for about three weeks and got progressively worse. She had a history of rheumatoid arthritis and had been treated with corticosteroids for a long time. The steroids reduced her body's ability to fight infection.

She had an infection in her blood and the antibiotics did not get rid of it. The last week she was in the hospital we could see she was in a lot of pain, and she stopped eating. She died on a Sunday morning. The staff was sad, but at the same time we were relieved that her suffering was over.

November 16, 2000

I am still on staff part-time at the rehab hospital and at the hospital where I had my first full time position. But I need to be full-time at a hospital, so I can get health insurance and other benefits. I went to the hospital where I first worked as an RN and asked if they had a position for me. The SNU unit there was closing within a month. All staff will have to be transferred to other units. I told the nursing director I could not work the evening shift because I need to be home at night with my daughter. I told her Susie is dyslexic and I needed to help her with schoolwork. At first, she said there was nothing but second shift available. I asked if I could work in the float-pool, but she said I did not have enough experience. She said I might be able to work on the oncology unit, but there was no position open on the day shift. I asked about the weekend shift. I knew the hospital had some nurses who worked twelve-hour shifts on Saturday and Sunday and got full-time benefits. She said there were no weekend day shifts open on Oncology. I asked if I could work weekend nights. At first, she said there were no openings. I was disappointed and said I would have to look somewhere else for a job. She said to wait a minute and she called the oncology manager, Sharon. She said Sharon would be calling me back and there might be an opening for me on the weekend night shift.

T W O

ONCOLOGY

February 5, 2001

I am working the weekend night shift on the Oncology unit and still work one or two days a week at the rehab hospital. We have four nurses on our shift, but we can only use three, even if we are full. Every shift one nurse must float to another unit. If we do not have enough patients for three nurses, then two nurses must float.

The charge nurse on our shift is Shelia. She is an experienced nurse in her forties with short light-brown hair, fair skin and freckles. She has been a nurse for a long time and is always willing to help new nurses learn. She would make a good nursing instructor. No matter how busy we are, anyone can go up to her with a question and she will stop whatever she is doing to find an answer.

After a few weeks, one of the nurses on our shift quit and moved away because her husband was transferred by his job. So now there are only three of us left. Nursing staff for our shift is Shelia, Marian, and me.

Marian is a young married woman with two little girls. She is from India, as many of our nurses are. Our hospital is part of a large non-profit health care system that recruits staff from India and other countries. She is nice to everyone and almost always has a smile on her face. She gets tired late at night and often falls asleep at her computer while she is charting. Her husband calls her a lot while she is at work. I do not know what her husband calls about because she does not speak English to him.

Marian told us she is too busy to sleep much during the day. She said her husband insists she prepare all meals from fresh food. She is not allowed to use anything frozen, from a box or a can. She told us she usually gets about two hours of sleep each day on the weekends. Even though she works Saturday night, she must get her girls ready for church on Sunday morning, and then fix a meal after church before she can sleep. Then she must work on Sunday night.

She told us her husband is jealous and abusive. Sometimes she goes into the employee bathroom and cries. But when she comes out, she always puts a smile on her face and takes care of her patients.

February 12, 2001

One of my patients last night was a frail Hispanic woman in her eighties. Several family members, well dressed and professional-looking, were in the room. She complained that the staff in radiology were rough with her and inconsiderate. The nursing supervisor was called and came to talk to the family. When I went into the room, she quietly but tearfully told me about how they had treated her badly. She was so sweet, and I knew she had terminal cancer.

I wanted to do everything I could to make her comfortable. She did not ask for any pain medication, but at about 10:30 PM she asked for something to help her sleep. She said she had gotten it the night before. She did not know what it was, but it helped her sleep. The only thing she had ordered that would help her sleep was Ativan. But when I tried to get it for her, I noticed the order had expired. It is a narcotic, and I could not give it to her without a new order.

I paged the doctor on-call. The answering service called him twice before he called back. He sounded like I just woke him up, and when I asked for the order all he said was: "Yes." Then he hung up. I wrote the order and gave the medication to her. About fifteen minutes later he called back. He was angry and wanted to know who had paged him at 11:00 at night, and why he had not been called earlier.

I told him I was the one who called, and I did not know why the day shift had not called him to renew the order, but there was a note for a doctor about it on her chart. He asked me if I was a "regular" on the unit and I said: "Yes, but I just started a few weeks ago." Then he said in a grumpy tone: "Are you all going to need anything else from me tonight?" Of course, that is a question I could not answer, but I just said: "I don't think so." I told the other nurses and they said I should have just given the medication and made sure there was a note to re-order on the chart. I told Marian and Shelia that I hoped I did have a good reason to call and wake him up again. He was rude, and I thought it was wrong to expect me to give medication, especially a narcotic, without a valid order. I would be putting my nursing license at risk just for the convenience of a physician who was on-call but sleeping.

February 19, 2001

Last night I only had four patients at the start of the shift. One sickle-cell, one cancer, one bowel obstruction that was post-op, and one diabetic dialysis patient who just had a big toe amputated and had a foot wound. I had to do dressing changes on the post-op bowel obstruction patient and the patient with the amputated toe and foot wound.

The patient with the foot wound had a hole about as big around as a quarter on the underside of his foot. It was packed with a dressing that looks like ribbon and is made damp with sterile normal saline before packing it in the wound. I try to get everything needed set up on a sterile area and make sure nothing becomes contaminated. Then I remove the old dressing with regular gloves. I put on the sterile gloves when I am ready to pack the wound with the new dressing.

The hole in this man's foot was surprisingly deep. I packed about half of a bottle of ribbon in it. I could have used a little less, but I would have had to cut the ribbon with my scissors. Even though I cleaned them with an alcohol pad, I did not want to use them unless I had to. It would be nice if we could have a sterile scissors to use for every sterile dressing change. I can see how wounds like this get infected if the nurse changing the dressing is in a hurry. I have seen nurses do a dressing change without putting on sterile gloves and using their scissor, pulled out of their pocket.

The patient is a thin black man, about sixty years old. He has been on our unit for about two weeks. He usually stays in bed with the blanket pulled over his head. I noticed he had not touched his supper tray. He refused to eat because his wife was going to bring barbecue. It was already 10 PM, and I did not think she was coming. I tried to get him to eat but he told me to take the tray away. There was a brownie on it, and I was hungry, so I ate it. His wife did not come.

After midnight I was talking to Shelia about other hospitals in the area. She told me she works part-time at another hospital, and she liked it. I said that I might apply there to make some extra money. She told me they pay more for part-time work than the hospitals I am working at now.

February 21, 2001

I was scheduled to work at the rehab hospital from 7 AM to 3:30 PM yesterday but was called at 6 AM and canceled. The supervisor called back later and asked if I would work 3 PM to 11:30 PM. I said I would think about it and let her know. I called back in about fifteen minutes and said I would work 3 PM to 7 PM, and she said that was good. About halfway through the shift she asked me if I would stay until 11 PM, and I said I would.

I had ten patients on the 300 unit. It is a small unit on the opposite end of the hospital from the large unit where most of the patients are. Staff was only me and one aide. She spent most of the shift on the phone or talking to other aides that came to visit. I think they come over to this unit to hide and not have to answer call lights on their unit.

My aide seemed upset and told me she was close to having a breakdown. She left the unit for about twenty minutes, and when she came back, she was crying and asked me for some Tylenol.

One of my patients was a young woman, only twenty-two years old. She had long blond hair, pale skin, and looked frail. In report I was told she had a congenital heart defect. She came here from another state and had been living with her aunt. She has a four-year-old son.

She was working at a deli-sandwich shop when she passed-out and fell. She was unconscious for twenty minutes, and it caused cerebral hypoxia (low oxygen to the brain). Now she is child-like, with no memory of what happened to her or how she came to this hospital.

When I spoke to her, she asked me where she was and how she got here. She said: "I don't feel good." I told her she was in a rehab hospital, and she had passed-out at work. She said: "You mean I had a job? I don't remember it." I asked her if she remembered her parents and she said she did. She also remembered where they lived. I asked her if she remembered anyone else, thinking she might remember her son, but she said: "No." I did not mention him because I thought it might upset her.

I took her to the bathroom once. She got out of the wheelchair herself. She was wearing an adult diaper. I changed her and helped her to bed. Her bed has plastic and nylon mesh all around and zips up. It is made to keep a patient from getting out of bed without having to use restraints. About ten minutes later, she was standing in the hall in front of the nurses' desk and asked me to help her find her shoes. They were next to her bed. She had found a way to unzip the nylon mesh from the inside.

February 27, 2002

I worked at the rehab hospital today and was on the 300 unit again. I had the same young woman. In report I was told the patient remembered her son and talked about him. Today I discharged her to a nursing home in this area. Her parents live in North Carolina and had refused to take her or send her to a nursing home there. She asked me if her parents knew where she was being sent and I told her they did. Her son was sent to live with his father. I helped her pack her things into two large plastic bags. I felt sad for her. I hope she gets better at the nursing home.

March 22, 2001

I applied and was hired at the hospital where Shelia works part-time. Now I am on staff at three hospitals. I usually work about five days a week. I do not like the hospital where I just started, but I think I might get used to it. The nurses' work area is so small it is hard to find any place to sit down and do paperwork. They do not use computers for charting. It is all done the old way, on paper. The units are too busy, and I always must stay at least an hour late. All the full-time nurses complain about staffing and scheduling. They make less per hour than the part-time nurses, and sometimes they act rude to us.

Yesterday I was on the medical/surgical unit working the day shift. One of my patients was a confused older white man. He had problems with blood circulation in his feet and one of his toes had been amputated. I was going past his room, and I saw him walking to the bathroom. He was not steady on his feet.

One of the nurses' aides had been standing in the hall talking to a housekeeper for the last fifteen minutes. She was responsible for taking care of this patient's bathroom needs, so I asked her to help him to the bathroom. She is a large strong young black woman, and I did not think she needed my help to do it.

About ten minutes later my pager rang and said to go to that room. I found the patient on the floor, unable to get up. He was covered with liquid stool from head to foot. The floor had stool all over it and he was rolling around, trying to get up. It took three people to get him up and into bed.

The aide helped to clean him and change the linen. The dressing was off his foot where his freshly amputated big toe had been. The wound was open and looked like someone had just taken a butcher-knife and chopped the toe off. I cleaned it with soap, water, and antiseptic, and put a dressing on it.

The aide told me the patient had fallen and she could not hold him up. I did not believe her because there was liquid stool all over the bathroom floor and half-way to the patient's bed. She probably left him alone in the bathroom, and after he fell, he tried to crawl back to bed. I did not say anything, but I was a little upset with her.

April 20, 2001

Yesterday I worked at the rehab hospital. I had a bad day and turned in my resignation before I went home. The patient load is just too much for how they staff. When patients call to go to the bathroom there is always a long wait. One of the nurses told me I should only answer call lights for my patients. If I tried to help every patient who asked me for assistance, I would not have time to do my patients' care.

There was a class for the aides. They were all gone for about two hours. I had seven patients and an admission who had arrived just before the class started. The call lights were going off and no one was answering them.

Only an RN can do an admission assessment, and I was the only RN at the hospital except for the supervisor. I was trying to get caught-up on giving my afternoon medications. Some of my patients were in physical therapy and I had to go to the gym and look for them.

I passed by one of my patients' room and the door was open. The call light was ringing, but no one was answering. The patient saw me and asked for help to the bedside commode. She was a sweet little old lady who was too weak to get out of bed by herself. I was holding medications in my hands for two patients in the gym, and I told her to just go in the bed and we would clean her in a few minutes.

One of the hospital's social workers walked by the room and could hear the lady crying. She saw me coming back from the gym and asked me to help the patient go to the bathroom. The patient did not have a diaper on and was fully dressed. She was already soiled. I felt bad, and I stayed to clean and change her.

Shift change was at 3 PM and I passed the admission on to the next RN. She was mad at me, but I just told her the aides had a class and I did not have any help.

May 1, 2001

Saturday night my son, Alex, was in an auto accident. When I came home from work on Sunday morning, I was making eggs when the phone rang. It was my ex-husband. He said Alex was in a car accident and had been taken to the county hospital. He said Alex had hurt his neck and I needed to go.

My stomach felt like it was tied in a knot, and I was really scared. I told Allen and Susie we had to go. I felt weak and unsteady. I had a shot of bourbon to calm my nerves; Allen drove.

When we got to the hospital Alex was in the ER. He was alright, except for a badly broken right arm and leg. His neck was not hurt. When his father was there earlier, he had been wearing a neck brace that is put on victims of auto accidents. He was awake and talked to us, even smiling. I was so happy.

I stayed at the hospital all day and took off work that night. There was no patient room available for Alex, and at 5 PM he was taken to the post-op unit so his bed would be available for another ER patient. Since it was Sunday evening, there were not any scheduled surgeries, and there were empty beds in that area. Usually, only hospital staff and patients are allowed there. But I still had my uniform on, and I told the nurse I was Alex's mother, so she let me in. It was a large open area with ten beds and each bed had curtains that could be pulled around it. Alex was in pain and the nurse gave him some IV pain medication. We talked for a few minutes. Alex still had pieces of glass in his back from the accident, and she gave me supplies to remove the glass and clean it. At 7 PM there was shift change, and the new nurse was not as nice. She told me I had to leave. She said Alex needed to sleep, and he was scheduled to have surgery on his arm and leg in the morning.

We went home, and I came back myself in the morning. I spoke with Alex's doctor, and he said Alex would need pins in his arm and a long rod through the bone in his upper leg to hold the bone together until it could heal. I sat with him in the pre-op area, waiting for him to go to surgery. After surgery he got a semi-private room. His roommate was an older man, and Alex said he was "kind of weird."

I asked if Alex could have a private room, or a room with one of his friends who were in the accident with him. There were five boys in the SUV that crashed. Two of them were on Alex's floor. One had gone by helicopter to another hospital. He had a bad head injury and was in a coma.

The charge-nurse said she could not put Alex in a room with another one of the boys from the accident because they required too much care, and it would not be fair to a nurse to have two of them. I told her I was an RN, and said all Alex needed was pain medication, and possibly antibiotics. I said that was not a lot of care for a patient. I told her Alex was covered by my insurance, and if it did not cover a private room, I would pay the difference. She said she did not know if a private room was available, but she would see what she could do.

The next morning Alex complained to me that he had to ask for pain medicine when he needed it, but the nurse always took at least an hour to bring it. I talked to his doctor and told him I wanted Alex to have a pain pump. That way, he could push a button for a dose of pain medicine. The pumps have a computer that only allows the patient to get a certain amount of medication, so they cannot overdose if they push the button too much.

He ordered the pain pump and about two hours later Alex was put in a room with one of his friends. That made him happy. One of the other boys was just down the hall and able to visit. A lot of kids visited the boys. I went to see Alex as much as I could, and I would wash him and help him get comfortable.

Alex spent about five days in the hospital and then I went to pick him up and take him to his father's apartment. I wanted to take him home with me, but I would be gone to work a lot. His father and girlfriend had a young son who stayed at home, so I knew one of them would usually be home to take care of Alex.

When I went to pick him up, I thought someone would help me get him into the car. Since his right leg and right arm were broken, he had to use a wheelchair. After his discharge papers were signed, we waited at the front desk for someone to help take him out. I was going to get the car and pull up to the front door. That is the way it is done at most hospitals. But at the county hospital no one would help us. The nurse said I would have to take him from the unit to the car myself. I was not sure I would be able to get him in the car without assistance, but we made it okay. When we got to the apartment, Alex's little brother was playing outside and happy to see him.

All the boys in the accident recovered, although one boy lost a finger. Alex told me the accident happened when they left a party on Saturday night. Alex was in an SUV with four other boys. Friends were in a car behind. They were on a country road they drove on often. There is a little hill on the road and the boys liked to go over it fast, so the car would go up in the air at the top of the hill. They had always driven over the hill in a car, but one of the boys from the party had an SUV. When they drove over the hill they went up in the air, came down and rolled.

Their friends in the car behind saw the accident and called 911. The boy who had the head injury was thrown out of the SUV. His twin brother was in the car behind. He found his brother with part of his scalp ripped off. He took off his shirt and held it tightly over his brother's head to stop the bleeding. His brother was taken from the accident by helicopter, and he was in a coma for a week.

September 6, 2001

I worked the day shift today at the hospital where Shelia works part-time. I was sent to the skilled nursing unit there. The charge nurse told me they have a good nurses' aide, but today was her day off. They did not have a replacement for her, so I had to do all my patient care. Most of the patients needed to be helped to the bathroom. Some wanted a bed-bath or shower. They all had medications, and some were diabetic. I had two or three of my patients calling at the same time and no one helped me. At the end of the shift, I turned in my resignation at this hospital too.

October 18, 2001

Today I am working an extra shift at the hospital where I am full-time. It is the only one I am on staff at now. The hospital is paying bonuses to work extra shifts and I am on the Neurological Unit. This is my favorite unit to work on. The patients here have had seizures, and they are admitted for testing to determine the cause of their seizures.

They are connected to electrodes placed all over their heads. The electrodes send a signal to a monitor. A tech watches the patients on a video camera and records their brain-wave patterns. The patients are taken off all their seizure medications and are then sleep-deprived, to induce a seizure that can be recorded. They are kept awake all night, and if they do not have a seizure, in the morning a strobe light might be used. After the seizure is recorded for a minute, the RN will give IV Ativan to stop it.

I like working here because the patients are healthy, except for the seizures, and I do not have to give many medications. I usually have only four or five patients. Staff for the unit is one RN, a monitor tech and a PCA. I have been working here often on the 3 PM to 11:30 PM shift and it is easy, especially since the patients almost always have their seizures in the morning. Other nurses in the hospital are afraid to float to this unit because of the seizures, so I am getting a lot of shifts here.

The unit is quiet, and I ate lunch at the desk of the nursing station. I brought the newspaper to read because I have time here to relax.

October 25, 2001

I am on the neurological unit again today. The patients are all quiet and I brought my bills and checkbook to work with me because I have time to get my bills ready to mail out. The monitor tech today is a young black man. One of the patients he is watching on the monitor and by video camera is a young white woman. She has been on the unit for three days now. He has had to go in her room a few times to put electrodes back on her head when they came loose. He can talk to her through the intercom, and she knows he is watching her on camera.

He complained to me and the PCA. He said: "She's doing it again! I can't just sit here and watch that!" The patient was masturbating in full view of the camera. The PCA said she had seen her doing it several times since she has been here. We just laughed about it. The patient was not breaking any rules, and I do not think she would listen to me if I told her not to do it anymore.

December 3, 2001

I worked on Oncology Saturday and Sunday night. Shelia told us she is transferring to the day shift. She said she cannot sleep good in the daytime and it's too hard for her to stay awake at night.

On Sunday night one of my patients was a white woman in her sixties who had cancer and had been a chemotherapy patient. All her hair was gone, and the cancer had spread to her lungs, but she still went out to smoke with her daughters. At least one of them was always with her. Her son stayed last night, and the daughters went home to get some rest. He is a large man with shaggy hair, a long beard and a beer-belly. His mother was made a DNR (do not resuscitate) and she was not expected to last much longer. She was wearing an oxygen mask and her breathing was labored.

I went into the room at about 2 AM and the son was asleep in a chair. I went in because before, when I walked by the room, I could hear her wheezing from the hall. But now it was quiet, except for the slight hiss of oxygen coming out of the mask. I felt for a pulse on the side of her neck, and I could feel a faint slow heartbeat. I listened to her lungs and there was no movement of air.

I called Shelia. She woke the son and told him: "It's time to say goodbye to your mother." He jumped up and yelled: "Oh no! I fu---- up!" He was supposed to call his sisters if there was any change in her condition. Now it was too late.

We told him it was alright. There was nothing he could have done. He called his sisters, and they came in. We called the funeral home, completed information for the death certificate, and she was taken away.

December 17, 2001

A third nurse was hired for our shift and started last weekend. Her name is Jackie. She is a young white nurse who has been working at an oncology doctor's office for the last two years. She gave chemotherapy there and has her oncology certification. Marian and I are not certified to give chemo, so it had to be scheduled around our shift. It was usually given on the day shift.

Jackie is married and has a young son. She is nice and easy to work with. The three of us get along well and make a good team. We do not have a charge-nurse. Marian has seniority, but she has no interest in being charge-nurse. I do not want the responsibility, especially since it does not pay more. We divide up the patients as we see fair and take turns with admissions. Sometimes we flip a coin to see who will get the next admit.

May 20, 2002

Things have gone okay on the weekend for the last few months. Marian's problems with her husband are getting worse. His constant calling during our shift is a nuisance. Last night he called several times when Marian was gone to the pharmacy to pick up medications. I answered the phone when she was on her way back to the unit and put it on hold. When she got off the elevator, I told her that her husband had been calling repeatedly, and she said: "Tell him I went outside with a doctor, and he was cute." I told him that, and I knew it was a mistake as soon as I said it. He became angry, talked to his wife and then called back several more times. Marian had to go to a patient's room, and when she came back, she refused to talk to him. He asked to talk to me. I told him that Marian told me to say what I did, and it was not true. We just thought it would be funny. I told him Marian was not the kind of woman who would do something like that. She had told me how she grew up in India, living at a Catholic boarding school where her parents sent all their children. She had never dated and had an arranged marriage. He was angry, so I said I was "sorry" just to get him off the phone. I did not want to get involved in their marital problems.

September 21, 2002

I am working my usual Saturday night shift on Oncology and my mother called from South Dakota at about 8 PM. She said my father is in the hospital and his nurse told her that she should call family members. He has had cancer for a long time.

I told the nursing supervisor when she was making rounds and she asked if I wanted to leave. I told her it was a long drive, so a few hours would probably not make a difference, but I would like to take a vacation day on Sunday if she could find someone to cover my shift. She said I could take off work tomorrow. I called Allen and he said we could leave in the morning when I get home from work.

September 29, 2002

My father died early this morning. My mother was with him at the hospital. When we arrived in South Dakota last week my father was alert and in good spirits. He smiled and joked with the doctors and nurses. He always had a good sense of humor. My mother said he was scheduled to have a feeding tube placed in his stomach that afternoon, but he did not want it. We talked about it and decided we should respect his wishes. We spoke to a young doctor who was covering for my father's regular doctor, who was out of town. He told us my father's cancer had spread to his bones and chest, and there was nothing that could be done about it. Even with the feeding tube, he would not live long.

We discussed my father going home for a few days. I told the doctor I was an RN, and I could give him pain medicine at home. My mother said that was okay with her, but she knew I would have to go back to work soon, and she could not take care of him herself.

We considered putting him in a nursing home, but we knew he would hate that. With IV fluids and liquid feedings going in through a stomach tube, he would probably live for a few weeks. But he was in a lot of pain from the cancer, and we did not see the point of making him suffer in a nursing home with no quality of life.

After discussing the situation with my mother and brother, we decided it would be best to just make sure my father was comfortable with pain medicine. We talked to the doctor about our decision, and he said my father could stay in the hospital for a few days, and we would see what happened.

The nursing staff at the hospital were very good to us. They gave my father a large private room with a couch that pulled out to a double bed. One of us was with him all the time. Sometimes my mother and I spent the night, and one night Allen stayed with me so my mother could get some rest at home. My father was born in South Dakota and still had family members living there. He had brothers and sisters, nieces and nephews who came to visit him.

He was happy and able to talk to everyone for a few days. He even told Allen about a family tree book I did not know existed. He was allowed to eat and drink whatever he wanted, but that was not much. My mother or I would call the nurse every two or three hours to ask for a shot of morphine. The last two days he was on a morphine drip, and he quietly passed away in his sleep.

October 7, 2002

Last night I was working on Oncology and one of my patients was a little old white man with Alzheimer's. The first time I went into his room, he had his IV line pulled out and was playing with it. The IV pump was still running, with the fluid dripping out on the floor. He was supposed to have wrist restraints on, but he had managed to get one of them off. When I asked what he was doing he said: "I was going to walk to the store, but it's too windy out there. I think I'll just stay here."

Another of my patients was a younger white man who was not allowed to eat. He had a continuous tube feeding going into his stomach through a PEG tube (a plastic tube inserted through the skin into the stomach). He called for morphine frequently, and I had already given him a dose when he called later for another one. I went in and saw him sitting on the side of his bed, with his penis in the large 70 ml syringe that is used to put medication in the PEG tube. He was urinating into the syringe, and the urine was squirting out the tip into a trash can. He must have thought the syringe was his urinal.

I noticed his IV line was gone. He asked me for morphine, and I laughed and said: "You can't have any morphine, because you took your IV line out." He acted surprised and looked at his arm where the line had been. He said: "I didn't know." He found the line in his bed and held it up. I said: "It's no good now. I'll have to put a new one in later. I don't have time right now." He looked sad, probably because he was going to have to wait for his morphine.

October 22, 2002

Marian told us on Saturday that she must resign. She is going on vacation to India with her husband and children. She will be gone two months. Our manager, Sharon said she could not give her that much time off. I think she might have given her the time off if Marian's husband was not calling all the time.

Marian told us her husband asked her for a divorce, and he told her that all she had to do was sign the papers. She signed them, but then changed her mind and tore them up. She has no family in this country and does not know what to do.

December 2, 2002

Last night I had five patients to start and two admissions. One of my patients was a Hispanic man in his sixties. He had a CVA (cerebrovascular accident, also called a stroke) and had been unresponsive in the ICU. His breathing tube was removed, and he was sent to our floor to die just before the start of my shift.

He had a lot of family with him. There were children and grandchildren. The waiting room was full all night. He had a temp of 105, even with getting a Tylenol suppository every six hours. His family asked about the high temp, and I told them I did not know if it would go down. He was on oxygen with a mask. He was unresponsive with labored breathing and his lungs started filling up with fluid. They asked me what would happen, and I told them he would just stop breathing. They asked me when it would happen. I said I did not know; it might be minutes, or it could be days.

Another patient was a ninety-year-old white man with Alzheimer's and a bowel impaction. He was also a DNR, but he was getting better. He had some large bowel movements on Saturday and on Sunday night he was feeling better. He was talking and started to move around. I was afraid he would pull out his IV line or his Foley catheter, so I gave him some things to keep his hands busy. I gave him a suction canister, some mouth swabs and clean towels that I asked him to fold. When he finished folding the towels, I would thank him for helping me and take them out to the hall and mess them up. Then I would take them back into the room and ask if he could fold some more. It kept him busy, and I did not have to use restraints on him.

One of my patients was on a chemo drip. Even thought I was not certified to give chemo I could take care of this patient because his bag of chemo was started on the day shift and would run over twenty-four hours. He was a white man in his fifties and had been a patient on our unit for a long time. His wife and teenage daughter were with him. He had not eaten for about a week and had IV nutrition running continuously. Even though he had no food in his stomach, he was vomiting (only a little saliva, but he was retching). I gave him nausea medicine, but it only helped a little. I had to call the doctor and was given the order to stop the chemo. The patient is always nice, even when he is not feeling well.

December 9, 2002

Saturday night I was on my regular 7 PM to 7:30 AM shift. One of the patients in my group had just died at 6:50 PM. The patient was an elderly Hispanic man, and there was a large group of people singing and praying in the room. They seemed to be having a religious service, so I left them alone.

Hospital policy states a body must be removed from the room within two hours of death, but I did not think it was necessary to make an issue of it. At about 10 PM they said they were going to take the body back to Mexico. I never had a family ask to take a body with them before, so I called the nursing supervisor. She said a body could only be taken out of the hospital by a person sent from a licensed funeral home.

The family had not made plans for a funeral home, and they needed to wait until the next day so family members could agree on what to do.

I told them we would put him in our morgue, and he could be picked-up after they made their arrangements.

The family left at about 10:30 and the PCA helped me tag and bag the body. While we were doing that, an elderly oriental female patient who had just come up from the ER about two hours earlier, and was in the room next door, died. She was a DNR, and I had expected her to go at any minute. I called her family, and they came quickly. It was almost funny, because as we went in and out of the Hispanic man's room, getting him ready to take to the morgue, the oriental woman's family would peek in when the door was open. An older oriental man said: "Is he dead too?" I just said: "Yes."

We had to call a security guard to bring the stretcher we needed to transport the body and unlock the morgue. The security guard refused to help us lift the body onto the stretcher. All he would do was walk with us to the morgue and unlock the door. He would not even go in. A female PCA and I had to lift the body and put him in the drawer ourselves. I was glad he did not weigh too much.

Sunday night I got an admission from the ER. She was a large white woman forty-four years old and was admitted for asthma. She was put in the same room the oriental woman had been in the night before. When she first got to the unit, she was wheezing but I thought the respiratory therapist would get her breathing under control. I gave her a dose of the steroid ordered, and I thought she would be okay. But she did not get any better and started getting worse.

I asked her a few questions trying to figure out what was going on with her, and she told me the wheezing had started after she ate at a restaurant. I knew she had a history of asthma, but I thought she might also be having an allergic reaction to something she ate. I called the doctor and the nursing supervisor, and quickly transferred her to the ICU. My PCA helped push her in the bed with oxygen on. She was heavy, and we had to push up a long ramp that is between the old section of the hospital and the new section where the ICU is.

When we got back to Oncology, I was breathing hard and sweating.

I told Jackie I was glad I had a can of deodorant in my locker, because I needed it. I was going to take a break, but I had another elderly Hispanic man who was a DNR in the room where the man had passed-away the night before, and he had just died. It was a busy night.

Jackie and I are the only nurses on our shift now. If we have enough patients that staffing requires another nurse, one is sent from the float pool or another floor that has extra staff. The other nurses in the hospital do not like coming to our unit.

Last weekend a nurse from the rehab unit had to float here. She is an experienced black nurse, about my age. I have worked with her before, and she is a good nurse to work with. One of her patients who was not a DNR died, and it was not noticed until a PCA went in to check vital signs. A "code blue" had to be called. We got the crash cart and started CPR. Doctors, the nursing supervisor and the rapid response team all rushed in and worked on the lady, who was already blue and very dead. The rehab nurse said she was never coming back to our unit again.

January 6, 2003

I heard on the weekend that two nurses have been hired for our shift. One is a white male nurse who used to work at our hospital two years ago and is coming back. His name is Joe. I do not know him, but some of the other nurses do. The other is a white female nurse named Helen. She has already started and is working Thursdays and Fridays from 11 PM to 7:30 AM. She also works Saturday and Sunday from 7 PM to 7:30 AM. She is in her forties and has been a nurse for a few years. She would like to work on the weekends as much as possible because we get paid extra then.

Our unit holds twenty-one patients. At night staffing is less than on the day shift. With up to sixteen patients, we have two nurses. With seventeen or more patients, we get three nurses. The extra nurse or nurses must go to other units.

Saturday night while working on Oncology, I became a little

emotional. I admitted a twenty-eight-year-old young man who I had also admitted the Saturday before. His hemoglobin level was 3.5. Normal would be 13.5 to 18. Hemoglobin in the blood cells carries oxygen from the lungs to the cells of the body and carries carbon dioxide out. This was the lowest level I had ever seen. He had orders to get four units of blood.

He has sarcoma, a cancer of the epithelial cells (skin cancer). It was diagnosed about a year ago in his left arm and the tissue was removed. He went through chemotherapy but now the cancer is in his left lung, causing a hole that has been bleeding into his lung for months. He has pain that is getting steadily worse. His skin is pale, and his weight is down to 120 pounds. Even with the tattoos on his arms he looks younger than he is.

His mother and sister were with him when I took in the consent form for the blood transfusion. He had signed his DNR papers in the ER. His mother and sister were softly crying, and he seemed kind of angry, but I thought he was just afraid. When I came out of his room, I told the PCA we were going to transfuse four units of blood and she was surprised. We usually only transfused one or two units. I told her why he had to have four units, and my eyes started tearing up. She said: "Are you crying?" I said: "No" and quickly turned and walked away. I was embarrassed to look unprofessional like that.

I made sure he got pain medicine as often as he could have it. But at 6 AM he was in pain and could not have another dose until 8:30 AM. I called the doctor who wrote his admission orders, but he said he was only seeing ER patients, and I would have to call the attending physician. I paged the attending physician, but he did not call back with the order until 8 AM. We had already done shift change, and I told his new nurse I had gotten the order, and to please give him the pain medicine.

On Sunday night I had a patient who looked like a middle-aged biker. He had long hair worn in a braid, a beard, and several large tattoos. His daughter and two cute little granddaughters came to visit him Sunday night at about 8 PM.

He had a stroke that caused weakness in his left leg and arm. He also had a history of chronic back pain and epilepsy. He asked me for pain medicine at 7:30 PM and I gave it to him. He complained to me that the day shift nurse would not give him anything when he asked for it.

At about 1 AM I heard a loud noise that sounded like something rattling. It was him having a seizure and shaking the bed. I called the PCA and told her to stay with him while I got some IV Ativan. I put it in his IV line and the seizure stopped. He was still sleeping, and I do not think he even realized he had a seizure.

I went back to the desk, but about twenty minutes later I heard the rattling noise again. I ran to his room, and he was having another seizure. I just watched him, because I knew it was too soon for another dose of Ativan. I knew he needed it, but my orders said he could only have it every four hours. He was so tense he stopped breathing. I was watching his chest to see if he was going to take a breath. He stopped shaking, and was just rigid, and not breathing. I called to him and shook him trying to wake him up, but he was unresponsive.

I ran out, called a "code blue," and ran back in with the crash cart. I was only out of the room a few seconds, and when I went back in, he had started to breathe again. Jackie asked if I wanted to cancel the code, but I said: "No." His breathing was not regular, and I was afraid he might stop breathing again. Within minutes the room was full of nurses and a doctor. They gave him oxygen with a mask and had electrodes on his chest to monitor his heart rhythm. The doctor ordered another dose of Ativan.

After I gave the Ativan, the seizure stopped, and everyone left. He sat up and asked for a cup of coffee. He did not remember the seizure, but he said: "I feel like someone hit me all over with a baseball bat." He had a bad headache and muscle pain. I gave him a cup of coffee and some pain medicine.

February 10, 2003

Saturday night the new male nurse started on our shift. He is young, tall and looks like he lifts weights. He has light skin and is shaved all over (that is what he said). Anyway, there is no hair visible on his head or arms, which have large tattoos. He wears two earrings in each ear. We wear white uniforms, and he looks like "Mister Clean" from the old TV commercials about the floor-cleaning product. He seems to be an experienced nurse and is friendly. He has a southern accent and a sense of humor the female patients like. He makes even the oldest of them giggle.

March 17, 2003

Now that we have four nurses again, one or two of us must float to another unit each shift. We really hate to float because we are often sent to a unit for four hours and then to another unit for the last eight hours. That means we have twice the patients to assess and do charting on. I have been floating almost every Saturday because Helen and Joe work on Friday night, and the regular Monday to Friday night nurses make them float. They say that counts as their turn, so on Saturday night they will not float. Jackie and I complained to Sharon about it, and she said that from now on Helen will always have to float because she was not hired as a weekend nurse.

May 12, 2003

Helen got sick of floating all the time and transferred to the Telemetry unit about a month ago. Now there are only three of us.

I think Jackie is having money problems. She had to take off work one weekend because the check she sent to the nursing board to renew her license bounced. She said it was just a mistake. We sometimes order food to be delivered, but Jackie never orders anything. She works all the extra shifts she can get, usually two or three every week. But she drives an old car with no air-conditioning. She must bring her uniform with her and change when she gets to work because she is wet with sweat from the drive.

Joe and Jackie spend a lot of time together talking. On Sunday night Jackie was upset and Joe had his arm around her when I walked by. Jackie told me what they were talking about so I would know he was just comforting her. She said Joe had raised the question of where all Jackie and her husband's money was going. She said her husband controlled all the money, and he did not tell her how he spent it. They quarreled and decided to split up all the household bills and each pay half. But her husband did not pay his half of the bills and would not account for what he had done with his money. Jackie said if her husband would not pay his half of the bills, she was leaving him.

July 21, 2003

Jackie and Joe have become close. They sit together and play games on the computer late at night when the unit is quiet. They often give each other back-rubs, and sometimes in the early morning hours they go down to the vending machines together. When the shift is over, they always leave the unit together.

Last night Joe's live-in girlfriend came up to the unit and they had a loud fight in the breakroom. There was yelling and things being thrown. One of the PCAs is friends with Joe's girlfriend, and she told about Jackie.

August 11, 2003

Joe and Jackie have not been sitting close to each other as much lately because they do not know when Joe's girlfriend might show up. But the doors to the hospital are locked after 10PM. Visitors can leave but not enter, except in the ER. Last night I floated to the rehab unit and came up the back stairs to get something out of my locker at about 3 AM. They were at the desk, sitting close and facing each other. The lights on the unit were turned down low. He had his knee between her legs and her hand was on his leg. They looked like two people in love.

August 25, 2003

On Monday morning a week ago, Joe, Jackie and I were standing at the desk waiting for the day shift to come out of report (We leave a written report and wait for the day shift to go over it before we leave). The lights were all on and I noticed Joe's pupils were dilated. It was noticeable because he has blue eyes. I thought his pupils should be small in the bright light, not large. I did not say anything about it, the day shift came out of report, and I went to my locker to get my purse and go home.

Saturday night about 9 PM, I went into the staff bathroom, and I noticed a small round yellow piece of plastic on the floor. I picked it up, and I knew what it was. It was the top of a 30 ml vial of IV pain medicine that goes in a pain pump. It would be taken off only when the vial was put in the pump. It should not have been in the bathroom.

I thought about it, and I remembered Joe sitting in a chair in the breakroom, just outside the bathroom, when I went in. I thought about how his pupils had been dilated the week before. I suspected him of using the pain medication. But I was not sure about it, and the shift was busy. I knew he and Jackie were close, so I thought she would know if he was taking drugs at work.

Jackie has been made charge nurse because she is certified to give chemotherapy. I don't mind. We have more chemo patients now and someone who can give chemo needs to be on the unit. Jackie does not float to other units anymore. Joe and I take turns floating, but he works Friday nights and is usually floated to another unit then. So, if anyone must float on Saturday, it is me.

September 8, 2003

Jackie told me she is transferring to the ICU and is going to work the day shift. I know ICU nurses make more money than we do. The hospital is going to give her training and she will be able to find a better paying job anywhere with ICU experience. I told her I was happy for her.

I thought she was trying to keep her family together, and that is why she wanted to work on another unit. Later I heard that one night when I was working on another floor, the supervisor was making rounds and could not find her or Joe. They got in trouble and one of them had to transfer off Oncology.

September 22, 2003

Jackie is gone from the unit and another nurse, LeeAnn, has been hired. She is scheduled to work Sunday through Thursday 11PM to 7:30 AM. She is not a weekend person, and the Monday through Friday nurses work eight-hour shifts. This complicates our schedule because we do not have a third nurse for Saturday, or the first four hours of the shift on Sunday.

It is becoming obvious that Joe is taking drugs while working. Last night I found two vials of morphine and a vial of Phenergan (nausea medication) on the floor by the desk he was sitting at. They had dropped off his clipboard. I picked them up and asked him about them. He said he was planning to give them to patients.

Later in the shift, I was reading my newspaper and I heard him go in and out of the narcotics medication room three times. I could hear the beeps that the narcotics machine makes when it is dispensing drugs. I was watching to see if he went into a patient's room, and he did not. Instead, he went into the breakroom. The staff bathroom is entered through the breakroom.

After a few minutes he came out and said: "I'm going downstairs for a while." I knew he did not smoke cigarettes, so that was not the reason. It was about 4 AM and the unit was quiet. I went to the narcotics machine and printed a report on all the narcotics he had taken out that shift. It was a long list. I put it in my pocket and sat down to do some charting.

One of the PCAs sat next to me and I asked her if two of Joe's patients had been asking for pain medication. She said: "I have not heard a peep out of either one of them." Joe had taken out narcotics for both the patients several times during the shift.

I felt sick to my stomach and angry. Now that Jackie was gone, I felt responsible for the unit during our shift. I went to the breakroom and called the nursing supervisor, intending to tell her what I thought. She was not in her office. I decided I would wait and tell her in person before I went home.

I sat down at the desk, and I was steaming mad. Joe walked by and said something, and I just could not hold it in. I said: "I have to talk to you." I walked to the medication room and when he came in, I shut the door. I pulled the report out of my pocked and said: "What's this?!" He said: "I didn't take the medicine!" Then he tried to tell me how upset he was because he and his girlfriend had another fight. I said: "I don't want to hear it!" I was yelling at him, and he asked me to lower my voice so everyone would not hear. I told him I would not look the other way when I knew what he was doing. He stuck to his story that he was just trying to make his patients comfortable. I did not have any way of proving he took the medication himself. I told him if I ever suspected him again, I would go straight to the supervisor.

October 13, 2003

Now I am the only nurse on our shift except for LeeAnn, who works with me Sunday night from 11 PM until 7:30 AM. Joe was fired last week. He was working on Friday night, and something happened between him and the charge nurse. No one will say what happened, only that it was "serious." He was escorted out of the hospital by a security guard and told he could never come back again. I am glad he's gone.

When I worked on Saturday night one of my patients was a middle-aged white lady who was on pain medicine. She was unsteady on her feet and had to be helped to the bathroom a few times during the shift. She was in a room close to the nurses' desk and kept the door to her room open all the time. I was not aware she was listening to what staff were saying.

The unit was full that night so two nurses were floated from other floors. One was a nurse who had worked on the old SNU unit before it closed. She has red hair and a voice that can carry across the unit. She talks and laughs a lot. At the end of the shift a few female staff members were at the desk and the subject of ex-husbands came up. The women were joking and talking a little too loudly.

Sunday night at the start of shift I was told I could not have the lady with the open door as my patient again. I was also told I had to see the director of nursing in the morning. I did not know what I had done and was worried about it all night.

Monday morning at 7:30 AM I was called to the nursing office. When I went in, the director of nursing asked me if our manager had talked to us about customer service. I said she had. Then she told me a patient had heard me give report to a nurse on Sunday morning and I said she (the patient) was an "ass." The patient also said she had called to go to the bathroom, and no one came for about an hour. Then she was taken without her slippers on, and her feet were cold (I always put her slippers on her feet before getting her up).

I told her we do not give a verbal report, we leave a written report. She acted angry and said: "Are you calling the patient a liar?!" I said: "No, but I did not give a verbal report. The patient was on pain medication. She might have been confused." She said: "If you are lying! You didn't talk to Shelia at the desk Sunday morning?!" I said: "No, and I didn't have a problem with the patient. But even If I did, I would not have called her that." She seemed to calm down a little, and said she was going to talk to my manager, and everyone involved.

When I got home, I called Sharon and talked to her about it. I told her I thought the patient might have heard the conversation about ex-husbands and somehow thought the nurses were talking about her. The only person who could clear me of the accusation was Shelia, and she left for vacation before anyone asked her about it.

Tuesday, I worked an extra shift on the Oncology unit. The patient who made the complaint was there and still had her door open all the time. I had the patient in a room next to hers, and she saw me in the hall walking by. About 10 PM she stood in her doorway and called me to come in. I went to the door but told her I could not go in. She said she was so sorry, and she thought she might have gotten me in trouble. I said: "Yes, I know." She said she made a mistake and she had been so "needy" that she thought I said something about her. I told her what she heard was not about her and it was not me giving report because I left a written report. She said she had to go to the bathroom in the morning and no one came to help her. I told her I did not know she called, and I probably had gone home by that time.

She said again how sorry she was. I asked her to tell the right person so I would not be in trouble. She called the nursing supervisor on duty and told her. The next day she called Sharon into her room and told her it was not me she heard talking. Sharon said she would send a memo to the nursing director.

I never got an apology for being accused of misconduct. Early the following Monday morning, the nursing director came to our unit to check if we had the correct information on boards in patient rooms. She smiled at me and acted as if nothing had happened.

October 18, 2003

It is Saturday night, and Sharon was in earlier cleaning out her office. The Oncology unit is going to be remodeled starting on Monday. A few rooms at a time are going to be closed for the work, and Sharon's office and the break room are going to be moved. I asked her who was going to be charge-nurse now that Jackie is gone. She said I was. I will not get paid any more, but it will look good on my resume.

Tonight, we have three nurses, two PCAs and a secretary until 11 PM. One of the nurses is from the float pool and the other is a nurse who was on the day shift and is just coming back to work after having a baby. She will be working weekend nights with us. Her name is Beth. She is tall and thin with long very curly blond hair. It is hard to believe she just had a baby. She is well-educated and told me she got a degree in micro-biology before going to nursing school. Her father is a doctor. She is going to work the weekend night shift so she can stay home with her baby during the week. She and the float pool nurse are both breast-feeding, so they need to pump every few hours.

I have six patients and they are all old ladies. One of them has COPD (chronic obstructive pulmonary disease). She has been smoking for fifty-six years, since she was sixteen years old. She wears oxygen all the time, even at home, and takes Xanax for panic attacks. Her roommate is a confused woman with an alarm on the bed so we will know when she gets up. The alarm goes off every time she gets up to the bed-side commode.

We have a new tube system that connects with the pharmacy and lab. We can send lab samples or get new medications without having to leave the unit. It should save us a lot of time and walking during the night.

October 26, 2003

It is Sunday night, and I am on Oncology. The unit is still being remodeled and six rooms are blocked off. Staffing is me and Beth with one PCA. One of my patients is a little old Hispanic man. He is thin and contracted. He stays in bed with his knees almost up to his chest. He keeps yelling in Spanish, but when someone goes in, he seems okay.

Our PCA tonight is fluent in Spanish. She asked him what he wants, and he said he wants some crackers. He has pneumonia and is not allowed to eat anything. His doctor thinks the pneumonia might have been caused from getting food or fluid in his lungs. He is scheduled for a swallowing evaluation tomorrow. He is getting IV fluid and antibiotics.

Another patient is an eighteen-year-old Hispanic boy. He cannot speak English and came to the ER today with appendicitis. He went to surgery at about 8 PM and came back to the unit at about 10:30PM. The patient has three friends with him and none of them can speak English. When he was brought back to the unit after surgery he was sleeping, and then he started shivering. He told the PCA he was cold. We covered him with blankets but then found he had a fever of 102, so we took the blankets off. The PCA explained to him that his temperature was too high. At about 1 AM his fever broke, and he started sweating. That is good; it means his fever is coming down.

I asked him if he had pain and he said: "Poco." I am learning a few words of Spanish. I knew he was saying he had a little pain, so I gave him a small dose of Demerol. He was thirsty and I gave him some ice-water. The surgery had gone well, and he should be fine.

Another patient is one of our frequently returning cancer patients. He has been here quite a bit lately. He was admitted again yesterday. He has a colostomy which drains liquid stool to a bag. He also has two urostomies, one from each kidney, that drain urine into separate bags. He has a supra-pubic catheter that is clamped-off and a gastric tube draining to a bag. He also has an implanted medication port with IV fluids running. He was transfused two units of blood today and seems to be feeling good.

October 27, 2003

I am waiting for my sister Jessica to pick me up at a ferry boat dock in Washington State. I left today for a short vacation to visit her. I planned it over two months ago and bought airplane tickets over the internet. My mother is visiting her now and I booked a ticket for my mother to fly home with me. Then she will stay with me through Christmas.

Since my father died last year, I have been helping with her travel plans. She is still spending winter months in south Texas and the summer in South Dakota. But now she is also trying to stay with me in the Fall and visit each of her other two daughters when she can. My sisters live in Washington state and Idaho.

Jessica is going through a divorce. She is forty-seven years old with a ten-year-old son and a five-year-old daughter. She has been married for eighteen years. She and her husband bought land in the mountains of Washington after they were married. Recently she discovered that her husband has a girlfriend. Now she has filed for a divorce and is going through a very stress-full time. She has not been able to eat much lately and has lost weight. I have not seen her for about eight years. I thought she had a good marriage and a great life living in the mountains with land and horses.

October 28, 2003

When I woke up today, I saw three deer in front of the house. The mountains are beautiful. We took a long walk and picked a few apples off a neighbor's tree. Jessica showed me the one-room cabin where they lived for years while they saved to build a house. They had burned wood for heat and only ran a generator for a little while each day. We stopped to visit a neighbor and she gave us a large smoked salmon and two jars of home-canned tuna she made from fresh fish.

November 8, 2003

It is Saturday night, and I am working my regular shift on Oncology. We still have six rooms blocked off. Staffing is me and Beth with one PCA. Beth has a patient who has been here for about a week and will be here at least a week longer getting IV antibiotics. He is a tall clean-cut white man in his early forties who has a history of drug abuse. He has infection from a back surgery. He goes out to smoke about every hour or two, and when he comes back, he always goes by the nurses' station and asks for pain medicine. He only wants IV medication, not the pills. If it is time that he can have it, he always gets it. If a patient says he is hurting, we must give the medication whether we believe him or not. The last time he went by he asked for ice cream. I told him where it was, and he took three containers of it.

Beth said when she was trying to start a new IV line on him, he told her just where to put it. His veins are so scarred that she had a hard time finding a place to start it. She could not see the vein he was pointing to, but she tried it anyway and he was right. She said it is probably the only good vein left in his arms.

November 9, 2003

It is Sunday night and staffing is me and Beth with two PCAs. One of my patients is a twenty-three-year-old nurse who works at this hospital and is a recent graduate of nursing school. She is married and had an infected IUD that was removed. She is being treated with IV antibiotics. She is in severe pain. I gave her Demerol and Phenergan about 10 PM, but it did not help. I called the doctor on-call, and he raised her dosage of Demerol.

About 1 AM she called and said she could not urinate. She said she had not gone since about 8 PM and felt like she needed to go but could not. She has IV fluid running at 125 ml per hour, so I knew her bladder should be full. I asked her if she ever had a Foley catheter before, and she said: "Yes, when I had my baby." I paged the doctor again and he said to put a catheter in.

This is the first time I have put a Foley catheter in a young woman. I have put a few in old women. On the first try I missed the urethra and it started to go in the vagina. I am careful to follow sterile procedure because it is easy to get a bladder infection with a catheter. So, I threw away everything and started over with a new set. This time I got it in the right hole, and she put out about 700 ml of urine immediately. She felt a lot better, and with the increased Demerol dosage she went to sleep.

November 10, 2003

It is Monday morning, and I am glad the weekend is over. Last night the unit filled up except for the six beds that are blocked. An alarm went off in the construction area and I went to see what it was. There was an electrical panel that said PROBLEM. I called Engineering and someone came and looked at it, but he did not know what it was or what to do about it. He did manage to get the alarm turned off.

We were busy. I had two admissions and Beth had one. In the morning I was finishing up the paperwork from my second admit. He is a nice older man admitted with pneumonia in his left lung. He also has a history of cancer, and I think it may have spread to that lung because he was in severe pain. It hurt every time he took a breath or moved. I gave him 4 mg of morphine every two hours, but it was not enough to control the pain, so I also gave him hydrocodone two times and Advil once.

I also had a younger man with lung cancer and a hole in his left lung. He had a chest tube draining fluid to a canister. He needed pain medicine a few times. I had six patients at the start of the shift and eight by morning. I ate lunch at the nurses' desk and was just able to take a few bites at a time between answering patient calls.

At 7:20 AM lab called and told me the sputum sample from my newest admit had been lost. It was supposed to have been collected in the ER, but I do not think they did it. If a patient is going to be admitted to a unit, they almost never collect urine, stool, or sputum samples. Sometimes when we tell a patient we need one of these samples, they say the nurse in the ER gave them the container and instructions on what to do with it, but no one picked it up. I think lab samples just sit in the ER room until the patient is sent to a unit and then are thrown away when the room is cleaned.

I was busy with the unit's morning paperwork, much of which could be done by a secretary. The day shift nurses were in report, and I still had to finish my admission paperwork. The unit secretary who is supposed to start at 7 AM was just standing around and talking. I told her the sputum sample was lost and asked her to put the order in for it to be collected again. She told me to put it on the nurses' orders as a specimen to be collected. That is exactly what I was asking HER to do. She was already clocked in, and we do not have a secretary at night after 11 PM. I knew she was supposed to start working at 7 AM, but she never does. I got mad because every Monday this woman clocks in at 7 AM, and then eats breakfast or just stands around talking until 7:30 AM, when the day shift nurses come out of report. She will not even answer the phone for the night shift. I was angry but did not say anything to her because I knew she would argue with me, and I needed to focus on my admissions.

It took me until 8 AM to finish my work. Then I called the nursing supervisor and asked her what time the secretary starts her shift. She said 7 AM. I told her our secretary would not do anything for the night shift, and Monday mornings I really needed a secretary at 7 AM.

November 14, 2003

I worked an extra 3 PM to 11:30 PM shift yesterday on Oncology. I had the young RN with the infected IUD again. She had surgery yesterday morning. They did an abdominal laparotomy (surgical incision, often done on an exploratory basis) and found adhesions (scar- tissue that binds together two anatomic surfaces which should be separate from each other, usually in the abdomen, and can form after abdominal surgery, inflammation, or injury). She had to be opened-up. One of her ovaries and the fallopian tube to the other ovary were removed. She has a Demerol pump for pain control.

When I went in to see her, she was obviously in pain, and I asked her why she was not pushing the button for medication. She said the day shift nurse had remarked that she was pushing the button a lot, so she was trying not to use it. I told her to go ahead and push it. I said that was what it was for. Her mother was in the room, and she agreed. The poor girl was in so much pain she was almost crying. So many patients abuse narcotics that I think some nurses are no longer sympathetic to real pain.

November 16, 2003

It is 3 AM Sunday. The unit is finally quiet. An elderly confused female patient had been yelling in a high-pitched shrill voice since about 9 PM. Her daughter is in the room with her and has calmed her down for now. The patient had both hips replaced over ten years ago and is having a lot of pain in the left hip now. The doctor suspects a hip fracture or a dislocation of the artificial hip. She also has other medical problems including chronic low blood pressure and glucose in her urine.

No one was able to start an IV line on her. Even the supervisor tried. Her doctor came up at about 11 PM and put in a central line (large IV line that goes almost to the heart). She is not my patient, but Beth asked me to give her a shot of Haldol (anti-anxiety medication) IM (a shot given in a large muscle, usually the buttocks). Beth does not like to give shots like that. We could not use the central IV line until we got an X-ray back showing it was in good position.

We have twelve patients and staffing is me and Beth with one PCA. One of my patients is a healthy-looking 18-year-old boy with a left hand that was fractured three weeks ago. He had to have pins put in the hand and now it is infected. He went to surgery this evening to have the pins removed and the dead tissue cut out. He is on a morphine pain pump but not using it much.

He came back to the unit from surgery about 7 PM and slept until 9 PM. He started waking up when a girl came to visit him. My PCA told me he has not urinated since he came back from surgery. I put a urinal next to the bed and told him to try to use it. At 11 PM he still had not urinated and I told him he needed to try. One of his friends was in the room and asked what would happen if he did not go. I said he had to urinate, or I would have to put a catheter in. The patient said he would go in a few minutes, and he did.

I was reading his chart and saw he fractured his hand when he punched a tree. Pins were put in and the hand got infected. He went to his doctor two days ago when his hand started swelling up. He was prescribed antibiotics but never had the prescription filled.

Another of my patients is a woman about my age with Burkitt's lymphoma, a kind of cancer which usually forms a large tumor in the jaw area. She is on a high dose of continuous chemotherapy and her hair is starting to fall out. When I went in the room at about 8 PM her husband was there with their ten-year-old son. The boy was sitting on the bed playing cards with his mother. I really hope the chemo works for her.

November 17, 2003

It is Monday morning, and I am home from work. Last night we had eleven patients to start and got two admits. Staffing was me and Beth with one PCA. At 11 PM they tried to give us a third admit. I called the nursing supervisor and asked her if she could send us another PCA because staffing with fourteen patients should be two nurses and two PCAs. She said she did not have another PCA, but she would send the third admit to another floor.

The confused patient who was yelling Saturday night was yelling again. The day shift nurse said she yelled all day. Her daughter said she has been yelling like that for months. She yells: "Help me! Hurry!" over and over. Beth said the only way to make her stop yelling is to give Ativan. That makes her sleep. But the family said they do not want it to be given anymore because it makes her sleep all the time.

She tries to get out of bed, but she is not strong enough to stand. She has IV fluid running to a central line, and I was worried she would pull it out. I gave her a shot of Haldol IM in the hip again last night. This time I gave her double the dose that I gave her the night before. She is not my patient, but I have been giving IM shots for Beth's patients.

The boy with the infected hand was transferred to the orthopedic unit Sunday morning. He came to our unit at about 9 PM and asked if he could be moved back. He said that whenever he called for something it took about forty-five minutes before anyone came. And when he had friends visiting, he was told his friends could not sit on his bed. I told him he would have to talk to his doctor about it, but the orthopedic surgeon usually wanted all his patients on that unit.

One of my patients is an older man who is confused. At about 10 PM his daughter asked me to go in and tell him where he was because he did not believe he was in a hospital. He has been in the same room for days, but he does not remember.

He kept taking off his gown and covers. He can use a urinal, but he has been urinating in the bed. We had to change the sheets at least twice each night. Sometimes he calls to go to the bathroom and the PCA gets him up and walks him there.

Another of my patients was a sixty-seven-year-old man with lung cancer. He had a chest tube removed a few days ago. His son stayed with him last night. At about 5 AM we got a call from the telemetry unit, and they said they had one of our patients. He had left the unit and wandered across the hospital. A telemetry PCA brought him back in a wheelchair. The patient was alright but the dressing where his chest tube had been removed was soaked with clear yellow fluid. I cleaned the site and changed the dressing.

His son said the patient had been getting up all night and had walked into the room of the woman with Burkitt's lymphoma and woke her up. The son was not able to stay awake all night and watch his father. I told him we would put a bed alarm on his bed so when he got up, we would know.

At 3 AM one of my patients had an IV antibiotic due. She is a nice white lady in her 70s with an accent from the north-east, maybe New Jersey. She always has her hair fixed nice and her make-up on. Saturday night she told me a story about the time she left her hair-dresser's place after dark and got lost. She usually does not drive at night. She ended up at the airport and police stopped her. She told them she was lost, and they made sure she got home.

She has two toes that are infected and have turned black. She thinks they can be treated with antibiotics, but I can tell they will have to be amputated. When I went in to start her antibiotic, I saw her IV line was not working. A regular IV line usually lasts only about two or three days.

I removed it and told her I was going to start a new one. I got it in on the first try and was pleased with myself. She has good veins and I said: "I think this is the best IV line I have ever put in." She said that was good, and she was glad I enjoyed my work. I said: "Yes I do, most of the time."

About 5:45 AM the phlebotomist (lab technician who draws blood for lab tests) went into one of Beth's patients' room and found the patient on the floor. She was a large older woman who had fallen while trying to get up to go to the bathroom. The floor was wet with urine. The patient said she had been on the floor a long time and her leg hurt. It took all three of us to get the woman up and back to bed. We paged the doctor to get orders. I was sure she would need an X-ray on the leg she said was hurting. It was swollen and red.

The ER called and said they were sending another admit. The room the patient was supposed to go in was not cleaned yet. Housekeeping had been called to clean it, but they never came. I called housekeeping and ordered a "stat clean." I took report on the admit at about 6 AM and told them the room was not ready yet, and I would call them when it was. I stalled until about 7 AM so the patient would not get to the floor until after shift change.

The secretary I had reported last week came in at 7AM and did not start to work until about 7:30 as usual. We were busy and we needed bed alarms ordered for two patients. The phone was ringing constantly, and she would not answer it until after the day-shift nurses came out of report.

Surgery called and said they were coming for my patient with

Burkitt's lymphoma. I did not know anything about her going to surgery. I just said "okay" and then asked the patient about it. She told me her doctor said her surgery had to be postponed because her white blood cell count was too low, due to the chemo she was on. I called surgery back and was told I needed to call the surgeon and tell him. I was told his name and I asked the secretary to page him. She said it would be a few minutes because she was busy paging other doctors (probably for the day shift nurses).

A little later the surgeon called and was upset because no one had notified him about the surgery being canceled. He gave me his cell phone number and said he wanted me to call the other doctor and put him through. I do not even know how to do that (I have never been trained on the secretary's phone system). I wrote the number with a note and gave it to the secretary. I checked the patient's chart to make sure I had not missed anything. There was nothing written about the surgery being ordered or canceled. I told the day shift nurse and left.

November 19, 2003

I worked an extra 3 PM to 11:30 PM shift yesterday on Oncology. We had three nurses, one PCA and a secretary. We had twelve patients to start and got three admits. The patient who had been yelling all the time finally stopped. She seemed calm and knew where she was. She talked, sat up and ate supper. The confused patient who had wandered off the unit was discharged home at about 5 PM, just before the supper trays came to the floor. I was hungry so I had his tray.

The IV site I placed in the woman with the necrotic toes was no good when I started her IV antibiotic, so I removed it and tried to place another one. This time I could not get it. Her vein would just roll away when I tried to get the needle in. I called the nursing supervisor and the same thing happened when he tried to do it. Finally, a young nurse who recently graduated from nursing school, and is charge-nurse on this shift, got it in.

The woman who fell Monday morning has a broken femur. The X-ray showing it was just done yesterday. On Monday the doctor who was notified only ordered X-rays of her hips because she has had hip replacements. The hips were fine, and no one thought to X-ray the leg that was hurting, red and swollen. She is scheduled to have surgery on it tomorrow.

November 21, 2003

I worked another 3 PM to 11:30 PM shift yesterday. I had the lady with the gangrene toes again. Her doctor told her tonight that the front half of the foot would have to be amputated. I went into her room to give her Darvocet for pain just after he told her. She said she just felt sick about having half of her foot cut off. She did not know how she was going to be able to walk. I tried to make her feel better. I told her she would be able to walk with a cane or a walker, and the necrotic tissue needed to be removed before she could get better. She accepted that, and said she already had a wheelchair at home. Then she called her family and told them. Her surgery is scheduled for tomorrow. I took her consent form in, and she signed it.

The female patient who had been yelling on the weekend was still calm. She even used the call button when she needed something. She sat up in bed at supper time and I cut up her chicken up for her. After supper she had to have a BM and I put the bedpan under her. Our PCA was on her lunch break. I needed to collect a stool sample for a lab test. I got a specimen container and a plastic spoon and put a glob of the stool in the container. She said: "Oh my God! What are you doing with that?!" I told her I had to have a sample to send to the lab. I cleaned her bottom and made sure she was comfortable. She said her hips hurt and I gave her some Tylenol. She wanted something stronger, but her doctor wrote "no narcotics" on her chart because of her yelling spells. She is scheduled to go to the rehab unit tomorrow.

November 23, 2003

I am working my regular Saturday shift on Oncology. It's midnight and finally quiet. Staffing is me and Beth with one PCA. We have twelve patients including two admits that are already here. We could get one or two more admits.

My patient with the gangrene toes has not had her surgery yet. It was postponed until Monday because her surgeon had to do an emergency heart surgery yesterday, when she was scheduled to have her amputation. She has a lot of pain in the foot, but she still gets up to the bedside commode herself. I gave her Darvocet for the pain at 8 PM.

I have another patient who has been here before. I think she is dying. She has cancer that started in the breast and has spread. She had a mastectomy, but it was done too late. She has family in her room, and they are talking about making her a DNR. I hope they sign the papers before she stops breathing. Otherwise, we will have to call a "code blue" and try to resuscitate her. Pushing on the chest during CPR often breaks ribs, especially in older patients. Then she would be sent to the ICU and probably be intubated. That is an unpleasant way to die, and it just prolongs the death process.

Another of my patients transferred from PCU (Progressive Care unit) today. It is a unit with a level of care between our unit and ICU. She had abdominal surgery recently. She has a vertical incision with staples in her abdomen and a colostomy draining liquid stool to a bag. Neither me nor the PCA were told she had a colostomy, so I am glad I noticed it before the bag got too full.

It is 8:15 AM now and I am home. The second half of the shift was crazy. We got a third admit and they tried to send a fourth. Our fax machine and tube system were both not working. I went to Rehab and sent new orders to the pharmacy using their fax machine. While I was on Rehab, I heard a familiar voice calling: "Help me! Help me!" It was the lady who had been yelling so much last weekend but was better on Tuesday and Thursday. A PCA told me she acts more confused than she really is just to get attention. She pretends to have anxiety attacks and said she has "closet-phobia."

Both of my admissions last night were "total care" patients (they cannot do anything for themselves; they are incontinent, cannot turn, eat or drink without assistance). The first was an old Spanish-speaking man who had a mass in his left lung, renal failure and a stroke three years ago that caused left-sided weakness. He was trying to cough up fluid from his lungs, but he was too weak to do it. His lungs sounded coarse, he had a sore throat and trouble swallowing. He had a Foley catheter draining urine that was the color of Coke.

My second admit was a young man from a group home. He has cerebral palsy, is developmentally delayed and has a history of seizures. He seemed happy and just smiled at me when I talked to him. He was admitted because of vomiting, but the ER said they had not seen any vomiting. Our PCA told me that when a caregiver at the group home wants to go to a party or something, he will make up an excuse to take a patient to the ER. Once he turns the patient over to a nurse there, he is free to go, and if he does not go right back to the group home no one will know. I did not find anything wrong with the boy (other than his baseline medical problems).

November 24, 2003

It is Monday morning 5:30 AM and I am on Oncology. We got two admits and now the unit is full. Staffing is me and Beth with two PCAs.

I discovered the young man I admitted last night with cerebral palsy can understand what is said to him. He moves his eyes from right to left for "yes" or up and down for "no." He was here three weeks ago and had a feeding tube placed in his stomach. The reason he vomited was probably because too much of the liquid nutrition was being put in at once. He does fine with half a can at a time, but his doctor ordered one and a half cans at a time. That amount makes him vomit. He will be going back to the group home in a few hours.

I have the lady with the gangrene toes, and she is scheduled for surgery today. Her IV site had to be changed again. I tried using a smaller size IV needle and got it started on the second try. She is worried the infection is spreading up her foot to her leg. I assured her the IV antibiotics would get rid of the infection if it did spread to her leg. I gave her Darvocet three times, and she is sleeping now.

November 28, 2003

Yesterday was Thanksgiving and we had a big family dinner at our house. My mother Lynn is visiting, and Allen's mother Nikki was also there. Alex, Susie and my brother Jim were there. Allen's brother came with his wife and two boys. Nikki's husband John did not come this year. He has recently been diagnosed with Alzheimer's and he is not comfortable around a lot of people. This was the first year in a long time that John has not cut the Thanksgiving turkey. I cooked a large one and we had plenty of food. My mother baked apple pies with apples from her trees and Nikki brought chocolate and lemon cream pies.

Tonight, I am working an extra 3 PM to 11:30 PM shift on Rehab. The patient who yells is here. She started yelling at about 6 PM and told her nurse to call her nephew. He said he would come to see her by 8 PM. He was a few minutes late and she started yelling again. When he arrived, he pushed her around the unit in a wheelchair and she was happy.

November 29, 2003

It is Saturday night 11 PM and I am on Oncology. We only have nine patients, so staffing is just me and Beth. We will probably get admits later but it is quiet now. I have the lady who had the gangrene toes. She had surgery four days ago and is doing okay. She still has pain in that foot and seems depressed. She had family visiting tonight at about 8 PM and that perked her up some. Her son, his wife and a teenage granddaughter came from out of town. She is going to start physical therapy tomorrow and should be able to walk again before she goes home.

I also have the little old Hispanic man I admitted last weekend. He is breathing better now. He has a NG tube (nasal gastric tube, a plastic tube that goes in through the nose and down to the stomach and can be used to suction out fluid or give medication and nutritional feedings) with a continuous feeding. He still has a Foley catheter but now his urine is yellow. He is alert and has not complained of any pain.

November 30, 2003

It is Sunday 9 PM, and I am on Oncology. We have ten patients. Staffing is me, Beth and one PCA. We have a secretary until 11 PM. One of my patients was a transfer today from PCU (pulmonary care unit). She was admitted because she took an overdose of phenobarbital. It was prescribed for her dog because it has seizures. The day shift nurse who had her was Shelia. She told me she thought the lady has bipolar disorder (a major psychological disorder characterized by episodes of mania, depression, or mixed mood). Shelia asked her if she was bipolar, but the lady said: "What are you talking about?" Shelia said the patient was manic all day. She was constantly walking around in the room while talking on her phone. But she is alright now and should be discharged in the morning.

The little old Hispanic man said to me: "Hi, how are you doing?" It surprised me because I did not think he spoke English. I think he picked up that phrase since he has been here. He seems a lot better.

The lady who had her toes removed said her doctor checked her foot today and did not like the way it looked. I cannot see it because it is covered by a dressing that is only changed on the day shift. She is still on IV antibiotics, and I hope it will be okay. Often if the incision does not heal well, especially if there is poor blood circulation, the patient must have surgery again and have more cut off. Dead tissue will never heal and must be removed. I gave her Darvocet for pain.

December 04, 2003

I am working an extra 11 PM to 7:30 AM shift on the Telemetry unit. All the patients here wear a monitor that sends a signal to the nurses' station where a tech watches their heart rhythms on a screen. It is a large and busy unit. The shifts are stressful, and staff turnover rate is high. The staffing on this unit should be about five patients per nurse, but over the last year it has usually been seven patients per nurse. Most of the nurses on our unit do not like to float here.

One of the day-shift nurses who works from 7 AM to 7:30 PM forgot to give report on one of her patients before she left. I got the patient at 11 PM but could not find who to get report from. Then I discovered he did not have a nurse for the last four hours. It was a good thing he had a heart monitor on, so at least the tech was monitoring his heart rhythm. He is diabetic and missed his insulin and other medications at bedtime. He was alright so I did not tell him what happened, and I gave him everything he missed at about 11:45 PM.

One of my patients has HIV, Pericarditis (fluid around the heart) and end-stage renal disease. He is a young black man only thirty years old. The monitor tech is concerned about the height of his ST wave. I do not know what that means, but the charge nurse knows I am not trained for this unit so she will take care of any heart related problems. The tech told me she hopes the patient does not code on us. I checked on him and he seems okay.

Another of my patients is a nice middle-aged woman who had a cardiac catheterization (a tiny scope is used and enters a main artery at the groin. It is threaded through the artery to the heart to look for problems) done today. The patient is doing fine but they found she needs to have a heart valve replaced.

I also have a confused older man. Earlier this evening, before I got here, a PCA found him sitting on the floor in urine and stool. He had a bed alarm that should have gone off when he got out of bed, but it did not work. A new alarm was ordered and when I went in to put it on, I noticed that the old one had just not been attached correctly. And the patient was out of bed again. The side rails of the bed were all up and he had gone over them. It was lucky he was not hurt.

December 7, 2003

It is Sunday night, and I am on Oncology. We have fifteen patients, and the unit is full. The areas where remodeling is being done are starting to look nice.

Our unit does not have a manager anymore. Sharon was demoted to float pool nurse. No one will say why, but I think it is because of Joe. I guess the director of nursing or someone in administration blamed her for hiring Joe, or for not monitoring him closely enough. I heard he did something wrong while employed at his last job, and I think his nursing license was suspended for a while. Sharon probably was giving him a second chance. The manager of another unit is doing our scheduling now.

Last night, Saturday, was too busy. I did not slow down all night and left an hour late in the morning. One of my patients was a sweet older man who has prostate cancer and had blood in his urine. He had a three-way catheter with normal saline irrigation running in continuously through his penis to his bladder. There were new orders on his chart that were written on the day shift but not signed-off by his nurse.

The doctor had written to slow the rate of the irrigation and manually irrigate the bladder with a syringe and sterile water every six hours. Then he changed his mind and wrote to disregard those orders and manually irrigate every six hours. I stopped the irrigation and called the pharmacist to ask him what he thought the doctor wanted done. He agreed with me that the continuous irrigation should be stopped, and the manual irrigation done every six hours.

I irrigated the patient's bladder about every three hours all night because he was passing a lot of blood and I was afraid it would clot and clog the catheter. At about 4 AM when I was checking all the orders for the day, I read the order over again and thought I might have made a mistake by stopping the continuous irrigation, but I was not sure. I had problems with other patients and got the call from ER that I was getting a second admit. I did not have time to worry about the bladder irrigation. Even if it needed to be re-started, I did not have the tubing I would need.

In the morning when Shelia came in, she asked me about the patient. When I told her what I had done she knew right away that the doctor did not want the continuous irrigation stopped. She had been talking to him when he wrote the orders, but she got busy and forgot to sign them off before she went home. She called him and he was upset. He told her to file an incident report on me. He had wanted the continuous irrigation and the manual irrigation both done.

I stayed late and watched Shelia do the manual bladder irrigation. I had been putting the sterile saline in the Foley line and letting it drain back out into the bag. She was putting the saline in and then drawing it back out into the large 70cc syringe that we used. The syringe would fill up with saline, blood and clots. Then she would empty the contents of the syringe into a basin, re-fill the syringe with sterile saline and start again. She did this several times until it looked like the bladder was flushed out well. I learned how to do a manual bladder irrigation. Thanks to Shelia's experience the patient was fine.

My first admit Saturday night was a twenty-one-year-old man with a ruptured appendix. He came to the ER in the afternoon and had emergency surgery. He was okay when I got him at about 10 PM, but the nurse giving me report said he had not urinated since before he went to surgery. He was sleeping for the first two hours after he came to our unit, but at 1 AM I made him get out of bed and sit in a chair. He was sore from the surgery and did not want to get up, but I told him he had to get up and urinate.

His pregnant girlfriend and two male friends were in the room with him. Over the next three hours I went into the room a few times and asked him if he had urinated. He said he could not go. I told him to get up to the bathroom and leave the sink running. Hearing running water sometimes helps. At 4 AM I told him to go back to bed. I called the doctor and got an order to place a Foley catheter.

This was the first time I had put a catheter in a man. It is easier than placing one in a woman. But it is something I had never been instructed on. I found that the best way to do it was to grip the shaft firmly with my left hand to keep it straight, while holding the catheter in my right hand. Otherwise, the shaft would bend, making it hard for the catheter to go through. And of course, it is important to use lubrication. It was left in place until about 4 PM today, when the day shift nurse removed it. The boy was finally able to urinate tonight at about 10 PM. He is very sore because they had to open him up when his appendix was removed, but he is going to be alright.

I have the patient who had the gangrene toes removed. She had to go back to surgery and her leg was amputated just below the knee. I was a little angry at her doctor for not acting quicker when the infection was just in her toes. Hopefully the leg will heal, and she will not have any more problems with it. She is doing okay, and her sister was here to visit her tonight. Her sister has the same accent and is very nice. She brought a box of chocolates and offered one to me when I went into the room.

The little old Hispanic man who was a DNR went home on Friday. He was doing much better.

One of my patients tonight is a young Hispanic woman. She has been gaining weight around her abdomen lately and having pain. She came to the ER, and they found a mass on her spleen the size of a football. She will probably have surgery Monday or Tuesday. Hopefully the mass is just a cyst or a benign tumor and not cancer.

Her IV infiltrated (IV fluid leaking out or into surrounding tissue) and I started a new one in her hand. She has not complained or asked for pain medicine. She talks on her cell phone with her family most of the time. I can tell she has been crying although she always tries to smile when I come in to ask how she is doing. I know she is nervous about what they will find when she goes to surgery. They will not know what the mass is until after it is removed.

I was helping pull a patient up in bed and strained my right shoulder. It was another nurse's patient and she asked if I could help. We each got a grip on the fabric pad we keep under patients who are incontinent or must be turned and pulled up. She said: "one, two, three" like we usually do before we pull up a patient, but when we pulled, the patient did not move. Then I noticed the nurse had not put the bed down flat. The patient's back was up at a slight angle. That would have been okay if the patient was light, but this woman was heavy. I am careful about how I lift and pull up patients, but this time I was in a hurry and the room was too dark for me to see the bed was not flat.

December 15, 2003

It is Monday morning, and the weekend is over. I worked an extra shift Friday night from 3 PM to 11:30 PM on the Rehab unit. The lady who had her toes and then lower leg amputated is there now. She was not my patient, but I thought about stopping by her room just to say hello. I got an admit and was busy for the rest of the shift, so I did not get a chance to.

On Saturday night I had another patient with a bladder irrigation. This one was a Hispanic man who did not speak English. He had an abscessed prostate. He had irrigation running into his bladder through an incision in his abdomen. The dressing where it went in was bloody. The irrigation fluid drained out through a Foley catheter in his penis and into a bag which could hold 3000 ml and could be emptied as needed. His urine was bloody with a lot of clots. I was glad I stayed late last week, and Shelia showed me how to do manual bladder irrigation.

At about 9 PM he started complaining of pain. His wife and several adult children were in the room with him. I gave him pain medicine twice, but the pain got worse. At about 10 PM I realized the irrigation fluid was running in, but it was not coming out. He did not have orders to manually irrigate his bladder, but I knew it needed to be done so I did it. But it did not work. The Foley line was completely clotted off. I stopped the irrigation fluid and IV fluid and called the doctor. He told me to do manual bladder irrigation, and I told him I had already tried it and it did not work. Then he told me to change the Foley catheter and put in the largest size.

The patient's children had left but his wife was staying the night. She turned her head the other way while I removed the old catheter and put the new one in. He was in a lot of pain. When I got the new catheter in, bloody urine squirted out. I managed to get it connected to the tubing draining to the bag without getting any on my uniform, but the bed got wet. The line drained well after that. It got clotted-up once, but I did manual irrigation and got the clots out. I am starting to feel like an expert with bladder irrigation.

Sunday night was busy. We had to move a patient to another room because the second phase of the remodeling is going to start Monday morning. Another six rooms are going to be worked on, and we were supposed to have all the hospital furniture and equipment out of the rooms that the work was going to start on in the morning. The day shift on Sunday had an extra nurse who was supposed to coordinate the moving, but they did not get it done. I did not have time to worry about it on the night shift. Staffing was me and Beth with two PCAs. I had six patients at the start of the shift, spent a lot of time on my bladder irrigation guy and then got an admit.

My admit was an old lady from a nursing home who had been here before. She had a bad urinary tract infection. She also had Alzheimer's and chronic heart failure. She opened her eyes but did not speak or move. When a PCA from the ER brought her to our unit, she told us the patient needed her teeth brushed. I could see what looked like rotten food between her teeth. It looked like it had been there a long time and most of it had turned black. She had a diaper on that was full of stool, so we had to wash and change her when she got to the room. She had a Foley catheter draining a little urine that was cloudy and concentrated.

The ER doctor ordered IV fluids and antibiotics that needed to be started. He also ordered a nasal-gastric tube to be put down through her nose into her stomach so that she could be given her regular medications. I really did not want to put the NG tube in. I was afraid she would gag and vomit. She could choke on the vomit and die. A patient must sit up and cooperate when this kind of tube is put in. This lady was like dead weight and not breathing well. I was not sure if she would even make it through the night.

About an hour after I started the IV fluid and antibiotics, I noticed she seemed to have more trouble breathing. I listened to her lungs again and they sounded a little wet. I thought fluid was getting into her lungs because her heart was not strong enough to pump fluid through her body like it should. This happens often to patients who have CHF (chronic heart failure). I called her doctor and he said to turn the IV fluid rate down. I told him I did not think I could put the NG tube in. He said if I could not get it in, we could hold her oral medications until she could swallow. I wrote the order that way, but I did not try to place the NG tube. I did not think it was safe to try in the condition she was in, and I did not have time anyway.

One of Beth's patients was a white woman in her forties who inhaled a thumb tack into a lung. She said she was standing on a stepladder while putting up Christmas decorations. She had a thumb tack between her lips she was going to use to place something on the wall. She slipped and her mouth came open. She must have taken a deep breath because the tack ended-up in her lung. It had to be removed. Now she has a chest tube and is in a lot of pain. She will be alright but probably need to stay in the hospital for several days.

At 7 AM when the day shift came in, I was still doing patient care and paperwork. The manager from one of the medical-surgical units is managing our unit and came. She was on our unit to see that equipment was moved out of the rooms where remodeling was going to be started. The construction workers were on the unit promptly at 7 AM and the rooms were not empty yet. When the first six rooms were worked on, some of the equipment in them got lost. So, when the equipment is taken out of rooms today, it is supposed to be placed in a storage area.

No secretary showed up this morning and the phone was ringing, with no one to answer it but me. Also, the day shift's staffing was a nurse short. Beth was moving things out of the rooms that are going to be worked on, but I did not have time to help. She did not get an admission last night.

At 7:30 when the day shift came out of report, the phone was still ringing, and the call lights were going off. Our temporary manager, who I have never met, was helping Beth. I was wondering if the manager would ask me to stay and help. I would have stayed for a while if she had asked me to, but she did not speak to me. I just finished some charting and left.

December 20, 2003

It is 3:30 AM and I am working an extra 11 PM to 7:30 AM shift on the Rehab unit. We only have eleven patients with two nurses and one PCA. It is quiet now. The hospital had Mexican food for the staff tonight. We took turns going down to the cafeteria to get our plate.

The patient with the gangrene toes and amputations went home today. I asked about her and was told she is doing well. Her husband cannot get out of bed without help, so they have a home health person to take care of them at home.

I spent the last two days putting new floor tile in our first-floor bathroom. Allen and I did it ourselves. He did most of the work, but I helped. We called a plumber to put the toilet back in place when the floor was done. Our house was built in the 1960s and is starting to need work done on it.

We were so busy working on the bathroom and going Christmas shopping that we had not checked our e-mail for about a week. Our friends Bill and Teresa sent us an e-mail a few days ago about Bill. He had a biopsy done on his tonsil and the results showed cancer. Bill and

Teresa are a married couple our age, and we usually meet them about once a week at a club that has karaoke. They both smoked when we first met them, but they stopped about a year ago. Then Bill started again. I do not think he ever quit completely but he tried to cut down. Teresa said he would go outside to smoke.

Bill works for the railroad and Teresa does computer programming from her home office. Bill is going to work for two more weeks and then take off for a while to have testing done to see if the cancer is in his lungs. I am worried about him. Even though I work on an oncology unit, I do not know much about cancer and the different kinds of it. I hope the cancer Bill has, is one that can be cured.

December 24, 2003

Tonight is Christmas Eve. My mother is here visiting, and Jessica is here from Washington with her two kids. Jessica is staying for about two weeks. My younger sister drove here from Idaho with her three boys. She will be staying with us for a few days until her husband can get off work and fly here. Then they are going to visit his family.

My mother baked a ham but miscalculated the cooking time and it was not ready for supper. I took some frozen precooked chicken out, and we had it at about 6 PM. We had to eat early because everyone wanted to open presents, and I had to take a nap before going to work. I signed-up to work 11 PM to 7:30 AM on Rehab. The late-night shift on Rehab should be easy and I will get holiday pay for tonight.

December 25, 2003

It is early Christmas morning, and I am on Oncology. I signed up to work on Rehab, but when I got to work, I was told to go to Oncology instead. Staffing is me and Ruth, the charge nurse who was working with Joe the night he was fired. We have one PCA.

I heard tonight that Joe was found in his apartment, dead from an overdose. I feel sorry for his parents, losing a son just before Christmas.

One of Ruth's patients died tonight. It was expected. He was an old man from a nursing home and a DNR. The patient was brought to the ER on December 23rd and sent to our unit. The ambulance staff had put him in a body bag, leaving the top unzipped. They probably thought he would not make it to the hospital alive, but he did. The staff in the ER left him in the body bag and brought him up to our unit that way.

The PCA for the patient that night was the laziest one on our unit, a woman in her fifties from India. She had told Ruth, who had the patient that shift, about the patient being in a body bag. Ruth told her to get the other PCA and take him out of it. They did not do it and he was still in the bag when the day shift nurse went in. He had a Foley catheter, so the bag did not get wet. The day shift staff took him out of the bag and placed it on the countertop by the sink in his room.

Tonight, he died and was put back in it. His son came in to sign the consent form to release the body to a funeral home, but he did not even peek in the room. He just signed the form at the nurses' station and left.

Ruth admitted an older woman who fell at home, causing a cut on her arm. Then I admitted the woman's husband in the same room. He has chronic bowel problems and was admitted for vomiting and diarrhea. They have been married fifty-seven years and still get along well. They were pleasant and cooperative. Their son stayed until they were both settled into bed.

January 4, 2004

It is early Sunday morning, and I am on Oncology. Staffing is me and Beth with one PCA. The shift has been crazy. One of my patients died before I even got to see her. Then I got an admit who is dying and in severe pain. She has cervical cancer that has spread. She is in renal failure and the area from her abdomen to her toes is so swollen that she looks like a balloon. Her legs are stiff and hard. Her feet are swollen and mushy. She is only thirty-seven years old. I have been giving her morphine every hour.

Admitting just called and I am getting another admit. We have thirteen patients and one coming. One of Beth's patients pulled out her Foley catheter and it took all three of us to put in a new one. The PCA and I each held an arm and a leg while Beth put it in. The patient was fighting us, but we got it done.

January 5, 2004

It is early Monday morning. I am on Oncology with Beth. We have ten patients and one on the way from ER. Tonight, we have the lazy PCA from India. She will sit at the desk and read a magazine when there is work that needs to be done.

The patient with cervical cancer I admitted yesterday is still alive and has a room full of family and friends. Her doctor has told her family that she is not expected to last more than two days. I am giving her hydromorphone (concentrated form of morphine) every hour or so. She is still awake most of the time and is very uncomfortable. Her family members talk to her, but she cannot respond except in moans. She reaches out to them, and they hold her hand.

When I went in to give hydromorphone and check her oxygen saturation, which is starting to drop, she was frantically grabbing at the shirt of a woman who looked like she might be her sister. She pulled on the shirt and the woman laughed and said: "You're going to show everyone my tits if you keep pulling on my shirt like that!"

The family members seemed fascinated by the instrument that checks the oxygen saturation level by putting it over a fingertip. Everyone had to check their own oxygen saturation level with it. No one seemed sad.

But I knew they were all grieving, and I am sure there had already been a lot of crying. A person can only cry for so long in a situation like this. Then it is just a matter of waiting. When it is over there will be tears of sadness and relief.

When I get off work Allen and I are taking my mother to south Texas where her winter home is. It is in a "Snow-Birds" trailer park, which is only for people over fifty-five years old and mostly has retired couples who live up north and spend the winter in South Texas. There is a nice swimming pool with no kids or teenagers around. There are activities like movies, card games, parties, and pot-luck meals. I do not have to be back to work for five days. I am looking forward to getting some sun and going swimming. We will probably go shopping in Mexico.

January 12, 2004

It is Monday morning, and another weekend is over. I worked my regular Saturday and Sunday night shifts on Oncology. Saturday night was busy. I had two admits and Beth had one. Sunday night started out okay, but then Beth got an admit who wanted narcotics. The ER doctor had written on her chart "absolutely no narcotics." The patient was a young woman who has been here often. She is only twenty-seven years old and has diabetes, which causes a slowing of her gastric system. That causes pain in her abdomen.

Her last admission was only five days ago, and the doctor admitting her wrote for her to have IV fluid and hydromorphone for pain. She got it for a few days and then was discharged. Now she is back, and she wants the hydromorphone again. The ER doctor who admitted her this time does not believe she has enough pain to need narcotics.

She got only one small dose of pain medicine in the ER, and by the time she came to our floor she was screaming constantly. It was waking up all our patients and she would not stop. Beth called the doctor and got an order for one dose of Ativan to calm her down. That stopped the yelling for about two hours but then she started again. Beth and I tried to calm her down, but it did not help. She started crying and yelling:

"Mommy! Mommy! I want my mommy!" Beth called the doctor again and got an order for one dose of a non-narcotic IV pain medicine. That helped for a while and then she started crying and yelling again. Finally, at about 7 AM one of the oncology doctors was called and gave the order for hydromorphone.

One of my patients was a nice lady who is a librarian. I admitted her on Saturday with vomiting and bloody diarrhea. It was so bad that at one point she was sitting on the bedside commode with diarrhea while her head was leaning over the bed, and she was vomiting into a basin. I gave her some IV Phenergan and it helped. She was started on IV antibiotics and fluids.

Sunday, she had to drink a gallon of laxative called Golytely (it comes in powdered form, is fruit flavored and added to a gallon of water) so she could be scoped on Monday. She started drinking it Sunday at 3 PM and finished it at 8 PM. She had to sit on the bedside commode most of the time until about 10 PM. She was nauseous and I gave her more Phenergan. Her IV site needed to be changed and I started a new one. I got it placed on the first try. She had good veins. Transport from the GI department came to get her at 7 AM this morning.

When I admitted her on Saturday, she said she had been having stomach pain off and on for about two years. She should have seen a doctor about it a long time ago. I asked about her family history for the admission paperwork, and she told me her father had stomach ulcers and her mother had colon problems.

Yesterday Allen's daughter Sarah called and said her son, Jason has pinkeye and cannot go to day care. Usually, she could work at home when she cannot go to the office, but Tuesday she has an important meeting. Her husband works for the federal government and is out of town for a few weeks at a training camp. We are going to drive to their home this afternoon so we can baby-sit for Jason tomorrow. He is nineteen months old and our first grandchild. I am looking forward to taking care of him.

January 15, 2004

It is 3 AM and I am working an extra shift on Rehab. We had a good time with our grandson. It turned out that he did not have pinkeye after all, but just allergies. We stayed with him on Tuesday and came home that night. The weather was warm, and we pulled him in his wagon to a nearby playground. It was nice to spend some time outside in the sun.

Tonight, Rehab staffing is two nurses and one PCA. We have fifteen patients. It is quiet now except for a patient of mine who is confused. He is ninety-one years old and has been talking to himself all night. He is incontinent and we have already had to clean and change him twice. The last time, when I bent over to put a fresh gown on him, he coughed right in my face. I hope he does not have a cold.

Another of my patients is a 350-pound woman who has a fractured leg. The PCA called me in after the lady used the bedpan. We had to put fresh pads under her, and the PCA wanted me to see the patient's yeast infection. It is the largest yeast infection I have ever seen. It has been treated with medicated cream for a few days, so it is better now than it was. It is not bright red anymore, but it still looks painful. The rash extends from her lower abdomen down through her groin area and around her buttocks. It also covers the inside of both thighs. She is only fifty-eight years old. I asked her how long she has had the rash, and she said she got it from lying in urine on the surgical unit after she had surgery for her broken leg. I know the medical/surgical unit is busy, but a rash like this is caused by days of neglect. It should not have been allowed to happen in a hospital.

February 4, 2004

It is 3 AM and I am working an extra shift on Rehab again. My right shoulder has been hurting. I have been trying to use that arm as little as possible. I have not missed any work, but my doctor gave me a prescription for a muscle relaxer and said if the pain does not get better soon, I should have therapy. I do not have time for that.

Tonight, I have a patient who has been on Rehab for about two weeks. He is a young Hispanic man who fell off a ladder while working on a construction site. He hit his head and was in a coma for a long time. The accident was about four months ago. Now he can move his arms and legs and tries to speak. He has a tracheostomy and a nasal gastric tube. He keeps pulling out his IV line and NG tube, so sometimes his hands are tied down. There is a lot of fluid coming out of his trach. I can hear the gurgling noise it makes from out in the hall. He must be suctioned about every hour, or he would probably choke on the fluids. I do not know why he is on the rehab unit. He is not ready to exercise yet.

Rehab is quiet tonight. We have eight patients and two nurses. We do not have a PCA. One of my patients is a very confused older white woman. She is doing well and expected to be sent home tomorrow. But I need to sit where I can see her room because I am worried that she will wander off the unit. She has a bed alarm that rings when she gets out of bed, but it upsets her, and it wakes up other patients. I turned it off for now.

She has no short-term memory. Earlier in the evening she kept asking me what time it was. She would go in her room for a few minutes, and then come out to the hall and have no idea where she was.

She would ask what time it was again. She does not realize I am a nurse, and she is in a hospital. The last time I put her back to bed she said: "Do you have enough cover? You need to go to bed." I said: "I have some work to do. I'm going to stay up a little longer." I guess she thinks I am a family member.

Another of my patients is an older man who was admitted after a heart attack. He had compression sleeves on his legs that are supposed to help with blood flow. He does not understand what they are, and thinks we are angry at him and punishing him by making him wear them. I tried to explain what they are, and told him we were just following doctor's orders, and they were good for him. But he laughed and did not believe me. He asked me: "What have I done to you to deserve this?!" I told him I would take them off for a while, but I had to put them back on later. He wants to get out of bed, but it was all I could do just to turn him. I told him someone would get him up in the morning.

The remodeling is still going on in the oncology unit. The new counter tops are in place at the nurses' station, and they are nice. There is more room and more computers than before. We also have new chairs that are comfortable. The only thing I do not like is that the breakroom is so small only four people can sit in it at once. And the new lockers are tiny. I cannot even fit my clipboard in one.

We have been getting more chemotherapy patients than before. I had to give chemotherapy last Saturday night because it was due and there was no one certified to give it in the hospital. The following Monday morning the day shift charge-nurse heard me talking to another nurse about it and she said I should have refused to give it. I talked to the manager who is in-charge of our floor until we get our own manager, and she said she would try to schedule a chemotherapy certification class soon. It is usually a two-day class. Sharon will probably teach it.

Last Sunday night Beth had a patient who needed chemotherapy at 1 AM. I told her to call the supervisor and see if there was a chemo certified nurse in the hospital. Beth has taken the chemo class, but she has not been signed-off yet (a certified chemo nurse must watch her give chemo the first time and sign a form that states she did it correctly). Even if she is certified and signed-off, Beth could not give chemo because she is breastfeeding. She will not go anywhere near chemo for the next few months.

Jackie was working on ICU, and she was sent to hang the chemo. It was nice to see her again and we talked for a few minutes. I did not mention anything about Joe. I asked her if she liked the ICU and she said it was "different." The patients there are usually unconscious. I think she misses having patients she can talk to. She looked sad. She used to have long hair, but she cut it short. It looks more professional now.

One of my patients Sunday night was a woman whose husband bit her hand so bad he broke a blood vessel, and X-rays showed a fragment of some kind in the hand. It is not clear what the fragment is. It could be a piece of bone or a piece of her husband's tooth. She is a quiet black woman thirty-nine years old, with a seventeen-year-old daughter who stays with her most of the time. The supervisor told us the police have not found her husband yet, but he knows what room she is in. He found her car in the parking lot and broke out all the windows. We were told if she is not discharged in the morning, she will be moved to a different room under a fake name.

February 8, 2004

It is 2 AM on Sunday morning and I am working my regular shift on Oncology. Last Friday I had an appointment with the manager of the long-term acute care unit at our hospital. I wanted to see about working there part-time because I heard they pay more than our unit. But I found they pay the same, and I am not qualified to work there because I do not have ACLS (advanced cardiac life support) certification.

I worked Wednesday night on Rehab, and I looked at their schedule and noticed there was only one nurse scheduled for Friday night. I asked the manager on Thursday morning if she needed someone, and she said: "Would you like me to call you?" I said: "I would be glad to work it." Then she said: "I'll put you down." I only wanted the shift because it would be overtime and pay time and a half.

The nursing office called me Friday and left a message that they needed a charge nurse on Oncology from 3 PM to 7 PM. Later they called again and left a message that they needed a charge nurse from 7 PM to 11 PM. I did not take either shift because I thought I was scheduled on Rehab from 11 PM to 7:30 AM.

Friday, I took a nap at 4 PM and slept until 7:30 PM. Then I got up and helped Allen fold clothes for his mother. Her dryer was broken, so he had picked up the wet clothes from her house. She sent over a pot of beef stew, and we had it for supper. I ran on our treadmill for about 30 minutes and then showered and got ready for work. Allen was going out to our favorite karaoke club after he took his mother's laundry to her.

I left for work without calling to make sure I was on the schedule. That was a mistake because when I got to Rehab, I was told that I was not on staffing. I called Allen at his mother's house before he left for the club. I told him to meet me at home and I would change clothes and go with him. When I got home there was a message from the hospital saying they needed a nurse from 11 PM to 7:30 AM. I returned the call and was ready to go back to the hospital but was told they had already found someone to cover the shift. Allen and I went out to the club and had a good time.

Tonight, we have two nurses and two PCAs. I started with seven patients and got an admit. The next admit will be Beth's and I hope we do not get a third one. I had one patient getting chemo and one getting blood at the start of the shift. The one getting blood is a seventy-three-year-old white man with lung cancer and pneumonia. He talks just like Billy Bob Thorton in the movie "Sling Blade." At the start of the shift, he told me he hoped his doctor would discharge him tomorrow. His wife is on the 4th floor, and he has not seen her in three days. I asked him what she is in for, and he rattled off a long list of things. She has CHF, Diabetes, blood clots and then she fell and broke her shoulder.

Later he called for his nurse and when I went in, he had his IV line in his hand. He said: "I just took this thing apart and I don't know why I did it." It was okay, and I just screwed it back together, put up fresh tubing and a bag of IV fluid.

Another patient is a large sixty-nine-year-old white man who has been here before. He came in this time with an allergic reaction to a medication. It is the worst reaction I have ever seen. He has a very red rash covering almost his entire body. His back is completely red, and the rest of his body has splotches all over. He asked me for something to help stop the itching and I gave him IV Benadryl. I started to leave, but then I stopped and asked him if he would like some cream or ointment. He said: "yes." I noticed a bottle of lotion he had brought from home. The label said it was for burns, rash and itching. I started putting it on his legs and as I got to his thighs, I could see his groin was even redder.

He had boxer shorts on, and they were saturated with drainage from the rash. I said he needed to take them off and let his skin get some air. He did, and I got a hospital gown for him and put lotion on his groin. His skin there was bright red and blistered. He yelled that the lotion was burning him there, so I grabbed a towel and started to wipe it off. That hurt more so I let him do it himself. The skin was too sore for him to wipe it, so he just held the towel there. I asked him if he wanted lotion on his back and he said he did. I put lotion all over his back, stomach, chest, neck and arms. I used at least half of the bottle.

February 09, 2004

It is 3 AM Monday morning and I am on Oncology. Tonight, we have three nurses and one PCA. I do not have the patient that sounds like Billy Bob, but I went in his room about midnight because I heard the alarm on his IV pump beeping. His bag of IV fluid was empty and his nurse was busy, so I replaced it. I noticed his lungs sounded like they had fluid in them. I could hear it even without my stethoscope. I thought he might be getting too much IV fluid and it might be leaking into his lungs.

He had a young nurse who floated from another floor. I told her what I thought, and she checked him, but she did not think it sounded too bad. She called Respiratory Therapy and asked them to give him a breathing treatment.

The therapist came and started an inhalation treatment, but after a few minutes the patient was short of breath and started gasping for air. His oxygen saturation level was checked, and it was in the low 80s (it should be between 96 to 100%). He was sitting up on the side of the bed gasping hard for air, while the therapist tried to calm him and keep an oxygen mask on him.

The poor guy was like that for about an hour. His nurse called the doctor, but he never returned her call. After about forty-five minutes she called a respiratory doctor who had been consulted. He gave orders to stop the IV fluid and give Lasix (medication that helps get rid of excess fluid).

I had stopped the IV fluid when the patient first started being short of breath. Our PCA stayed with him and held his hand to try to calm him while he struggled to breathe. I checked on him every few minutes. The respiratory therapist was with him for about half an hour. In the first hour after getting the Lasix he urinated about a liter. After that he started breathing better and went to sleep. He was exhausted from trying so hard just to get enough air.

February 17, 2004

It is 3:30 AM and I am on Rehab working an extra night shift. I was expecting a quiet shift, but we have eighteen patients with two nurses and two PCAs. Nine patients each for nurses is too much on any unit.

One of my patients is a nice white man in his sixties who takes Coumadin, which is a blood thinner. I think his blood got too thin, because the blood vessels in one of his legs started leaking. Now he has large blood blisters all over that leg from the knee to the ankle.

I had to change his dressing because it was saturated. When I took off the old dressing a few of the blood blisters broke. Bloody fluid started running out. I had to grab some towels quickly to keep the bed from getting wet. The leg looked terrible, but I told him it was not as bad as it looked. I told him it should heal up fine after all the blisters drain. I gave him two pain pills, and he said his leg felt much better after some of the fluid drained out. He said it took the pressure off those spots. He slept the rest of the shift.

February 19, 2004

Tonight, I am working an extra 11 PM to 7:30 AM shift on Oncology. We have three nurses and one PCA. Two admits came last shift in my group of patients, but the nurse who had them was an LVN, and he did not do the admission paperwork. Only an RN can do an admission assessment. The nurse is from a foreign country and does not speak English very well. We usually do not use LVNs at our hospital except in Rehab. He must have been floated from there.

The charge nurse last shift was Ruth. She should have made sure the admissions were done, but she was having a hard time with her own patients. She is an over-weight older white nurse, and she just came back to work after having knee surgery. She was limping and complaining about how much her knee was hurting, so I did not say anything about the admissions.

One of my patients tonight is a fifty-six-year-old black woman who looks much older. She has multiple medical problems and lives at an assisted-living home. At the start of shift, she called and wanted help to get comfortable in her bed. She was sitting on the side of the bed and when I started to help her, I noticed she was soiled with BM. I told her I had to get some wet wipes to clean her, and she acted like she was surprised that she was messy. Since we only have one PCA I cleaned her myself.

Later I was checking all my patients' charts and I read her history. She eats dirt out of flowerpots at the assisted-living home. She told her doctor she started eating dirt when she was a little girl in Louisiana, and she saw her mother eating it. There was information in her chart about Pica (eating things that are not food). It said eating clay is so common in some south-eastern states, that clay sold to be eaten can be purchased at markets.

Another one of my patients is the young Hispanic construction worker who fell off a ladder at work. I had him two weeks ago on Rehab and he is on our unit now. He is not a cancer patient, but the rehab doctor finally realized his medical problems were too serious for him to be on that unit.

He is doing much better now. He still has a trach that needs to be suctioned sometimes, but not as often. He has a gastric tube with suction draining excess fluid from his stomach, and a tube going into his small intestine with liquid nutrition being pumped in continuously. He also has a Foley catheter.

He opens his eyes and likes to watch TV. When I went in the room at the start of shift, he was watching a "Girls Gone Wild" commercial and rubbing his penis with the hand he can still move. He was soiled with stool, and I called for the PCA to help clean him. He had a wrist restraint that was not on, and I thought it would be alright to leave it off. But later the respiratory therapist told me he was pulling on his Foley line, so I had to put the restraint back on.

The nursing home he was at before he came here has refused to take him back. The hospital has contacted his family in Mexico, and they want him to come home. The hospital will have to arrange and pay for medical transport to Mexico if no one here will take him. The hospital would be willing to do that if it is the only way he can be discharged.

March 1, 2004

It is Monday morning, and I am home from work. The last few weeks have been busy. I worked three extra shifts each week for the last two weeks. The construction work on the unit is still going on. There is one section left to be done. All the rooms were open for a few days, but then the last section was closed.

When the rooms were all open, a week ago, Beth and I were the only nurses on the weekend night shift. On Saturday I had eight patients to start and then got an admit. On Sunday Beth had eight patients and got an admit. She was not happy about staffing and said we should refuse to take more than eight patients each. It is hard to keep up with patient care and get all the paperwork done on nine patients, especially if one is an admit.

I got a little upset one night because staffing called for two PCAs, but we only had one. I called the nursing supervisor about it, and she said she could not find another PCA. The PCAs on our unit are usually willing to work an extra shift. Their shifts are only eight hours, and they will often stay and work a double shift if asked to. But because the patient load has been so heavy lately, they do not want to work extra. The supervisor did not start calling to try to find another PCA until I complained at 11 PM, when I saw the staffing for the 11 to 7:30 shift. Then she sent us admissions when she knew we were already understaffed.

There is a box for comments. I wrote a note saying that every Saturday and Sunday night patients come to the ER and then are admitted to the units. Why is the person doing staffing not taking this into account? We always must start a shift with the number of staff based on the number of patients we have at that time. But everyone knows we are going to get admissions. And patients rarely leave at night unless they are sent to a funeral home or the morgue.

I am really getting sick of nursing. I can see why so many nurses are unhappy and burnt-out. At the same time, I am becoming more confident as I learn more nursing skills. And I feel good about helping people who are suffering. It is just so frustrating when you are running between patients as fast as you can, trying to take care of them all, and then you get an admission. It is also frustrating when we are short a PCA, and patients are calling to go to the bathroom or needing things done that the PCA usually does. It becomes impossible to do everything.

Lately I have had to keep a list when patients call. I answer the most urgent calls first. The wait time for me to answer a call can be more than forty-five minutes. Then I run in, out of breath and do what they need as quickly as possible. I do not like working that way, and I am afraid mistakes could be made. Also, patients who are not strong enough to get up by themselves often will not wait for twenty minutes or longer to be assisted to the bathroom; they will try to go by themselves. Being short-staffed is not safe.

I had the Hispanic patient who fell off a ladder again this weekend. He should have been discharged but no one will take him. He has a niece in this area, and she was supposed to come and be shown how to take care of him at her home. She probably took one look at his condition and realized she could not care for him alone. He is doing much better, but he cannot get out of bed, is incontinent of stool and still has a trach that needs to be suctioned at times. He also has a feeding tube and a Foley catheter.

One of my patients needed chemotherapy during our shift. Sharon has been promoted to shift supervisor (nurse who is in-charge of all hospital staff during her shift). She is supervisor tonight until 11 PM. I called her and she said Beth should hang the chemo with Jackie, who could come from the ICU. That way Beth could be signed-off and be able to give chemo. Beth is still breast-feeding, and she refused to do it. She was angry at Sharon for expecting her to do it because she had already told her she was still breast-feeding. Beth printed a copy of the hospital's policy which states nurses who are pregnant, or breast-feeding should not administer chemotherapy. She showed it to the nursing supervisor who came on duty at 11 PM.

Jackie came to hang the chemo and told me she has gotten hired at a hospital closer to home. I think she wanted to get away from this hospital and get a fresh start someplace where people do not know about her and Joe. She told me she is getting a $5000 sign-on bonus and is going to make $3 per hour more. This will be the last time she can come to our unit to hang chemo.

March 4, 2004

It is 8:30 AM and I am home after working an extra night shift on Oncology. A patient we had last year is back. He is a young white man about twenty-five years old, and his sister works at our hospital as a secretary. He lives with his mother and sister. Last June he was admitted with what looked like a spider bite on his back. It was probably a Brown Recluse. The tissue around the bite got infected and then the infection spread to other areas of his body. His colon became infected and burst. He had to have a colostomy (surgery that cuts through the colon and brings an end of it out the abdomen so stool empties into a bag). He also had a feeding tube placed into his stomach and was getting liquid nutrition. He had skin grafts taken from his thighs to replace the tissue lost from his back.

He was on our unit for about two months and seemed to be doing well. His sister would visit him every day. When he was discharged home, he was supposed to get outpatient care at the county hospital. He was scheduled to get care for his wounds at the burn unit there. The doctors at the county hospital were going to reverse his colostomy so he would be able to eat and have normal bowel movements again.

Last night he came back to our hospital. His mother called an ambulance because he had been refusing all medical care, including dressing changes since November. He stayed in his bedroom at the apartment he shared with his mother, sister and her son. He had not taken a bath or changed his clothes in months.

The ER staff had to soak his clothes in water just to be able to cut them off. Even then a lot of skin came off with the cloth. He had dressings on that were dated in November. His back was black, mushy and gangrene. He had bedsores on his buttocks and heels. The feeding tube was still in his stomach, though it had not been used in a long time. The site where it went in was infected. The tube was made of a clear plastic and dried black remains from an old feeding could be seen in it.

When he first arrived on Oncology, we thought he must be on our unit by mistake. None of us had ever seen an infection covering as much of the body. He was not a DNR, and we did not think we would be able to keep him alive. We thought he should be in the ICU.

He was my patient. The smell within twenty feet of him was overpowering. It was the smell of rotting flesh. It seemed as if the infection (a flesh-eating bacteria) had invaded his entire body.

He was alert and oriented. He said he had been eating regular food, but he was emaciated. He weighed about 100 pounds. He told me he was angry with the doctor at the county hospital because he refused to do the colostomy reversal until after his wounds healed. And he was upset because he had to wait for a long time to be seen whenever he went to the burn unit. He was also upset because he applied for disability benefits and was denied. He was told he could get a part-time job.

He got depressed, angry and locked himself in his room. He stayed in bed all through December, January and February. His sister said she tried to change his dressings, but he refused. His mother finally called an ambulance because she was worried that he was going to die. His infection is so bad now that I do not know if he will ever recover. He will probably be in the hospital for months.

He is a nice young man, although very needy. I do not mind taking care of him, except that I don't see how I will be able to give him the care he obviously needs, when I already have a heavy load of patients. I hope I do not have to change his dressings. He is in pain when just laying still. I am sure turning so dressings can be changed will be hard to do. Removing his dressings and packing his wounds will be excruciating for him. He will have to be given Morphine or Hydromorphone before any dressing change.

I wore a gown, mask and gloves every time I went in the room. I gave him morphine twice and started his IV antibiotics. He was ordered three units of blood. I talked to him for a few minutes to get information I would need for his admission paperwork, but I could not stand the intense smell.

Last night staffing was me and Beth with two PCAs. We started out with seven patients each and both got an early admit. Then we got two more admits at about 6:45 AM. The unit's cut-off time for our shift having to do the admission paperwork is 6:30 AM, so we did not have to do the admission paperwork on these patients. We made sure the late admits had their IV fluids started. We were out of IV pumps, so I had to go to Rehab to borrow one. By the time I got my admit settled in his room with his IV fluid running it was after 7 AM.

The day shift secretary made me angry again because of her misconception that she only works for the day shift. I told her at 7:20 AM when she finally came to the desk that we had admits. I put the admission orders and forms from the ER in front of her computer and she just walked away and ignored me. I printed the twenty-four-hour charting for all the unit's patients and was going to leave at about 7:50 AM. She saw me with my purse and lunch bag, ready to walk off the unit and said: "Is that your charting that just came off the printer?" She knew it was. She was inferring I needed to file it.

I was too tired to get into an argument with her, so I put down my purse and bag and started to file the papers. While I was doing that, the charge-nurse on the day shift asked me where my new patients' charts were. I told her I had left everything for the secretary.

I pulled my patients' information out from under the papers that had been thrown on top of them and handed it to the charge-nurse. She acted surprised and said: "You mean the bio (short for biological history, which includes the admission assessment and can only be done by the admitting RN) is not done for either one?" She acted like she could not believe I left so much work for her undone. I told her the patients just got to the unit at 6:45 AM and we did not have time to do it. She made some remarks about how one patient's son was gone now so it would be hard to get questions answered. The patient is from Nepal here visiting his son and does not speak English. By this time, it was after 8AM. The son had just left minutes earlier. If the charge nurse was so worried about getting the admission done, she should have talked to him before he left.

Our shift had only two nurses and two PCAs, but the day shift has three nurses, three PCAs and a secretary. Yet they seem to think we do not do our share of the work at night. I really do not care what they think, but it would be nice to go home feeling good about the work I do.

March 12, 2004

It is Friday afternoon, and I am home. I did not work an extra shift all week, and it was nice having a few days off to get things done around the house. But the nursing office just called and asked if I could work for four hours from 3 PM to 7 PM. They offered me a $25 bonus and I took it.

Last weekend was not too bad. The patient with the necrotic back who smelled so bad was supposed to be transferred to the county hospital, but he refused to go. He said he would leave AMA (against medical advice) if we tried to make him go. He got to stay but he was transferred to another floor.

We were happy we did not have to work with that smell anymore. Beth said she dreaded going to work because she might have him as her patient. I did not want to have him as a patient either. His dressings had to be changed twice a day and it took about forty-five minutes to do it.

The Mexican construction worker with the head injury was finally sent home to his parents. The hospital paid for medical transport to Mexico.

March 17, 2004

It is 3 AM and I am on Rehab working an extra shift. It has been quiet tonight. We have eleven patients, two nurses, and one PCA. All my charting is done. I had to do bladder irrigation on an older male patient with a Foley catheter. He had traces of blood in his urine, but he is not having any bleeding now.

Another patient is a Hispanic man in his fifties who fell from a cherry-picker (lift that a man stands in while working on something high) while working on a traffic signal-light. His lift was hit by a large truck, and he fell twenty feet onto his head. The accident happened about a month ago. He had a concussion and spinal injury, but he is doing well. He can talk and swallow. He moves his arms well and can move his legs a little.

He is oozing stool and cannot control it. He tries to urinate in a urinal, but he has no control of his bladder. He was wearing a diaper during the day shift, but the evening shift nurse took it off because his skin is getting too red. I put ointment and powder on him.

I was reading his chart and he is a Vietnam veteran. He was on a bowel program before he came here but his laxative was stopped because he had several small bowel movements. Now he is probably full of hard stool, and loose stool is oozing out around it. This is a problem I have seen often, because staff chart each small bit of stool as a bowel movement. When the doctor reads it, he thinks the patient is having diarrhea.

The rehab nurses have been giving this patient medication to stop the frequent stools. What he really needs is to resume his bowel program and get cleaned out. He has been complaining of abdominal cramps all day, and the rehab nurses have given him pain pills, Pepto-Bismol, and Lomotil. I gave him pain medicine and Milk of Magnesia. I also left a note for the rehab doctor that his bowel program should be resumed.

March 22, 2004

It is 4 AM on Monday morning and I am on Oncology. We started with fifteen patients and an admit on the way. I took the first admit. We have seventeen beds now and the second admit came at about 1 AM, so we are full. Beth called in sick Saturday night because she and her baby both have bad colds. She came to work tonight and worked four hours. The supervisor let her go home at 11 PM and sent a nurse here from another floor. The hospital census is down a little so there was an extra nurse.

I worked an extra shift last Friday night on Rehab and I had the patient who fell from the cherry-picker again. The first time I had him as a patient was Tuesday night, and before I went home on Wednesday morning, I told the day-shift nurse, a woman from India about my age, that I had given him Milk of Magnesia. I told her that I thought he was impacted. She said: "He can't be, because he was on a bowel routine." I said: "Yes, but then they stopped it." I tried to tell her how patients will continuously ooze stool when they are impacted, but she did not believe me. I was surprised she did not know anything about bowel impactions. It is one of the first things taught in nursing school. I think she is a LVN (licensed vocational nurse), and I guess she was not taught about that kind of problem where she went to school in India. She was charge-nurse on Rehab, so I did not see any point in arguing with her.

The patient continued to be treated for diarrhea until a GI doctor was consulted and checked his rectum. He found it was impacted with hard stool. He dug out some of it and ordered an enema followed by a suppository and laxative. He also ordered the patient be put on an aggressive bowel routine.

Saturday night on Oncology was busy. A nurse was floated here from PCU, and she was not used to having so many needy patients. I planned to take the first admit and give her the second one. After my admit came, one of the PCU nurse's patients was having chest pain and had to be transferred to Telemetry. She was busy with the transfer when her admit came, so I took both admissions.

Tonight, two of my patients have neutropenia (low white blood cell count). One of them is getting chemo running continuously at a slow rate. It was started on the day shift and the bag will last for twenty-four hours. Today was his first day of chemo and he is a little nervous about it. He asked me a few questions that I just gave general answers to. I did not want him to know I am not a certified oncology nurse.

He is a large cheerful white man fifty-eight years old. He is of Italian heritage and from the north-east, somewhere around New York. He is pleasant and optimistic about his treatment. He told me he was going to "beat it" (the cancer).

The day shift nurse who started his chemo told me he has eight sisters, and he is the youngest and only boy in the family. She said some of his sisters were here and asking a lot of questions about his treatment, but she was too busy to talk to them. She warned me they would be back. I stayed out of his room as much as possible until about 10 PM, and by then they were gone.

Half of my patients tonight are confused. One is a black woman who is blind and schizophrenic. Her son is staying with her, and I am glad he is here. She is too weak to walk, and I would be afraid to leave her alone because she might try to get out of bed and fall.

I have three patients who are confused old white women. Two came from nursing homes and one lives with her granddaughter. One of them was a new admission. She has a leg that is amputated below the knee and the other leg is red, swollen and painful. The ER doctor did not order any pain medicine, so I had to call and get an order for some. I gave her the pain pills about 8 PM and she went to sleep. At 10:30 I asked the PCA to change her diaper, but the patient said she did not want to have it done until she got more pain medication, because it hurt to move. She could only have the pain pills every six hours, so I took a dose to her at 2 AM. Her diaper, pad and sheets were soaked.

The other patient in the same room scratched the PCA when she tried to take her temperature. I had to hold her down and the patient got so agitated that I said to just forget about taking her blood pressure. The patient has a history of seizures, and I was afraid if we made her upset, she would have one. I tried to calm her down, but when I put a blanket on her she tried to kick me. Later we had to change her diaper and it took both of us. She was struggling and trying to hit and kick us the whole time.

March 22, 2004

It is 9 AM on Monday morning and I am home from work. We had problems with the dialysis unit again this morning. It seems to be happening a lot lately. The nurses on that unit want patients who are scheduled for dialysis to be brought to them by 7 AM. The hospital's transport staff does not start work until then and patients who have surgery scheduled will have priority.

Every Monday morning, they call our unit and tell us to weigh our dialysis patients and bring them to their unit by 7 AM. Our PCAs are busy in the morning. The vital signs for the shift and the intake and output amounts, including Foley catheters must be charted. Patients wake up and are calling for assistance to the bedside commode or bathroom. Often, we are getting new admits. We are just not staffed to have someone take patients to dialysis.

A dialysis nurse called at 6 AM and said we needed to have our three dialysis patients weighed and brought to their unit by 7 AM. I told her we did not have anyone available to take them and they would have to wait until after shift change. She said to just try to bring two of them, because she knew the schizophrenic woman could be hard to handle if she was woken up. I said we would do what we could, but I did not know if we would be able to bring anyone.

Dialysis patients must be weighed, vital signs taken, a special report form must be printed and completed, and all the morning medications put in a bag to be sent with. We were already pressed for time to do patient care and charting for our shift. I told the nurse who floated from PCU and the PCAs what the dialysis nurse said but told them just to do what they could. I planned to let the day shift get dialysis patients ready. They have more staff than the night shift and hospital transport could take the patients to dialysis.

Then a PCA from another floor arrived to take them. The dialysis nurse must have called the nursing supervisor and complained, so a PCA was sent. None of the patients were ready. The PCA wanted to take the schizophrenic patient first because she was awake. I said "okay," but I was on the phone with the Lab department when she came, and she had to get the patient up herself. I managed to get the dialysis form printed and completed using the vital signs taken at 4 AM. I got the medications ready, but I did not get the patient's weight. I thought the dialysis nurse could do that.

The PCA took the patient down and came right back for the other two. We had to rush getting their forms and medications ready while she got them up. One of them was a man with amputated legs who had a motorized wheelchair. He was able to follow her to dialysis while she pushed the other patient in a wheelchair.

A few minutes after they left the unit a male nurse from dialysis called and was angry that we did not get the weight on the first patient we sent. He wanted us to bring a bed-scale and weigh her. I told him she did not need a bed-scale because she could stand. He wanted to know why we did not get her weight. I told him we thought she was going later but then someone just showed-up to get her.

April 26, 2004

It is Monday morning, and I am home from work. We have a new manager now. His name is Jerald. He is a thin white man in his thirties. He was a nurse on PCU, but he was promoted to manager on Oncology. He does not have any experience in oncology, or as a manager. I think managers of other units were complaining about having to do manager duties on our unit. He always wears a suite and does not do any patient care. Our old manager, Sharon always wore scrubs and would help with patients if needed.

We had a unit conference last week and were told the Dialysis manager reported us for not having our patients ready. One of our PCAs, Elizabeth spoke up and said the dialysis staff were rude to us. Elizabeth usually works weekend nights with us because she is going to nursing school part-time. She is a young black woman whose parents are well educated. I think she said they are college professors. She is very outspoken and not afraid to say what she thinks. I said we already had as much to do as we could handle, and we could not spare a PCA to transport patients to Dialysis.

The remodeling is done now and Sunday night we were full, with twenty-one patients. Saturday night we had three nurses and we each got an admit. Beth is still pumping breast milk at least twice a shift. We have a new nurse on our shift. His name is Gary. He is a young black male nurse, and he has ICU experience. He is good at starting IV lines and always willing to help other nurses with patient care. He works

Friday, Saturday and Sunday nights. He must float to another unit if we do not have enough patients for three nurses.

I worked a double shift from 3 PM to 7:30 AM last Friday, and Gary had to float to Telemetry for four hours from 7 PM to 11 PM. It is hard to do that because you just have time to get your patients assessed and give them meds, and then you must leave and start all over again with another group. And you have twice the patients to do charting on.

Gary said Telemetry was crazy. The nurses there are taking six or seven patients and they might get two admits in a shift. That is the same as us, but Telemetry has a higher level of care. Their patients have heart problems and need to be monitored closely. They also have cardiac medication drips that need to be titrated (dose adjusted depending on heart rate, rhythm and blood pressure).

One of my patients this weekend was a young woman from India. She was admitted with an ectopic (in a fallopian tube) pregnancy. She is married to a man from India who looks old enough to be her father. They do not have any children yet. It was found she did not have an ectopic pregnancy, but a tumor on one of her fallopian tubes and a cyst on that ovary. The ovary and tube had to be removed.

The woman seems angry. She just lays in bed and does not want to move. She wants to be turned like someone who is unable to turn by herself. When I put her up in bed so she could take a sip of water, I had to hold the cup in front of her face with a straw in it. She acts like she cannot move her arms. She said she cannot swallow pills, so I must crush and mix them in frozen juice.

On Sunday night her Foley catheter had been removed and her doctor wanted her to be getting out of bed and going to the bathroom. Her PCA was nice young man from Africa. He took her to the bathroom, and she had a BM. He had left the room after he helped her to the toilet so she could have some privacy. She sat there when she was finished and called for him to come back. She was upset he had left her alone. He asked her what she wanted him to do, and she said: "I need you to wipe my ass!" He said he was not comfortable doing that, but she said someone had to do it because she could not. So, he wiped her butt.

I do not know why she could not do it herself. She is a slim young woman and capable of reaching it. She complained to me that he did not clean her well. She said she did not want him in her room again. I took her to the bathroom the next time and wiped her butt with soft lotion wipes. I told her he was going home at 11 PM, and she would have a female PCA for the rest of the night.

One of my patients on Saturday night was a white woman in her fifties who was dying. She had a cardiac catheterization done a month ago. It is a simple procedure to check for heart problems. But like any procedure there are risks. She had a stroke and went into a coma she never recovered from.

She was admitted to our unit for comfort care. She had a morphine drip and no other medications. She had a trach that had been put in after her stroke. Her adult daughter assumed control of her care. She wanted her mother to pass away as quickly as possible. The patient had been in a coma for a month and there was no hope of recovery.

At the start of shift the nurse who gave me report said the daughter wanted the rate of the morphine drip increased. It was already up to six mg per hour, but the daughter wanted it higher. When I went into the room, I could see the patient was not in pain. She was unresponsive and barely breathing.

The daughter said she had already told the other nurse to turn up the morphine drip. I told her if I turned the morphine up any higher her mother would die of an overdose. I explained we could give as much morphine as needed to keep her mother comfortable, but we could not purposely give her a dose that would kill her. That was against the law.

The patient's trach had a cap over it, and it was full of thick sputum. I took the cap off so she could get more air. The patient had a "significant other" with her. The woman wanted the patient to have more care, which might extend her life. But the daughter made it clear she was in charge, and she wanted her mother's suffering to be over. The daughter had refused to allow the day-shift nurse to do any suctioning of the trach.

While the daughter was out of the room I talked to the woman, who obviously was very attached to the patient. She thought the daughter might do something to end her mother's life more quickly. She and a cousin of the patient said they would not leave the daughter alone with her mother.

While I was talking to them, I could hear gurgling coming from the patient's throat. The patient seemed to be struggling to breathe and her trach was full of sputum. I could not just stand there and do nothing. I set up suction, and just when I was going to use it the daughter came back in. She said: "You're not going to deep suction her, are you?!" I said: "No, I am just going to clean it out a little." She glared at me while I did it but did not say anything else about it.

On Sunday night the patient was still alive. The daughter asked again to turn up the morphine drip and I refused. I suctioned the trach twice (not deep suctioning). At about 10:30 PM the patient started gasping for air. The daughter thought she was in pain and asked me again to turn up the rate of the morphine drip. I told her that her mother was not in pain, but her lungs were filling up with fluid. She told me the nurses in ICU had said there was no fluid in the lungs, but a little sputum around the top of the trach made it sound like there was. I listened to her lungs with my stethoscope and all I heard was gurgling. I told the daughter her mother's lungs were full of fluid. She was struggling to breathe, and the daughter said I had to give her something because she did not want her mother to suffer.

I said I could give her a little Ativan, which she had been getting about every eight hours. I only gave her one mg. More family members were called, and they were there within a few minutes. I walked out of the room to attend to some of my other patients, and I had an admit on the way.

About ten minutes later the cousin called me in and said the patient had been gasping hard and fluid squirted out her trach. Then she stopped breathing. I listened to her chest with my stethoscope and heard a faint heartbeat, but only one beat every few seconds. I knew her heart would beat only a few more times because her breathing had stopped.

While I listened to her heart one of the family members said she was gone. Then the patient gasped, and they said: "No! She's not!" About five seconds later she gasped again. Someone said: "She's not gone!" I told them it was just reflex muscles. I was listening to her heart with the stethoscope and still heard a faint beat every few seconds. Then it stopped. I looked at my watch for the time I would put on a form for the death certificate, and I told them she was gone.

May 6, 2004

It is 8 PM on Thursday and I am on Oncology working an extra 3 PM to 11:30 PM shift. I have been working more extra shifts than usual because we are going on vacation next week. Allen and I are taking my mother to her home in South Dakota.

Tonight, I have a forty-two-year-old white female patient with breast cancer. She was first diagnosed in January of 1991 and had a lumpectomy and chemotherapy. Later the cancer came back, and she had lymph nodes removed, another lumpectomy and more chemotherapy. Two weeks ago, she was at home and had a seizure. Tests showed the cancer has spread to her brain. At this point all treatments are failing. Her arm on the side with cancer is so swollen that it is about three times larger than her other arm, and painful.

Two of her daughters and granddaughters were visiting tonight. She asked me to change the dressing on her breast because it smelled bad. I noticed it when I first walked into the room. I removed the dressing and saw the breast was bumpy, hard and so swollen that the skin was tearing at the top, close to the collar bone. Over the entire breast the skin is cracking, and a yellow foul-smelling fluid is oozing out. She is on a Hydromorphone drip and gets six mg per hour. She also takes

Oxycontin twice a day. Even so, she is always in pain except when she is sleeping.

I have not had a breast exam in a few years but seeing this makes me want to get it done. I am going to schedule it for as soon as possible when I get back from vacation.

May 31, 2004

It is Monday afternoon. I worked my regular weekend on Oncology. It was one of the worst weekends in a long time. Beth had taken vacation for Memorial Day weekend, so it was just Gary and me on staff for nurses. Saturday night we had one PCA and a secretary from 7 PM until 11 PM. Then we had two PCAs for the rest of the shift. Sunday night we had two PCAs for the whole shift. Both nights we started out with 14 patients and then each got an admit. The problem this weekend was not just the number of patients we had, but the amount of care they needed.

Saturday night we both got behind at the start of the shift and then were running all night to try to catch up. Patients were calling continuously the whole shift and I was not able to do my admission or charting paperwork until after shift change in the morning. I left an hour late and Gary left about forty-five minutes late.

The patient who used the most of my time was a woman from India in her fifties who had terminal ovarian cancer. She should have been Gary's patient, but her family said she could not have a male nurse. She is dying and her family will not accept it. They will not make her a DNR or put her on hospice. They frequently called me in the room to ask questions.

The patient had IV fluid and a continuous feeding through her NG tube. She did not have a Foley catheter and she used a bedpan. She is a thin woman, but her abdomen is swollen with fluid and looks like someone who is seven or eight months pregnant. She had 1.75 liters of fluid removed on Saturday and one liter removed on Sunday. Monday she is scheduled to have more fluid removed. Her husband and adult children, a daughter and two sons hover over her and take turns dozing in the sleeper-chair.

Two of my patients on Saturday were older women who had breathing problems. One had terminal lung cancer and had been coughing up blood earlier in the day. She was okay on my shift and did not need too much care. The other was a Hispanic woman in her sixties who had severe asthma and had been using Prednisone, a corticosteroid, for a long time.

In the U.S. corticosteroids are only prescribed for short-term use because of the side effects caused by long-term use. But Hispanic patients sometimes use them continuously. They usually have a prescription given by a doctor at some time, and then when they have the same problem again, they just buy the medication at a Mexican pharmacy. Many medications can be purchased cheaply in Mexico without a prescription and are sent in the mail or brought to family members here.

The woman had severe wheezing and was short of breath, even while at rest and on oxygen. Her skin was thin and dry with open sores all over her body from the long-term steroid use. I put a thin dressing on her back where the sores were the worst. She asked me to put lotion on her back and give her a massage. I just put some lotion on quickly. She asked me to hit her back behind her lungs to loosen up the congestion, but I told her the respiratory therapist could do that when her respiratory treatment was given. Respiratory therapists are trained to do that.

I had another patient, a white woman in her fifties with a tracheostomy and a large brace that held her neck and head straight. I did not know what caused her condition because it was not on report, and I did not have time to read her chart. She could not talk but she wrote what she wanted on paper. She had pain that could not be relieved by medication. I gave her large doses of three different pain medications. But she was still calling for the next dose before it was due.

I gave her IV Demerol, Methadone pills and Lortab elixir. She got all her oral medications through a feeding tube going into her stomach. She also got feedings of liquid nutrition every six hours. She needed help to get up to the bathroom, and I spent a lot of time with her.

I also had a patient who is an obese white woman in her sixties. She had a cyst on her groin, and it became infected. The infected area had to be cut out. Her dressing was scheduled to be changed twice a day, and she had to be given pain medication before it could be done.

She was not getting out of bed, and she had a Foley catheter. The biggest problem I had with her was that she was incontinent of stool, and it was getting on the dressing. She had been constipated when she came into the hospital and had been given a laxative. Now she was having a lot of loose stools.

I noticed at about 8 PM that she needed to be cleaned. I gave her IV pain medicine and planned to have the PCA help me clean her at 8:30 PM. I was going to change the dressing then. But I got busy with other patients, and I could not do it. I asked the PCA to help me clean her at 10:15 PM, but then she was too busy. The PCAs work eight-hour shifts and she had to get ready for her shift change. She was the only PCA from 3 PM to 11 PM on our unit so she was busy. My patient had to wait until after the PCA shift change when we were scheduled to have two PCAs.

Another of my patients on Saturday was an eighteen-year-old boy who had a spontaneous pneumothorax (a hole in the lung that happens for no apparent reason). He had a chest tube draining a small amount of bloody fluid to a sealed container. He was getting IV antibiotics and doing well. He was able to pick up the container his chest tube was attached to and go walking in the hall with his father.

I got an admit at about 9 PM, a little old lady with hyponatremia (low salt level). I saw her and started her on normal saline IV fluid. I did not have time to do all her admission paperwork, but I got the information I would need and sent her medication list to the pharmacy.

By the time I got to see the last one of my patients it was 10 PM. He did not have any medications ordered and he had not called, so it just happened that I saw him last. I would have at least stopped to check on him, but I was running from room to room and the other patients were calling.

When I went into his room, I saw he was dead. I checked my report, and he was a DNR. I was glad of that. He had been sent to our unit with a GI (gastro-intestinal) bleed that could not be stopped.

He was a large white man in his fifties who had multiple medical problems, including a stroke that left him with weakness on one side and slurred speech. He had been sent to the ER from a nursing home and then sent to our unit to die. That is why he did not have any medications ordered. I felt his skin and it was still warm. I looked at my watch and noted the time. I made the required phone calls and completed the paperwork.

The only family contact written on his chart was an ex-wife. I called and got an answering machine. She called back about an hour later and seemed upset when I told her. Her husband got on the phone and asked me what happened. I told him: "He passed away." The husband said they would be right there.

I cleaned the patient as well as I could. He had a little blood around the sides of his mouth, and I washed it off. But his eyes and mouth were wide open. I closed his eyelids and they looked okay, but his mouth just came back open every time I closed it. I did not have time to worry about it. I had patients who were alive and calling.

When the ex-wife and her husband came, they had the patient's son with them. He looked like he was about eighteen years old. They opened the patient's door and then quickly closed it and gasped. The boy ran across the hall and started sobbing loudly. The stepfather came over to me and angrily asked me why the patient was not better prepared for viewing. He said: "His mouth is open!"

I told him I did the best I could, and I closed his mouth, but it just kept coming back open. He calmed down and went to comfort the boy. The son wanted to go back in and see his father. His stepfather and mother tried to stop him, but he said he needed to go in. He went in for a few seconds and then ran out crying.

I called a funeral home the stepfather chose, and the son signed the record of death as the next of kin to release the body. He was picked up within an hour. The family stayed until everything was done.

I finally got to change the dressing on the lady with the cyst at about 1 AM. The two PCAs we had after 11 PM cleaned her when they started their shift, but she was dirty again. I gave her more IV pain medication and gathered the supplies I would need for the dressing change. I had to cut off the old dressing and to my surprise, I found the largest wound I have ever seen. And she was oozing stool continuously, even while I was changing the dressing.

The patient had a hole that went from her left groin down the inner side of her left thigh. It looked like about two pounds of flesh had been cut out. The wound was completely open with no staples or sutures. It will have to heal from the inside out.

I talked to her while I did the dressing change and told her it looked good. She told me her groin was hurting a few days ago so she went to the ER. The doctor said it was good she came in when she did, because the groin and thigh had gangrene caused by a cyst. If she had waited any longer, they would have had to amputate the leg.

June 22, 2004

It is Tuesday morning, and I am home. The nursing director's secretary left a message on my phone today saying they are short of day shift nurses on Oncology this week, but I never called back. I am not used to getting up early in the morning and I do not like rush-hour traffic.

The patient from India with family who would not accept that she was dying, passed away two weeks ago. She was supposed to go home from the hospital on a Saturday, but when medical transport came to pick her up, her husband refused to let her go. He said he would sue the hospital if they tried to make her leave. She went home the next day. She had home health scheduled to treat her.

The day she left the hospital a PCA was sent to her room to remove her IV line. The daughter said to leave the line in and pushed the PCA away from her mother. The PCA is a large young black woman who outweighed the daughter by quite a bit, so it was a good thing she was able to control her anger, and just walked out of the room. The nurse went in and explained to the daughter that the IV line had to be removed before the patient left the hospital. Otherwise, we would be responsible for it if anything happened. The home health nurse would have to place a new line. The daughter finally agreed.

The last two weekends have been very busy, but that is normal now. I had a patient pass-away last Saturday night. He was an older white man from a nursing home with a GI bleed. He was a DNR, and I thought he was probably sent to our unit to die. He was almost non-responsive from the first time I went into his room, but his eyes were open, and he blinked sometimes.

He had very stinky dark blood coming out of his rectum. I helped the PCA clean him, and he was large and dead weight. The smell was so intense I had to put my arm across my nose and breathe through the fabric of my uniform a few times. I could tell he would die soon, and I wondered if I should call his family.

He died at about 11 PM, and when I called the family, his son answered and seemed surprised. He asked what happened and I told him his father passed away. I said I thought it was expected and he said it was. I asked if I should call his mother and he said: "No, don't do that." He came in alone about twenty minutes later, signed the form to release the body and told me which funeral home to call.

About thirty minutes later he came back with his mother and a brother. The funeral home pick-up man came at about the same time. The mother was a little old woman who was crying and obviously upset. Apparently, the patient had been awake and talking when they were visiting earlier in the evening, and they were not expecting him to die so soon.

Sunday night I admitted a young woman only twenty-six years old, with an abscess in her left breast that could be cancer. The breast is red, swollen and had discharge coming from the nipple. She weighs about three hundred pounds and is married with three children. She is Hispanic but speaks English well. She will be seen by a specialist and probably have a biopsy done.

I finally got certified to give chemotherapy. Sharon taught a chemo class last week. It was only an eight-hour class, and the last hour we took a test for our certification. I am still not supposed to give chemo until I do it with an experienced chemo certified nurse. But last Saturday I had to give it to a patient because there was no one else in the hospital who had chemo experience. I called the nursing supervisor, and she started the dose with me, but she is not chemo certified.

July 5, 2004

It is 5 AM on Monday morning and I am on Oncology. Fireworks could be seen from the windows of our unit last night, but I was too busy to watch them. Staff is two nurses and one PCA. At the start of the shift, I got an admit from Day Surgery: a young white woman, married and in medical school. She is in the early weeks of her first pregnancy. She came to the ER today with cramps and it was thought she might have an ectopic pregnancy. An exploratory laparoscopic surgery was done, and they found some fluid and drained it. She did not lose the baby. I had to do the admission paperwork, and by the time I was done with it she was ready to go home. Then I had to do the discharge paperwork. The patient was only sent to our unit because the day shift nurse wanted to leave, probably because it was the 4th of July.

Another of my patients was a man in his eighties who was sent to our floor this afternoon from ICU. They said he was brain-dead and stopped all treatment except morphine. The family said they could not stand to see him the way he was, and they stayed in the waiting room on ICU. They stayed there all afternoon and evening, waiting for the call from our unit telling them he had passed-away. A nephew came to check on him just before midnight, and he died about an hour later.

One of my patients is a young man with AIDS and Kaposi's sarcoma (cancer of the tissue and skin that people with AIDS often get). He was diagnosed with HIV just six months ago. His body is swollen and has purple splotches over most of it. His legs are very swollen and completely purple, with open sores draining yellow puss. He has a chest tube to a canister, and it is draining 100 to 200 ml of fluid every eight hours. His partner stays with him all the time, and they are nice young men.

I had to put lotion on the patient's legs, and his partner helped by holding up one leg at a time so I could get lotion on the under-sides. The patient is very weak, and I am glad his partner is here to help and call for pain medicine when it is needed. The patient gets nauseous and vomits at times. I gave him nausea medicine every few hours.

In the morning I am going to hang chemo with one of the day-shift nurses so I will be signed-off to give chemo on our shift. My yearly review was due about a month ago, but our new manager said he is too busy to schedule a time for it. Since I am charge nurse on our shift and will be able to give chemo, I hope to get a better raise this year than I have the last few years.

July 20, 2004

Last night I worked an extra shift on Telemetry. I took a night shift from 11 PM to 7:30 AM, but I agreed to come in an hour early because the nurse who I was replacing had been there since 7 AM and had to come back again in the morning.

When we sat down for report she started looking around and could not find her worksheet with all the information about her patients. She looked tired and flustered. One of her patients was an admit and she had not done the admission paperwork yet. She said to me: "Let's not make a long, drawn-out thing of report. I'll be here in the morning and take these patients back." I said: "okay" and she gave me a short report, just what she could remember about her patients. She said she had not even had time to chart, but she would do it in the morning. She told me she would do the admission paperwork on the new patient in the morning, but I said I would do it.

The new admit was a woman in her seventies from a nursing home. She was admitted with a GI bleed. Her blood pressure was low, and she had two units of blood ordered. She had a history of CHF (chronic heart failure) so we could not give her any IV fluid. It would just pool in her legs, and it could leak into her lungs. Her legs were already red and a little swollen.

She made it through the night okay, and so did my other six patients. One was a drug-seeking white lady in her sixties who was funny and sweet, but only if you let her think you would give all the pain medicine you possibly could. She was supposed to be on the rehab floor, but she did not like it there because they would not give her the pain medicine she wanted. She said that she had chest pain and was transferred to Telemetry.

Another of my patients had severe CHF. She was swollen all over. She was on a nitroglycerin (relaxes blood vessels so the heart does not have to work so hard) drip to help her heart pump the fluid through, but it was not working well. She had a fungal infection because of all the fluid. She was having a hard time breathing because the edema was putting pressure on her lungs.

The night went alright, but the next morning when I gave the day shift nurse report, she only had five of my seven patients. I did not have a good report ready on the other two. The nurse who I gave report to about them wanted every little detail. On top of that, the patient with the nitroglycerine drip had to be weighed every morning before the day shift came in and I did not know. The PCAs usually weigh the patients, but the one who had my patients had floated from another floor, and she did not know to do it. So, in the middle of report, I had to run and weigh the patient.

I could not get the patient up by myself and I had to call for help. I got her weighed and told the day shift nurse what her weight was. When she asked me about the patient's IV sites, I told her the patient had one line. After I left the unit, I remembered the patient had two lines.

I hope she does not report me for giving a bad shift report. I told her the other nurse had told me she would be taking my patients back, or I would have had a better report ready. I was upset because this was the first time I had worked on Telemetry in a long time, and I want to work more shifts there. I get a ten dollar per hour bonus.

August 30, 2004

I worked in Telemetry again last week and no one said anything about the bad report. They are still giving the ten dollar per hour bonus for extra shifts. I have been turning down shifts on Oncology during the week because our unit does not pay bonuses.

Staffing ratios changed for the med-surge floors including Oncology two weeks ago. We are getting less staff for the patient level on each shift. Sometimes they send the secretary or a PCA home halfway through the shift just to save a little money. Work has been a lot harder since they started using the new patient/staff ratios. Everyone is complaining, and if they keep staffing like this some people are sure to quit.

Beth and I wrote staff concern letters tonight about how bad staffing was last weekend. We had two confused patients who pulled out their IV lines and were trying to leave the unit. One was a little old lady in her late seventies who was trying to call a taxi. Someone had to watch her all the time or she would leave.

We also had some total care patients who had to be turned and cleaned often. Other patients needed help to the bathroom. And we had patients who called for pain med frequently. We only had three nurses with no PCA. It was crazy.

Last night was not any better. It was worse for me. We had fifteen patients at the start of shift with three nurses. We only had a PCA until 11 PM. I had two total care patients and two of our regular cancer patients, plus a late admit.

One of my regular cancer patients was the Italian man from New York who has eight sisters. He was always cheerful and optimistic about his cancer treatment. He had seemed in good health and never had any nausea or other reaction to the chemotherapy. He seemed to be doing well the last time he went home.

But when he was admitted a few days ago he was different. He had gotten a chemotherapy treatment in his doctor's office. It was supposed to be his last treatment and he was given two different chemo meds. He had a bad reaction. Now he is weak and confused. He slurs his words when he tries to talk, and he is too weak to stand up. He cannot even use his urinal by himself.

I did not realize how weak he was until about four hours into the shift. He was getting blood, and I thought he was just sleeping when he did not speak to me. I thought the PCA we had until 11 PM had been emptying his urinal, but when he vomited at about 10:45 PM and I changed his linen, I saw his bed was soaked with urine.

He was too weak to get out of bed, so I had to roll him to change his sheets. I knew I was going to have a hard time keeping him dry because he was getting Lasix, which causes increased urination. He was also getting IV fluid. He is a large man, and he was too weak to even turn himself.

About midnight, he and one of my total care patients started having bowel movements. I cleaned them both twice by myself. I had a lot of IV medications to give and I could not keep up with everything I needed to do. I did not have time for lunch, and I was tired and hungry.

I called the supervisor and asked if she could send us a PCA.

She sent a young PCA from Telemetry. They were low on patients and did not really need her. She helped me clean up my patients again and I asked her to answer the call lights so I could eat lunch. I went in the break room and took fifteen minutes. Before I finished eating, I was told I had an admit coming.

The new patient was on the unit about fifteen minutes later. She was a young woman in her twenties who had a red swollen area on her left thigh. She said she thought it was a spider bite. But when I asked her questions about her past medical history, she told me she had the same thing on her arm about two months ago. Then she asked me questions about MRSA (Methicillin resistant Staphylococcus Aureus). I explained to her that MRSA was a staph infection resistant to the antibiotics we usually use to get rid of staph. I assured her we had other antibiotics that would work. I looked at her thigh and thought it did not look like a spider bite. I suspect she has MRSA, but sometimes it is impossible to tell what caused an infection.

Beth helped me with the admission orders. She and Gary did the morning lab draws on my patients who had central IV lines (RNs can draw blood from a central IV line). I did not have time to do my charting. I heard from one of the nurses on another floor the hospital might be going back to the old patient/staff ratios where we almost always had one or two PCAs. I hope so, because working without a PCA is hard to do.

Gary told us he is transferring to PCU (Progressive Care Unit). The nurses there only have three or four patients, they always have a PCA, and the pay is better.

September 13, 2004

It is early Monday morning, and I am on Oncology. Staffing is Beth and me with one PCA. We started with twelve patients, and I got an admit. I heard the Italian chemo patient is on ICU, and they are thinking about putting him on a ventilator. His cancer is in remission, but his last dose of chemo that he got in his doctor's office caused neurotoxicity (damage to nervous system tissue). His doctor thought the condition was temporary, but now it looks like he will not recover. He was so optimistic about his treatment when he first came to our unit. I feel sad for his sisters. They treated him like the baby of the family even though he is in his sixties.

One of my patients tonight was a Hispanic woman in her sixties who was admitted Saturday afternoon. She lives in Mexico, but her family brought her here for medical care. She has smoked cigarettes since she was fifteen years old, and now she has stage four lung cancer. She was almost dead when she got to the ER on Saturday, and the family signed the DNR form. The nurse who admitted her on our unit expected her to pass away at any time. Her temp was 103 and she was unresponsive.

She has had many family members on the unit ever since she got here. Most of them are in the waiting room and they take turns going in her room. We have been giving them blankets and pillows so they can sleep and serving them coffee. I do not think anyone expected her to last this long, but now she is getting better.

She has been on IV fluids and antibiotics. She is awake now and her temp is down. Saturday night her family was hovering over her and crying most of the night. Tonight, most of them are still here but they are exhausted.

The patient has been sitting up and wanted to get out of bed. She got tangled in her IV line and pulled it out. I tried to start another one, but her veins are not good, and I could not get it. One of her sisters called the PCA and told her she needed to help me, because I did not know what I was doing. Beth tried to start a new IV, but she could not get it either. The supervisor finally came and got it started.

Another of the sisters asked me if the patient was: "very sick." I knew she was trying to get an estimate of how long it would be before her sister passed away. I did not want to give them false hope she would make a full recovery, because I knew her lung cancer was terminal. But her vital signs were stable, and she was looking much better. I told them: "Yes, she is very sick, but she is stable right now." The sister did not speak English very well, so I tried to be as clear as possible. I could see she was tired but did not know if she should leave or not. I said: "It could be a day or a week. It is hard to say."

About 5 AM I was called to the room because the patient was struggling to breathe and trying to sit up. She was talking in Spanish and her lungs sounded like they were full of fluid. I sat her up so she could breathe better and gave her some Ativan to calm her. I called Respiratory Therapy for a breathing treatment. Her heart and respiratory rates were fast, but then they suddenly slowed. I thought for a minute that she was dying.

One of the sisters asked if she should get the others from the waiting room. I said: "Yes, I think so." It looked like she had stopped breathing, and I said: "Get them fast." But then she started breathing and her pulse rate and blood pressure returned to normal. The Ativan had been effective, and she just fell asleep. I really felt stupid. I said: "She scared me for a minute, but she's okay now."

September 21, 2004

It is Tuesday morning 3 AM. I am home and not sleepy. Last weekend was a hard one as usual lately. I slept all day Monday until about 7 PM, so now I cannot sleep.

I had the Italian chemo patient again on Saturday night. I did not have him on Sunday night because he was sent back to the ICU on the day shift Sunday. Saturday night he had an oxygen mask on and had IV nutrition running because he cannot eat. He has been started on dialysis treatments and had his first one on the day shift Saturday. His sisters visit him during the day and one of them always stays through the night.

He had his wrists tied down at the start of shift, but I asked his sister if I could remove the restraints while she was in the room to watch him, and she said it was okay. He opens his eyes but does not speak much.

He seems anxious at times, and his sister said he told her his chest hurt. I gave him morphine a few times and Benadryl IV to help him sleep. Two times when I talked to him, he winked his eye at me. I think he still understands what is said to him, but it is hard for him to talk. We did not have a PCA after 11:30 PM and I had to get one of the other nurses to help me clean him.

I had five patients at the start of shift on Saturday and got an admit. Two of my patients had hepatitis C and one of them also had MRSA. Another patient had end-stage AIDS.

The patient with hepatitis C and MRSA was a Hispanic woman in her forties. She had severe asthma and a gangrene toe. She must have respiratory treatments often and wheezes so loud we can hear it out in the hall. She has open sores all over her back and upper arms. She asked me to give her a massage and I wanted to say no, but I told her I would put lotion on her back. I put two gloves on each hand and did it as quickly as I could.

About midnight she said she was having an asthma attack, and I called Respiratory to come and give her a treatment. She asked me if I would stay in the room with her until the respiratory therapist got there, and I had to refuse. I told to her I had an admit on the way and I had to take my patients' vital signs because we did not have a PCA. It is sad that I must choose doing tasks a PCA could do over taking care of a patient in distress. But I knew her "asthma attack" was more of a panic attack, and she would be okay. I still felt bad about leaving her alone.

My other hepatitis patient was a white man in his forties who had been in a motorcycle accident two years earlier. He lives in a long-term care facility. He has a caregiver in his room all the time, but the young woman taking care of him this shift could not handle him.

She came out to get me at the beginning of the shift and when I went in the room, I found him out of bed and on his way to the bathroom. He had an IV line with the fluid running. He paid no attention to it, and almost pulled it out. I came in the room just in time to disconnect it. His bed was covered in stool and urine, and he had a diaper on that was full. With the woman's help I got him cleaned and changed. He was very unsteady on his feet. He could speak but mostly mumbled and did not make sense. He has tattoos all over his body.

His caregiver told me she was leaving, and I asked her to wait a few minutes so I could get restraints and tie him down. I just needed to restrain him for a little while until the next caregiver from their facility came in. The person who replaced her was a large young black man who also worked as a PCA at a hospital. I took the restraints off when he got there, and he was able to take care of the patient himself for the rest of the shift.

Sunday night was not as bad as Saturday. Since I got the only admit on Saturday, I thought I would give the other nurses the first two admits on Sunday. We had three nurses and a PCA at the start of shift with sixteen patients. I took six patients and gave Beth and a nurse from the float pool, Monica each five patients. We had already been told two admits were coming.

Beth had a large female patient who needed total care and was very stiff. The patient had a urinary tract infection and a Foley catheter that was in place when she came to the ER. There was no way to know how long the Foley had been in, but it looked bad, so the doctor ordered it to be replaced.

Beth and Monica tried to put the new catheter in but could not get it. I am good at inserting Foley catheters, so I tried too. But I could not get it to go in. The woman must have had an obstruction. We called the nursing supervisor and she tried. But she could not get it in either.

About 4:30 AM the ER called to give report on our first admit. I thought it would probably be too late for a second admit before the end of shift so I flipped a coin to see if Beth or Monica would get the admit. Monica called heads and lost so it was her admit. I helped put the chart together for the new patient and Beth entered the orders in the computer system.

The patient I had with end-stage AIDS was a tall black man in his late fifties. He was down to ninety-eight pounds. He was getting IV fluids and his arm looked like it was starting to swell at the IV site. I knew I should start a new IV line on him. The thought of starting an IV on an AIDS patient makes me a little nervous. But I did it anyway and got a good line in on the first try.

December 7, 2004

It is Tuesday 6 AM and I am wide awake. I slept all day Monday as usual, then got up at 6 PM and made supper. I took a short nap between 8 and 9 PM, then stayed up until 2 AM, when I went back to sleep for a few hours. My mother is here visiting until after New Year, and I am sure she will be surprised I am up before her.

Work has been very busy. Management says they are trying to cut back on the budget, and they have reduced staffing. The PCAs and unit secretaries are being canceled or sent home early whenever the patient census drops below a certain number. One of our PCAs has started working part-time at a hospital close to where I live, and she told me that the nurse-to-patient ratio there is about one to five. We usually have from six to eight patients for each nurse.

It is getting close to Christmas, and some of the PCAs and secretaries are hurting financially because their hours have been cut. They never know when they will be canceled or sent home. The budget cut-back has not affected the nurses' hours, but the work is harder now. We have more patients and often are without a PCA. Even when our unit is full, we will only have one PCA.

We have three nurses on our shift now. A new nurse, Marlene, has been out of orientation for a couple of weeks. She is white, about my age and has been working in home health and hospice for the last few years. She is experienced and a good nurse to work with, but not as good at starting IV lines as Gary was. Sometimes Beth can get a line started on a patient who has bad veins, but I usually must call the nursing supervisor if I cannot get a line started.

Two of our regular cancer patients passed away in October. They had started chemo on our unit the same week and usually were in rooms next to each other, the rooms that are especially for chemo patients.

One was a schoolteacher and coach in his forties. He had a wife and young children. He would be admitted for a week or two at a time for chemo treatments. When he did not have the chemo running, he would walk around the unit fully dressed and did not look like a patient. When the remodeling was going on he would sometimes talk to the workers. One day a worker asked me about him, saying he did not look sick enough to be in a hospital.

The other patient was the cheerful Italian man with a lot of sisters. He became friends with the teacher/coach and joked about being jealous that the coach started his chemo a few days before he did and got to go home after the first round of treatment while he was still in the hospital. They both died the same week.

The patient census on our unit and the rest of the hospital has been low the last few weeks. I have had to float to another unit the last two weekends because Marlene said she was not ready to float yet. She is going to orient in Telemetry next weekend and then she will have to take her turn floating. I could have said I would not float because I was charge-nurse, but that did not seem fair to Beth. Our unit is one of the hardest to work on anyway, so I do not mind floating unless I must split the shift between two units.

Sunday night I floated to MS4, which is a medical/surgical unit on the 4th floor. They usually have a few telemetry patients. Their heart rates and rhythms are monitored by the monitor tech in the telemetry unit, which is next to their unit.

One of my patients was a twenty-one-year-old man who had been in a motorcycle accident. He had crashed into a concrete wall and got brain damage. It made me sad to take care of him. All he could do was open his eyes and make a sucking movement with his lips, like a baby. He had a trach with oxygen going to it, a tube in his stomach with continuous feeding, a Foley catheter and a central IV line. The accident was a little over two months ago so most of his injuries were healed, but the brain damage is probably permanent.

I got an admission about 2 AM who was a woman in her forties with Sjogren's Syndrome. She was nauseous and had abdominal pain. She has been in the hospital before for the same thing. I asked her about Sjogren's because I did not remember what it was. She said her stomach does not empty like it should. She has a special diet but still has problems with constipation, diarrhea and abdominal pain. Her potassium level was very low; it was half of what it should be. That is why she had to be on a heart monitor, because potassium affects the heart rate. A high or low potassium level is dangerous and can be fatal.

I was busy for the entire shift and not ready to give report to the next shift until 7:30 AM. That was alright because on that unit they give a verbal report, one nurse at a time, and I said I would go last. Their report procedure makes me nervous. I must go into the breakroom where the day shift nurses, and their manager are waiting and give a verbal report on all my patients. Someone always will ask a question I cannot answer, and it makes me feel stupid.

December 14, 2004

It is Tuesday, 2:30 AM. I am home and wide awake. Jerald asked me to work two extra eight-hour shifts each week, on Thursday and Friday from 3 PM to 11:30 PM. I am getting a fifty-dollar bonus for each extra shift, but I do not want to work these shifts. Our unit is too busy during those hours, and we have almost no PCA help anymore. But I agreed to work the extra shifts for a couple of months until he can hire and train more staff.

Saturday was Beth's last night. I just found out last Thursday that she has resigned. It is not surprising considering the way staffing has been lately. Two of the nurses who work Monday through Friday on the night shift quit too.

Jerald is making the day shift nurses work some night shifts to fill in when he does not have a night shift nurse. One of the day shift nurses told me he put her on the schedule working some night shifts without asking her or even telling her about it. She was surprised and upset when she saw the new schedule.

One of my patients last week was an old white man who was used to being well cared for by a private caregiver hired by his family. She would come into the hospital every night at about 8 PM and give him a bath, shave him and put pajamas on him. She would leave at about 10 PM when he was in bed and ready to sleep.

Thursday night he called and wanted to get up to the bathroom after she left. It took two of us to get him up, and then he did not do anything. A few minutes later he called again. This time it was 11:30 PM and I was leaving to go home. I knew the only PCA was gone, and the staff of the next shift would not start answering calls for at least another fifteen minutes. I walked by his room and saw he already had his legs over the side of the bed. I went in and told him no one could get him up to the bathroom just then and he would have to wait for a few minutes. I took his pajama pants and boxer shorts off him and put an extra pad under him. I put his legs up in the bed and put the side rails up. I told him if he had to have a BM, he would have to do it on the pad, and someone would clean him as soon as possible. He said: "Are you regular army?" I thought he was confused and said I was a nurse. He said: "Oh really, you're a nurse? You sound like regular army." I had to laugh because I realized I was barking orders like a drill sergeant.

February 28, 2005

Work has been busy lately. The flu season hit hard this year. Hospital staff are offered free flu shots as soon as they are available, usually in October. I always get one as soon as possible and I have not had the flu for a few years. But the hospital has been full most of the time for the last month. We have had a lot of older patients with the flu.

Some PCAs quit because their hours were being cut back in

November and December. And then there was a hiring freeze. So now we are short of PCAs. Some of the nurses quit because the work has gotten too hard and stressful without enough PCA help.

Last night was Sunday and staffing for our unit was Marlene, a day-shift nurse who stayed late and me with one PCA. One of my patients was a white man in his 40s with hepatitis C. He had been admitted with pneumonia and had a chest tube to suction in each lung. He had IV fluids and antibiotics. He moves around a lot and is confused and forgetful at times. Sometimes he gets out of bed and starts walking to the bathroom, forgetting about the tubes and IV line. Both chest tubes have had to be replaced because he pulled them out by accident.

At the start of the shift, I had to put a fresh dressing on one chest tube and tape on the other. While I was doing that, the patient said he saw smoke in the room. He said he was afraid there would be an explosion because he had oxygen on. There was no smoke I could see but the suction machine for one of the chest tubes was turned up high and felt hot. We have wall suction (built in equipment behind a wall with access in the room) in the patients' rooms, but it could only be used for one chest tube. The patient was in a private room, and it only had one suction connection. He need suction on both sides, so an old portable machine was brought in. It had a warning label on it that said there was a risk of explosion if used with an explosive gas. Oxygen is an explosive gas, and the patient's oxygen was turned up high.

I thought just to be safe I should call the doctor and ask if I could turn down the suction on the old machine. I told the doctor it felt hot, and the patient said he was seeing smoke. But the doctor said to leave the settings where they were because there was a risk of the patient's lung collapsing if I turned it down. He said to give the patient some Ativan to help him relax.

The patient was begging me to do something and was almost crying. He said he would not take anything that would make him sleepy because he was afraid that he would get blown-up in his sleep. I distracted him and gave a dose of Ativan through the IV line. He saw me and knew I was giving a medication. He was angry and said I tricked him. He yelled: "You shot me up, didn't you?! What did you give me?!"

I told him I gave him something ordered by the doctor. He kept asking me what I gave him, and I told him it was something to help him relax. He was upset but I did not have any more time to spend with him. I had other patients to see. I told him if he did not calm down and behave, I was going to tie him down. I had done it the week before when he was acting crazy and some of the other nurses had to do it too, so he knew I was serious.

He started crying but he stayed in bed. He said not to talk to him anymore and he was not talking to me. I left his door open and watched him from the nurses' station as much as I could. He sat up in bed, pouted and played Solitaire.

I had three isolation patients and I had to wear a gown and mask every time I went in their rooms. I had six patients total, which is not bad. But I wanted to have another group of patients, the ones I had when I worked an extra shift on Friday night. The day shift nurse who stayed late had them. She was supposed to go home at 11:30 PM, and I planned to take them back when she left and give my patients to whoever was sent to replace her. We were supposed to get a nurse from another unit.

The nurse going home had a Hispanic patient who died at about 8:30 PM. There were at least ten family members there and more were coming. The body stayed in the room until 11:30 PM and they could not decide which funeral home to call. We told them we could place him in our morgue, and they could decide what to do in the morning.

The day shift nurse who had stayed late put ID tags on the body, and I helped her put him in a body bag. By then it was 11:45 PM and she had been working since 7 AM, so I told her to go home.

I was hungry and I planned to have lunch before taking the body down to the morgue. I heated my food and was just going to eat when the security guard came with the stretcher to escort us to the morgue. He had the key to it and had to go with us to unlock and then lock the door. The security guards are all afraid of dead bodies. None of them will help us lift a body onto the stretcher or set foot into the morgue. If we ask for help to lift a body into a drawer they refuse, even though most of them are men.

Elizabeth was our PCA. Her shift started at 11 PM. She helped me take the body down to the morgue, but we were not able to lift it into the drawer. We had to call the supervisor and she sent two male PCAs to help us lift the body off the stretcher and put it into the drawer.

When I got back to our unit some of my patients had already called for pain and nausea medicine, and I had to give insulin to a diabetic patient. I was hungry and did not have time to eat. I was just going to heat up my food again when the nursing supervisor called. One of the nurses on the third floor had to go home because of a sick child. So now the nurse we had gotten from their floor at 11 PM had to go back to take the patients of the nurse who was going home. There were no nurses available, so we were sent a second PCA instead.

Marlene was upset. On Friday night she had nine patients, and the PCAs on that shift were not good ones. Some of the confused patients had bed alarms that would ring when the patients got out of bed, and she said the alarms were ringing all night. She had caught one patient just in time as he started to fall, and she had to ease the patient to the floor because he was too heavy to hold up. She told me she thought seriously about quitting and not coming back on Saturday night. Then staffing was short again.

Tonight, Marlene said if she had to take nine patients again, that was it, she was quitting. I told her I would take nine patients and she would have eight. The nursing supervisor said she would try not to send us any admits. I was really hoping she would not send one because I would have to give it to Marlene. I would hate to lose her because she is a good, experienced nurse.

We got through the night alright and did not get another admit. With nine patients the paperwork alone takes up a lot of the shift. It was lucky we had two good PCAs. We could not have done it without their help.

Elizabeth told us she is transferring to another unit. I am going to miss having her work with us. She did her job well and was always caring and friendly to the patients. She is leaving our unit because Jerald will not schedule her shifts so that she can go to nursing school during the week. Also, he called her in his office and wrote her up for not passing ice at the end of a shift. He did not care that she was the only PCA for the shift, when there should have been two PCAs. Or that there were several confused patients, and two patients fell in the early morning hours when she usually passed ice. She had tried to make patient safety a priority, but she got in trouble because she did not have time to pass ice.

April 9, 2005

It is 8:45 PM and I am on my usual Saturday night shift. Staffing until 11 PM is three nurses, two PCAs and a secretary. We have four open beds now and one that will be open soon because a patient just passed away. We have several DNR patients and one of mine will probably die this shift.

He was sent here from one of the more intensive care units. Whenever they have a patient who they know is going to die, as soon as the DNR form is signed the patient is sent to us. We have gotten used to patients dying on our floor. It does not bother me anymore. I would rather have a dying patient than one who is confused, trying to get out of bed, and pulling out his lines.

I had a patient for the last two weekends who has throat cancer and is very confused. He is a large, very pale man about sixty. His mouth and jaw were very swollen. His tongue was so big that it did not fit inside his mouth anymore and stuck out. He had a trach and a feeding tube. He also had a central IV line and a Foley catheter. He could not talk but he was strong and active. He kept getting out of bed and did not pay any attention to all the lines he had. He would frequently take off the oxygen line that was going to his trach.

His mother was always in the room with him. She is a little woman about eighty. We had a chair that pulled out to a bed so she could spend nights with him. She was a big help to us until the second weekend, when he was started on a morphine drip. It confused him but did not slow him down. She could not control him then.

He would not leave his hospital gown on. When we tried to put a gown on him, he would rip it off and his lines would get tangled in it. So, we just left him naked all the time. He would not leave a sheet or blanket on either.

One night when I had him, he pulled the inner cannula of his trach out, pulled the dressing off his central IV line and pulled it out about two inches. A male family member came to help the mother control him, but the two of them could not keep the patient in bed. I finally talked them into letting me restrain him by tying his wrists down.

I had him as a patient for several shifts, and he took up as much of my time as three other patients. Two days ago, he had surgery to remove some of the tumor and his huge tongue. After the surgery he went to one of the more intensive care units. I was glad I did not have him as a patient this weekend.

One of my patients, the one that will die soon is non-responsive. His body is still alive, but I do not think he will regain consciousness. At the beginning of the shift, I checked on him and I could hear him gurgling. His lungs are filling up with fluid. His wife and two daughters were in the room, and they asked me if he should be suctioned. I said I could suction him if they wanted me to, but his lungs would fill up with fluid again. I told them it would not change anything, and it might just prolong things. I asked them if they wanted me to do it. The wife did not answer so I thought I should just do it and started to reach for the suction equipment. One of the daughters said: "No, don't do it. Not right now."

It is 11:40 PM. I had to stop writing earlier so I could give medications. I am sitting at the nurses' station eating spaghetti and meatballs I brought for lunch. I am eating at the desk because our secretary went home at 11 PM and I am answering the phone and call lights while I eat.

About an hour ago the son of the dying patient came with his wife. They asked me if he had gotten any pain medication or if he was due for a dose. I said he could have some and I would get it. When I came back with the morphine, I saw the patient's mouth was full of white foam. The son had been cleaning around his father's mouth with a towel. I felt bad for him to have to see his father like that, and I suctioned the fluid out of his mouth. The son asked me if that would keep him alive longer and I said: "No, I was just cleaning him up a little." I showed him how to use the suction and told him he could do it if he wanted to.

I have three DNR patients tonight. One of them is a 100-year-old black woman. She is recovering from pneumonia and doing well. I think she will go home in a few days. She seems to be in good health. She has thick glasses and hearing aids, but that is to be expected at her age. She has large veins, which are one reason for her good health and long life. A person needs good blood flow to be healthy. Most of our chronically ill patients have small veins.

I must stop writing now. ER just called and I am getting an admit, a thirty-one-year-old woman with cellulitis (infection of the skin and subcutaneous tissue).

January 22, 2006

It is Sunday 2:30 AM and I am on Oncology. We have four nurses on the weekend night shift now. There is Marlene, me, and two nice young nurses from India. They are both married and have young children. They are both good nurses and always willing to help with patient care.

One of us must float to another unit every shift because we can only have three nurses, even when the unit is full. If we have fifteen patients or less, two of us must float. I am not really supposed to float because I am charge-nurse, and a unit is always supposed to have a charge-nurse there. But Marlene and the two young nurses hate to float. When one of them is scheduled to go to one of my favorite units I will take their place. I like the Neuro unit best, but I also like Telemetry and Rehab.

No one had to float tonight. One of the young nurses is off work because she hurt her back lifting a heavy patient. She has a name that starts with An and is hard for us to pronounce, so we call her Annie. She is small and probably weighs about 110 pounds, but she still tries to pull up and turn large patients. She tries to do it herself if no one is available to help her. I told her she should not do that.

The other nurse is Mary. She is also a small woman. She started working with us when she came back to work after maternity leave. That was several months ago and now she is pregnant again.

Tonight, we have one patient who is dying. He is Mary's patient.

There are several family members in the waiting room, and they keep pacing the floor between there and the patient's room.

I have the patient who had the necrotic back wound and the terrible smell almost two years ago. When I saw at the start of shift that he was going to be my patient, I said: "Oh no!" I dreaded the thought of it. I could still remember the overpowering stench of rotting flesh that he had the last time he was admitted.

When I went in his room, I was happy to see he was much better, and he did not even smell bad. He remembered me and said: "Do you want to see my back? It's all closed-up!" He was proud of the progress he has made. He turned over to show me, and where the big hole had been there was just a big scar. I told him it looked great, which it did, compared to the last time he was here.

His problem now is with his legs. On one leg he had a large sheet of skin taken off the thigh to be used as a skin graft on the other leg where the flesh had been eaten away by the infection. Where the skin had been removed it had not grown back yet. The dressing had to be changed twice a day, but it looked good. The flesh looked like fresh red meat, which is what it should look like.

He had an infection on his right ankle and foot. That is why he had to come back to the hospital. I changed the dressing there and saw he had dead flesh. He also had large dark-brown patches that looked like polished leather. The skin around the patches was white, as if it had no blood flow.

As I changed his dressings, he told me about a home health nurse who had been sent to his apartment to do wound care. She was in a hurry, and thought his skin graft was a dressing, and ripped it off. So now he has a large dressing on both thighs. I did not have to change the dressing where the skin graft was because it is only changed once every three days.

He still has a colostomy draining stool to a bag. But even with all he has been through, he has a positive attitude. He said his colostomy will be reversed as soon as he gets better. He told me it took him two years to get disability payments started but now he wants to get better and go back to work.

January 23, 2006

It is 5:30 AM on Monday morning and the weekend is almost over. The shift has gone well but we thought it would be a bad one. We had eighteen patients at the start of shift with three RNs, two PCAs, and no secretary. Our secretary was sent to another unit. Our PCAs were only scheduled until 11:30 PM, and there was no one scheduled to replace them when they went home. The hospital is short of PCAs, and the nursing supervisor asked all the PCAs here if anyone wanted to stay and work a double shift, but no one agreed to stay and work on our unit.

The supervisor said she would send us another nurse at 11:00 PM instead of a PCA. Two nurses who work the night shift on our unit during the week were scheduled to come in but neither of them showed-up. The nursing supervisor said she tried to call them but did not get any answer or return call. I wondered if Jerald asked them to work the shift or if he just put them on the schedule and thought it was okay.

One of them was supposed to go to the third floor and now that unit was left with only two nurses and one PCA. The supervisor said they could not take any admits, so we could expect to get admits that would normally go to their floor, as well as our own. We thought we would get three admits because we had three empty beds. And we still had no PCA.

But things turned out okay. The two PCAs that were supposed to go home at 11:30 PM agreed to stay an extra hour and take all the midnight vital signs for us. Then the nursing supervisor asked Bonnie, one of the PCAs who worked with me on SNU and now works on Rehab, if she would work the rest of the shift with us. She said she would. The rehab nurses were upset because that left them with no PCA. But they only had seventeen patients and they cannot get admits at night. We had eighteen patients and were expecting to get admits from the ER.

We did not get any admits, which was surprising for a Sunday night. I guess the only patients admitted from the ER were too sick for our floor and had to go to Telemetry or one of the more intensive care units.

A few weeks ago, I got an abscess under one of my arms. I put antibiotic ointment on it, but it did not go away. And then another spot came up. I went to my doctor, and she ordered an antibiotic. The spots went away. Two weeks later more spots came up. My doctor ordered more antibiotics. I think I picked up a staph infection, possibly MRSA, from a patient's bed rail. We have had a lot of patients with MRSA. I always wear a short-sleeved uniform because I get hot at work. After I got the red spots, I realized that my arms sometimes rub on the bed rail when I pull up a patient.

Now when I go in an isolation patient's room, I make sure to put on gloves and an isolation gown. I have always put gloves on, but if I was in a hurry or just helping to pull up a patient, I did not always put the gown on. Anyway, I am taking the antibiotics again and the spots are almost gone.

January 23, 2006

It is 9:30 PM on Monday night. I went to sleep about 10 AM this morning and got up about 6 PM. There was a message on my phone from the hospital asking if I could work tonight or tomorrow night. I did not call back. Allen said I should take a couple of days off. I have worked the last four nights.

Sharon also called tonight about 8 PM and asked if I could work. She said four nurses called in sick and she was short of staff. I told her I had worked the last four nights and my husband wanted me to stay home and spend some time with him. She said she understood and said: "Thanks for at least answering the phone." I think she has been leaving a lot of messages looking for nurses tonight. I felt kind of bad, but I did go in last Friday night when she called. Allen and I are going to our favorite karaoke club tonight, so I am going to stop writing and get ready.

January 25, 2006

It is 7:30 AM and I am in a day surgery room at the hospital we use (not the one I work at). Allen is fifty-seven years old and having his first colonoscopy as part of a complete physical exam. It is recommended that everyone have one at age fifty.

Yesterday he started preparation for the procedure. He took four laxative pills at noon and at 4 PM he started drinking 1/2 gallon of Golytely (flavored powder mixed in water). He could not have any solid food, just clear liquids and Jello. He could not have anything after midnight. He thought he would be starving by the time he was scheduled to have the procedure today, but he was not. I made a beef broth and a chicken broth from fresh meat. I bought white grape juice, apple juice, and Gatorade. I also made a bowl of Jello.

Allen was up all night and we had to be at the hospital at 6 AM. He has a private day-surgery room, which is nice for me because I can relax while he is gone for the procedure. His nurse started an IV on him and hung IV fluid at about 6:45 AM. The GI doctor came to see us at about 7 AM and said a prayer with us asking God that everything would go well. It is reassuring somehow that the doctor is a religious man.

Allen will be asleep and under anesthesia during the procedure. A tiny camera is inserted into the rectum and moved up through the colon to check for polyps. Any that are found are cut off and sent to the lab to be checked for cancer.

January 29, 2006

It is Sunday 5 AM and I am on Oncology. Staffing is Mary, Marlene and me with no PCA. We have fifteen patients. It has been busy even though we have not gotten an admit yet. We do not like working without a PCA, but we are getting used to it. We do not have any PCAs on the weekend night shift now, so if we really need one the supervisor must send one from another floor.

Annie is still off work because of a back injury that happened when she was trying to lift a large patient. A day shift PCA is also off work because of a back injury.

The hospital is short of staff, not because there is a nursing shortage, but because they will not hire new staff that are needed. Our hospital is part of a large, respected, non-profit healthcare system, with plenty of applicants for nursing and PCA positions. I am sure the hiring issue is due to executives in administration who do not see how the shortage affects staff and patients. Today, healthcare is all about money and the budget. I wish some of them would come to a unit on a day when we are short-staffed and see the problems it causes.

I worked extra shifts on Telemetry Wednesday and Friday nights. One of my patients was an old woman who was admitted after a fall at home. She had bruising and swelling around her forehead and left eye. She complained of severe pain when I first saw her, but I could not give her any pain medicine. She started crying and I felt sorry for her. I told her the doctor had changed her pain medicine from every four hours to every six hours, and it would be three hours before I could give it to her. She said she could not stand to wait another three hours. She screamed: "I hate them all!" I think she meant the doctors.

I reviewed her chart and saw tests were done on her head earlier in the day. The results showed a large mass behind her left eye. I went back to her room and checked the area. It looked painful. The patient said her doctor told her she could have more pain medicine. Apparently, the doctor had forgotten to write the order. I paged the doctor on-call for the night shift and explained the situation. She gave me the order to increase the dosage of pain medicine and shorten the time between doses.

Tonight, I have the young man who had a necrotic back wound that has healed and leathery brown areas on his foot. The brown areas will need to be removed, but the skin around them is looking pink, which is good. It looks like the blood flow to that foot has improved, so the foot might not have to be amputated. The foot is painful, but he has morphine ordered for it.

While I was drawing blood for morning labs from his PICC line (A large IV line that goes in through a vein in the arm and is threaded almost to the heart), I heard him urinating into his urinal. I looked away from his arm where I was drawing blood, and saw he was urinating about eighteen inches away from me. I did not flinch or say anything about it; I just hoped he did not splash me. He said he knew I had to add up the urine output for the shift since we did not have a PCA, so he thought he would have it ready for me. He also said his colostomy bag needed to be emptied. I had hoped to be able to leave it for the day shift because the PCA could do it then. I emptied it and he asked me to clean it good, so I did.

January 30, 2006

It is Monday morning 9:30 AM and I am home having a hot dog and a beer. I have worked twelve-hour night shifts for the last three nights and I am glad it is over. I want to take a few days off.

Last night we ended-up with nineteen patients after getting three admits from the ER. Staffing was Marlene, Mary and me with one PCA.

I called the supervisor just before 11 PM, when the PCAs have shift change, and asked her if we could have another PCA. With nineteen patients we are supposed to have three nurses and two PCAs. She said: "Yes, if you can find another one. I don't have another PCA to send you." I asked the PCA who was going home if she wanted to stay but she could not because she had class in the morning. She is in her last year of nursing school. I called Bonnie on Rehab, but she was already working a double shift there. I told the PCA who was leaving that if she passed any PCAs on her way out, to ask if anyone wanted to stay and work another shift. No one did.

The night was not too bad for me. We drew for first, second, and third admits. It seems fair that way. I just write 1, 2, and 3 on little pieces of paper, fold them up and put them in a cup. Then we draw. I got the first admit, which was good because we had a secretary until 11:30 PM. She was still there when my admit came. Mary got the second admit, who came about midnight, and Marlene's came at 12:30 AM.

Marlene had a bad night. Her patients called a lot, and she was not able to finish her admission paperwork until about 6 AM. I helped her a little by doing one of her blood draws and giving some pain medications.

I had two patients with staph infections, and both were young women. One of them had been my patient the night before. She had a large abscess on her left thigh. She told me it started as a little pimple that looked like an in-grown hair. It itched and she scratched it. She has artificial nails, which harbor bacteria. Her leg got red and swollen. She came to the ER and had to have some of the infected tissue cut out. Now she has a large wound with a wet-to-dry dressing (wound packed with sterile fabric made wet with normal saline and covered with a dry dressing) changed daily. She is on strong IV antibiotics.

The other woman is in her twenties and is a teacher. She has a staph infection causing abscesses in several areas. The largest place is on her left arm where the doctor removed some of the infected tissue. The dressing there is changed by the Physical Therapy department. They do the dressing changes on patients with the most serious wounds, but only during the day Monday through Friday. Nights and weekends, if a dressing needs to be changed the nurse must do it.

She has a smaller abscess on the same arm with a dressing that I changed last night. She also has two abscesses on her abdomen and one on her lower back. I also changed the dressings on them. They do not look too bad, but there is yellow fluid oozing out of them. The one on her back had fluid dripping out as I changed the dressing.

I asked her how she got the infection and she said she did not know. I told her most people do not know how they got an infection that starts on the skin. It could be caused by a bug bite.

She was not in too much pain. I only gave her pain medicine once. She is on the same antibiotic, Vancomycin, as the other woman. I made sure to wear a gown and gloves every time I went in their rooms.

Another of my patients was an old woman who had pain to her right abdomen radiating around to her back. I had her the night before and was told in report that she probably was getting shingles (An infection caused by the reactivation of the latent Varicella Zoster virus, also known as chickenpox). We see it often in older patients. It looks like a rash and may recur. The chickenpox virus hides in the body after a childhood infection and then reactivates when a person is in poor health. It is contagious and can be very painful.

We did not know for sure that she had shingles because there was no rash yet on Saturday, she just had pain. I talked to her about it, and she told me she had shingles in 1975. I looked at the area Saturday night and did not see anything. But on Sunday night the rash was visible. I started the isolation precautions. I am glad Mary did not have that patient, because a pregnant woman should never go into the room of a patient with shingles.

February 5, 2006

It is 9 AM on Sunday morning and I am having an egg sandwich and a beer. My legs were stiff and sore as I dragged myself to the car after work this morning. I felt like I did not sit down for the entire shift. Staffing was Mary, Marlene and me with two PCAs at the start of shift. We had sixteen patients and an admit on the way. We drew for admits as usual. I wrote on the slips of paper: 5 patients with 1st admit, 5 patients with 2nd admit, 6 patients with 3rd admit. I gave the person with the last admit six patients because that way staffing is more even if we do not get three admits. At the start of shift, we never know how many admits we are going to get. If I gave the nurse with six patients the first admit and we did not get another admit, she would have seven patients while the other nurses only had five.

I always let the other nurses draw first and then I take the last slip. I got six patients and the last admit, which I did not want because it is always busy at the end of shift. But it turned out to not be a bad draw because we got five admissions, which meant Mary and Marlene each got two.

The PCAs who were working with us at the start of shift were scheduled to go home at 11:30 PM. There was no one scheduled to replace them, and the hospital is still short of PCAs due to the hiring freeze. The nursing supervisor talked them into staying and working a double shift. Then she told us we were the only unit in the hospital that was fully staffed so she was going to fill us up. By the end of shift every bed on our unit had a patient.

One of my patients was a little old Korean woman who was admitted with a stroke. She spoke no English and her family went home before the shift started. At about 9 PM her granddaughter came to visit and called the nursing station to tell us there was blood in the woman's Foley catheter. The patient had gotten up alone to go to the bathroom and the catheter bag was dragged on the floor behind her. That happens a lot with older or confused patients.

I checked it and made sure the line was properly in place. I put a strap around her leg and attached it to the catheter line to keep it from pulling out. The granddaughter kept me in the room about twenty minutes asking questions about what was wrong with her grandmother, and what our plan of care was. She also wanted to know where the large bag of medications her grandmother brought with her from home was.

I looked for the medications and called the pharmacy to see if they were checked in. I had almost given up when I saw the bag sitting on the counter at the nurses' station. Apparently, it had been sitting there for the last two days and no one noticed. It was a large bag and had easily over $1000 worth of medication in it. I gave it to the patient's granddaughter, and she took it home.

I had problems with some of my patients and had to call doctors for orders a few times. One of my patients was an old black woman who was on dialysis treatments. Her red blood cells were low because she was bleeding from her GI system. She was oozing thick black stool that obviously contained clotted blood. She had been ordered to get four units of blood during dialysis on the day shift, but her blood type was not available then.

The blood finally arrived at 7 PM, but I knew I could not give her four units of blood. She did not urinate and that much fluid would be too much for her, unless she got it with dialysis. I called her doctor, and he changed the order to one unit. The other three units will keep until the next time she has dialysis.

She has casts on both legs, and she was moaning in pain at about 5 AM. I looked to see what was ordered for pain and there was nothing, not even Tylenol. I called the doctor again and got morphine ordered for her.

One of my patients had a colon resection done two days ago and her blood pressure was high. She had a NG tube draining the fluid from her stomach to a canister using low suction.

I went in to give her blood pressure medication at about 4 AM and noticed that the fluid draining from her stomach was brown with what looked like coffee grounds in it (that is what stomach fluid mixed with blood looks like). Also, she complained that she was having trouble breathing. I paged the doctor on-call and got NOW orders (not as urgent as STAT orders, but need to be done asap) for x-rays, lab tests, and blood pressure medicine.

She was stable, but while this was going on some of my other patients were calling for pain and nausea medicine. Also, my little Korean lady had to be helped to the bathroom. I had given her prune juice earlier and now it was working.

I took care of all my patients, but I could not get any charting done. I was late giving report to the day shift, and by 7:45 AM I had still not charted anything. I went to a computer, charted for about five minutes on each patient, and left.

February 6, 2006

It is 9:30 on Monday morning and my work week is over. I am exhausted but it is a beautiful sunny day. I wish I did not have to go to sleep.

Last night was a lot better than Saturday night. We started with twenty patients. Staffing was Mary, Marlene and me with a secretary and two PCAs. We only had one empty bed and I said I would take the admit because Mary and Marlene each had two admits the night before.

Within an hour I had an admit on the way and one of Mary's patients died. The funeral home picked up the patient who passed away and the room was quickly cleaned for a transfer from another unit. By 10 PM we were full. That was good because it meant we should get two PCAs for the rest of the shift, and we could not get any more admits unless another patient died.

The PCA for most of my patients was the lazy woman from India. She has been working at our hospital for many years and knows how to do her job, but she likes to knit or read more than work. I often must tell her to do patient care and then she says: "I didn't know."

One of my patients had a JP drain (a plastic tube with a suction bulb on the end, sutured into the tissue at a surgical site and excess blood and fluid collect in the bulb, which should be emptied every few hours).

When I went in to see the patient, I noticed the bulb was full. The lazy PCA had the patient since 3 PM, so she should have emptied the bulb at least once. I knew she had not emptied it because there was a paper on the wall with lines to write the time and amount each time it was emptied. I did it myself and then asked her when she last emptied it. She looked at her watch and said: "I checked it about two hours ago and it was only half full." I knew she was lying just by the way she said it. Whenever I ask her when she did something for a patient, she usually looks at her watch and says she did it about two hours ago.

I said to her: "You should have emptied it then. You know it will not drain when it is full." She acted like she did not know that. I do not think she checks her patient care orders like she should. I doubt if she even knew the patient had a drain.

There was no PCA scheduled to work from 11:00 PM to 7:30 AM. The lazy PCA said she would stay and work a double shift, and Bonnie was sent to our floor from Rehab. The Rehab nurses were not happy because that left them with no PCA. But we needed her more than they did.

About 1:30 AM I lost my temper with the lazy PCA. I had the old black dialysis patient with a GI bleed. She was on an air mattress because she was getting sores from being in bed all the time. She was oozing bloody stool. I told the PCA early in the evening that the patient needed to be cleaned and turned every two hours. Since we had two PCAs, I expected her to ask for help from the other PCA when she had to clean and turn the patient.

At about 10:30 PM I asked her when she had last turned and cleaned the lady. She said she had checked her, and she was not dirty. I said: "She's oozing stool. She's always dirty." I do not think she had been checked at all.

At 11:15 PM they finally cleaned the patient. She had a huge amount of bloody stool in her bed-pad. Her skin was looking worse with new skin tears. The lazy PCA told me that all the blood had just came out in the last few minutes. I did not think she was telling the truth, but it worried me enough to call the doctor. I got an order to give a unit of blood.

Two and a half hours later, I asked the PCA if she had turned and cleaned the patient again and how much blood she was passing. She told me she checked the patient, and she was clean. I did not believe it and I asked Bonnie to help me check her. The patient was in the same position she had been in over two hours ago. She had a bath towel between her legs and under her bottom. The towel had dried blood on it, and it stuck to her skin when I pulled it off, causing more skin tears.

Bonnie and I cleaned her and put lotion on her. Then I went and yelled at the lazy PCA. I told her I wanted the patient cleaned and turned every two hours, and I did not ever want her sticking a towel on a patient like that again. I stopped myself before I said too much, because it is better to have a bad PCA than no PCA at all.

Marlene got in trouble last night. She had the Korean patient I had the night before. The granddaughter asked what kind of progress had been made with her grandmother. She wanted Marlene to check the chart and tell her what the doctor had written. She wanted to know details about tests, medications and what was planned for the next day. Marlene was busy getting medications for other patients and told her she did not have time to look at the chart.

The granddaughter asked me if there was a form she could fill out for a complaint. I did not know where the form was. She asked for our manager's name and telephone number. I gave her one of his cards. Then I thought I should help her, especially since I was charge-nurse. I got the chart out and went through it. I answered most of her questions and she seemed satisfied when she left.

In the morning when Jerald came in, there was a message on his phone from her. She said Marlene was rude. Jerald asked me about it, and I told him Marlene was busy but not intentionally rude.

February 11, 2006

It is 9 AM on Saturday and I am having a hot dog and a beer before I go to sleep. I worked 7 PM to 7:30 AM on Telemetry last night. It was a good shift. The first five hours were busy. One of my patients was a large white man about sixty years old who is a regular patient at our hospital. He has a bad heart and complains of constant chest and abdominal pain. He can have morphine every four hours, but always calls for it thirty minutes early. The day shift nurse had given him a dose of morphine just before she left. I was busy and did not have time to check on him. I knew he would be calling for pain medicine, so I thought I would check him then.

I went in with his pain medicine at the earliest time he could have it, but he was angry. He said: "When did your shift start, at 7 PM? Aren't you supposed to check on your patients when you start your shift? Why haven't you been in here before now?!"

I told him: "Yes, we are supposed to check on our patients when we start, but I haven't had time to. It's been too busy. A patient down the hall was just admitted and she has not had any of her medications yet. I needed to get her IV fluid started. And we've had a lot of patients coming in and going home tonight."

I gave him his morphine and said: "Just call when you need another dose, and I will bring it right in. I have your night-time medications if you would like to take them now. Would you like your sleeping pill now or later?" He said he would have it in an hour and I said I would bring it in then. He was happy with that, and I did not have any problems with him the rest of the night.

I started an IV line on the new admission. She did not have good veins, so I just placed a small gauge one, but it was big enough to give her the antibiotics ordered. She was a large white woman about 200 pounds in her late sixties. She had chronic heart problems. The doctor had written an order to call results of the lab tests to him, but I did not see the order. The doctor called and asked for the lab results and was a little upset that I had not called him.

The patient needed a blood transfusion, and the doctor gave me the order. The IV line I had started for the antibiotics was too small to give blood through. I asked if any of the telemetry nurses wanted to try to start a larger line, and one of them did. I am not good at placing the larger gauge IV lines unless the patient has good veins. About midnight I got a transfer from another unit, a Hispanic dialysis patient I have had before. She is on isolation precautions for MRSA. She just had surgery; a catheter which could be used for dialysis was placed in her right chest on the day shift.

Her abdomen was distended and full of fluid. Her skin was jaundiced (yellow) and covered with sores. She was scratching herself hard and I told her to stop because it would get infected. She was tired from the surgery and having to transfer to another unit so late (they needed the bed she was in on PCU for another patient). She just wanted to go to sleep and was no trouble.

Later when I was checking my charts, I could not find an order for her to transfer to Telemetry. The charge-nurse checked the chart too and did not find an order. She said the patient might have to be sent back to PCU. But her bed was already taken, so we had to keep her and pass it on to the day shift to get the order to keep her or send her back.

The nurses on Telemetry ordered out for Italian food at 9:30 PM. They usually order out every shift. I ordered Lasagna. I did not have time to eat it until after midnight, but it was good. The night went by fast. Telemetry is always staffed better than our unit. I am considering transferring there, but I will need to be ACLS (advanced cardiac life support) certified.

The nurse who took over my patients this morning is just returning to work after having a heart attack. She is my age or a little younger and not overweight. We were talking about how stressful hospital nursing is, and she said her doctor wrote that she can only work eight-hour shifts for now.

February 17, 2006

It is 9 AM Friday morning and I am having a beer and a bowl of chili before I go to bed. I worked 7 PM to 7:30 AM on Telemetry last night. In the morning I asked the manager of the unit if I could transfer there permanently, and she said I would have to have telemetry experience first. I would also have to take an orientation class that is only offered once a year. And I would lose my weekend schedule. I would be scheduled about forty hours a week and work some weekend shifts. She did not sound like she really wanted me to transfer, so I think I'll just forget about it.

Last night just after the shift started one of my patients called. When I went in, his wife asked me what medications he had been given that day. The patient had been admitted at about 6 AM for a biopsy of his kidney because he was going into renal failure. The wife said she asked the day shift nurse what medications had been given, and the nurse just said: "I gave him everything he needed." She complained to me that the nurse would not take time to talk to her.

The wife told me her husband had taken all his daily medications at home and they had told that to the first nurse who talked to them. I said I would check and see what had been given. I got the patient's medication administration record and read to the wife what medications had been given and what time they were given.

All the patient's daily medications had been given by the day shift nurse at about noon. The wife got angry because she had already given her husband his meds in the morning, and he was only supposed to take them once a day. I talked to the charge-nurse, and she said the patient was alright because if he were going to have a reaction, he would have already had it.

The patient's wife wanted to make sure the mistake was reported and said she did not want that nurse again. She said the nurse was rude and would not even get water for her husband when he asked for it. She said they hardly even saw or spoke to the nurse all day.

This morning the nurse came back, and I told her what happened. She said she did not give all the medications but threw them away when she realized that they had already been given. She said she forgot to mark it off the medication administration record. When I told her the patient's wife said she would not take time to talk to her, she said: "I didn't have time to talk to any of my patients yesterday."

She seemed really stressed. I had noticed a mistake she made with another patient's medication, but it was not serious, so I did not mention it. She had charted she gave a patient a sleeping pill at 4 PM and it was not supposed to be given until 10 PM. I do not know if she really gave it or if it was just another charting mistake.

February 23, 2006

It is 3:30 AM on a Thursday morning. I am at home and wide awake. I have been having trouble sleeping at night when I am off work. Lately I do not get tired until about 5 AM.

I do not want to work as many shifts as I have been. Staffing has been the worst since I have been a nurse. There are only a few PCAs left at the hospital, not enough for staffing requirements. Those who still work here are often asked if they want to work a double shift. But now they are turning down the extra shifts because one PCA is often the only PCA on a full unit and expected to do the work that used to be done by two or three PCAs.

Of the few PCAs we have left, some of the best ones are nursing students and are going to graduate soon. Then they will be gone to nursing positions. I really do not know what management is thinking. People cannot be expected to keep working under this kind of pressure.

Last Saturday Oncology was almost full. We had nineteen patients with only three nurses and no PCA. Then we got two admits.

Sunday night was not quite as bad. We had twenty patients at the start of shift with three nurses and one PCA. Staffing called for two PCAs, but there was not another one available. We had one bed open so we drew numbers to see who would get the admit and Marlene lost.

The patient she got from the ER had a lot of orders and kept her busy. He was an alcoholic with a bad liver. He had been given contrast (liquid containing dyes, used to highlight organs, blood vessels, tissues, etc.) to drink before a CT scan, and now he had diarrhea. From the report Marlene got from ER, she thought the patient would have to be restrained. He was having alcohol withdraw symptoms, but he was calmer when he arrived. She did not have to put the restraints on him.

I had an alcoholic patient too. He is a thirty-nine-year-old white man who has been drinking alcohol every day since he was fifteen years old. He has a young wife who stayed with him. She took him to the bathroom and was a lot of help. He was in a semi-private room with another man, so I should have asked his wife to leave, but I did not even consider it. I needed any help I could get.

The patient has a large abdomen full of fluid. He hallucinates and is agitated at times. He was on oxygen, IV fluids and IV antibiotics. His wife told me he quit drinking hard liquor a few years ago. Now he only drinks beer, but he drinks about three gallons of it a day.

About 5 AM his wife had to leave to take their kids to school. She told me her husband seemed to be having trouble breathing. I told her that all the fluid in his abdomen was probably putting pressure on his lungs. I told her I would check his O2 sats (oxygen saturation levels) and ask the respiratory therapist to check him.

But then I got busy with other patients. About 7 AM the respiratory therapist told me the patient had taken off his oxygen line and his O2 sat was only 84%. That is not good, but it came up when the oxygen line was put back on. I told the therapist we would tape the line on his face if we had to.

One of the patients on our unit is an older white woman with cancer. She is a DNR, but her husband will not accept that she is dying. The weekend before, when her heart rate went up, he said he wanted everything possible done for her. We got an order to transfer her to a cardiac unit. It took her nurse on our unit about forty-five minutes to get the orders, have the supervisor assign a bed and call report. Then the patient's heart rate came down and the husband said to cancel the transfer.

He stays with her all the time and gets upset when her condition changes. The day-shift nurse who had her on Sunday said she was unresponsive for about twenty minutes. The husband shook his wife and yelled at her to wake up. He was so happy when she opened her eyes.

The respiratory therapist told me that after her treatments she sometimes spits up blood. That scares the husband, and he told the therapist to discontinue the treatments. The therapist tried to tell him that the medication in the respiratory treatments helps patients to cough up what is in their lungs, but the husband would not listen.

I was glad she was not my patient. I do not mind having a patient who is dying, but the family needs to accept it. Part of a nurse's job is helping the family deal with a patient's condition. But with the work load we have; it is hard to find time for family members. This couple's children live across the country and have not come to see their mother. I am afraid that when she passes away her husband will be alone and not handle it well.

March 17, 2006

Jerald called me at home on a Tuesday and said he had to talk to me. He would not tell me what it was about but said I had to make an appointment to see him. I said I could be there within an hour. When I got there, he was not in his office, so I waited. He came back with the manager of the rehab department who is a female. I knew she was with him as a witness so he could close the door to his office. He does that whenever he is giving a disciplinary action to a female staff member.

He pulled out a copy of my charting from Sunday night and it was very brief. The night had been extremely busy because of short staffing and admissions. I did not have time to chart anything until 8 AM, so I only did what is the minimum required charting. I had been told before by supervisors that patient care should come first, and it was okay to just chart the minimum required if that is all I had time to do.

But Jerald did not see it that way. He was a nurse on PCU before being promoted to Oncology manager. I do not think he ever worked on a med-surge or oncology floor before. On the unit he came from, the nurses usually had only three or four patients each. He expected us to chart like they did, spending about fifteen to twenty minutes writing about each patient.

I tried to tell him that I did the required charting on each patient, and even pointed it out on the copy of my charting he had. But he said he had never heard it was okay for a nurse to do the minimum required. He gave me a final written warning and told me I was on probation for six months. He said I could only work my regular weekend shifts and extra shifts on Oncology. If he did not need me on Oncology, I could work on another unit, but I could not have any bonuses for six months. I was upset but I did not want to say anything I would regret, so I just signed the form he handed me and left.

I knew why he was doing this. The week before he asked me to work extra shifts on Oncology during the week and I told him I wanted to keep my weekdays open. He knew I had been working on Telemetry during the week and getting a ten dollar per hour bonus. I knew he was angry because I had refused the extra shifts that he wanted me to work on Oncology.

A few days later when I worked an extra shift on Oncology, I was walking to my locker and Jerald was standing outside his office. He had a big smile on his face and said "Hello" to me. He even winked at me. He reminded me of "Cheshire Cat" in "Alice in Wonderland." I replied in a pleasant tone. I know he is happy because now I must work when he wants me to.

March 21, 2006

The hospital has started using agency PCAs. They are not as well trained as the hospital's PCAs, but they are better than nothing.

Last Saturday night I floated to MS4, a med-surg unit on the fourth floor that also has some cardiac patients who are on telemetry monitors. I was on Oncology from 7 PM to 11 PM, but I only had 5 patients. At 11 PM one of us had to float. The other nurses did not have experience with telemetry patients, and they did not want to go. So, at 11 PM I divided up my patients between the other nurses and I went to MS4. I had eight patients there. That meant I had thirteen patients to chart on, and I had to make sure to chart everything on each patient because Sam is checking it.

One of my patients on MS4 was a woman I have had as a patient before. She is in the hospital a lot because of chronic stomach problems. The last time she was a patient on Oncology, about a month ago, she had an NG (nasal gastric) tube. We used the tube to give medications, but most of the time it was attached to wall suction to drain fluid from her stomach.

She was not supposed to eat or drink anything. She had IV fluid and IV nutrition called TPN (total parenteral nutrition) going in continuously. Her NG tube was always full of a thick multi-colored drainage and her suction canister would fill up with it. It did not look like gastric fluid and the nurses suspected she was sneaking food into her room and eating it when no one was looking.

She would frequently ask to be disconnected from the wall suction so she could go for a walk. She would still have the tube going in through her nose, but the end could be clamped, and she could put it in the pocket of her hospital gown. Then she could get out of bed, push her IV pole with her and walk off the unit.

One night when she was my patient on Oncology, it was supper time and our unit secretary told me she saw her in the cafeteria. I went down and caught her just as she was going to pay for a large sandwich and a bag of chips. I threw it away and told the cashier and food servers that she was not supposed to eat anything, and if they saw her in the cafeteria again to call our unit. She was on contact isolation and should not have been touching things in the cafeteria anyway.

It was funny, the way she had looked going through the cafeteria line with the NG tube hanging out of her nose, her hospital gown on and pushing her IV pole. I told the secretary and the other nurses, and we all laughed about it.

I had told the patient she could not have any food, but she said she was still going to go outside to smoke. I got back to the unit before she did, and I went to her room and checked her bed-side table. It was full of crackers, cookies and candy. I put it all in a bag and when she returned, I told her she could have it back when she was discharged from the hospital.

Last Saturday night, when I had her as my patient on MS4, she was up to her old tricks again. This time her NG tube had been removed the day before, but she was still not supposed to eat yet. She was on TPN and IV fluid. TPN contains all the nutrition needed for twenty-four hours. It is expensive and costs about two thousand dollars per bag. She had an abdominal wound that would not heal and a new colostomy which should drain stool to a bag when she started eating.

The wound in her abdomen had a dressing over it. I was going to change it at 6 AM when I drew her morning labs, but I got too busy. I told the day-shift nurse when I gave report that I would change it before I left. I finally got to it at about 8:30 AM. The dressing was soaked, and the patient was holding a towel over it to keep fluid from dripping out.

I changed the dressing, and I knew what the fluid was. She was eating again, and the food was coming out of the wound in her abdomen. The wound never had a chance to heal because she was always eating.

When I finished changing her dressing I opened the drawers on her bed-side table. She yelled: "What are you doing?!" I said: "You are not going to get better if you keep eating." I took a big bag of candy out of the drawer and told her she could have it back when she went home. She yelled: "I just have to have something to eat! I'm going home tomorrow anyway! So, I don't care!" I am sure she will be back again soon, if she does not kill herself with food first.

April 10, 2006

Work has been busy as usual. Now that I must worry about charting a lot on each patient, I always stay an hour or two after the end of shift just to chart. It is too busy during the shift to do much charting. I am also checking my orders more carefully because Jerald has been writing-up staff for anything he finds wrong, and it is always a final written notice. He never gives a warning. The staff in general seems more stressed-out than it used to be, and more nurses have quit.

Since I am checking my patients' charts more carefully, I am finding more mistakes that were made on the day shift. The night shift is responsible for signing-off on all orders written over the last twenty-four hours. I usually find one or two mistakes each night. I just make sure the mistake is corrected. I am not going to run and tell Jerald like some nurses would.

It is partially the fault of the doctors that mistakes are made. Their handwriting is so bad I am surprised anyone can read it. Often the unit secretary and the nurses will pass around a new order and say: "What do you think this means?" The doctors usually write orders and then quickly leave. We must try to figure-out what the orders say. Sometimes even the pharmacist cannot understand what was written.

Last night at work staffing was Mary, Marlene and me. From 11 PM to 7:30 AM we had two of the best PCAs in the hospital. One was Vickie, a regular PCA on oncology. She is a tall young black woman who is going to nursing school part-time. She is always nice to the patients and does her job well. Bonnie was floated to our unit from Rehab, and she is great to work with. Marlene was charge-nurse. The hospital has started paying two dollars per hour extra to whoever is charge-nurse on each unit, so Jerald said I must take turns with Marlene. I do not mind, because it is not worth the extra two dollars to be responsible for the unit.

I started with five patients. Then I had one discharge, got two transfers and one admit. My first transfer was a patient being sent from CCU (Cardiac Care unit). He was expected to die soon.

I had him as a patient before. He has been in the hospital for a long time. He started getting better and was even sent to Rehab. Bonnie told me that when he was there, he got confused and pulled out his central

IV line. He tried to pull out his Foley catheter, but it got stuck. His nurse on Rehab tried to remove it but it would not come out. It had to be taken out by a doctor.

When he was sent to Oncology last night, he was unresponsive, and I could not feel a pulse. He was still alive, but his blood pressure was very low. He had several family members with him, and they had just agreed to make him a DNR. He was started on a morphine drip, and they expected him to pass away at any time. One of them asked me: "How will we know when he is …?" The woman could not say the last word, but I knew what she meant. She said: "He was wearing a monitor on CCU, but he doesn't have one now. How will we know?" I told her he would just stop breathing. The patient's ex-wife had power of attorney and she seemed more upset than the adult children. She was concerned he might be in pain. Her daughter assured her he seemed peaceful.

He passed away at 11:25 PM, just as I was going to take report on my second transfer. I told the nurse who was calling that I would call her back in a few minutes. I asked the family if they wanted me to call a funeral home. They said they did and gave me the name of one.

The ex-wife had brought pajamas and a robe from home and wanted us to dress him. She said she had promised him that he would not leave the hospital naked. She was upset and determined he be dressed, so I told her we would do it in a few minutes. She said the family would help.

I made the necessary phone calls to the doctor, nursing supervisor, organ transplant people (they must be called after each death even though they always refuse organs from our patients) and funeral home. Then I went to the patient's room and removed the Foley catheter and IV line. The son asked me about dressing his father and I told him we would, but we had never done it before. His mother asked me: "Never?" I told her we did not send patients out naked and assured her that he could keep the hospital gown he had on and his sheet too. I told her the funeral home could dispose of them when they dressed him. She agreed to that.

A young man from the funeral home came within forty-five

minutes. He signed the record of death as the person the body was being released to and he asked me if the body was bagged. I said: "No, do you want us to put him in a bag?" He said that he did. I told him we usually do not do that (I have only bagged patients who we were taking to our morgue). But I did not want to argue with him, so I said: "Okay."

I went to tell the family, but the ex-wife and daughters were crying, so I stopped myself before the words came out. I walked over to the son and said it in a whisper so they would not hear. The son shouted: "No way! We already talked to the funeral home about this!"

I said: "Okay, I'll tell him." I went out and told the young man that the family was refusing to have the man bagged. He became very flustered and said: "The family is here?! I thought the secretary said they were not here!" (He meant the person who takes calls for the funeral home) I said: "No, I told her they were here." He was obviously embarrassed by the situation.

I helped him get the body on his stretcher. The family was watching, and we were careful to do it in as dignified a way as possible. I let him keep the pillow and some sheets. The patient was a tall man and did not fit on the stretcher well. But with his head up on a pillow and his lower legs and feet wrapped in a sheet it looked alright. His ex-wife was kind of making a big deal out of the way he looked. She said this was the last time the family was going to see him. He was going to be cremated. As soon as they left, we called to have the room cleaned. Another patient was in it within two hours.

One of my patients was an older white woman who has been in and out of our hospital for years. She has a feeding tube going into her stomach with liquid nutrition running continuously. She does not speak or move herself anymore. Because of the continuous feedings she is having frequent loose stools. We try to keep her clean, but her bottom is red and excoriated. It is starting to bleed.

I happened to walk into her room to check her feeding pump and Vickie was giving her a bed-bath. We usually do not give patients baths at night, and it was nice of her to do it, especially since we were so busy.

The patient was awake, and Vickie was talking to her, even though she did not respond. I asked Vickie if she needed any help and she said: "No, I have been cleaning this patient myself for quite a while now." She thanked me for asking but said she was fine and could do it herself.

She must have cleaned the lady three times during her eight-hour shift, and always left the patient in a comfortable position covered with a sheet and blanket. The patient did not say anything, but I could tell by her expression that she appreciated it.

Another of my patients was a young black man with sickle-cell anemia and a blood clot in his right leg. He also has asthma and is in an early stage of congestive heart failure. The blood clot in his leg was painful. He kept his leg up on a pillow and hardly ever got out of bed. He had a urinal which he used and kept on his table. I emptied it every time I went into the room.

At about 4 AM I went in his room to replace his IV fluid bag. He was sleeping and I heard something beeping. He woke up and said: "Huh?" I said: "You have something beeping." He said: "Oh yeah, can I have my pain medicine now?" I said: "Yes, it's almost time. I'll get it." He had hydromorphone four mg IV ordered every two hours as needed. It was not scheduled every two hours; he had to ask for it. He always called for it at about one hour and forty-five minutes after the last dose.

I realized after I walked out of the room that the beeping I heard was his cell-phone alarm. He must have set it to go off every two hours so he would wake up and call for the Hydromorphone. When I was at the nursing station getting the medication, Marlene and Mary were there. I told them what he was doing, and we laughed about it.

In the morning I gave report to the nurse who was going to have that patient, and I told him about the cell-phone alarm. I stayed late to do my charting. Later the nurse told me he had asked the patient if he was setting his alarm to call for pain medicine and the patient said: "Hell yeah!" He thought it was funny. We both put it in our charting.

July 21, 2006

The hospital is using more nurses and PCAs from staffing services than ever before. Some of the people sent from the staffing services are good, but some are not. It puts more pressure on the regular staff because mistakes are being made.

Last Sunday night I had to float to MS3, the floor I dislike the most. I was scheduled to have my annual review with Jerald on Monday morning. I had all my paperwork done that I needed for it. I had ten examples of my charting and a record of all the hospital education I had completed over the last year. The night shift seemed to be going well, and at 5 AM I relaxed with a cup of coffee while I finished my charting. Then everything fell apart.

The PCA we had was sent from a staffing agency. He was a tall black man in his 40s. I think he was from an African country because he spoke with a strong accent. He seemed to know what he was doing and did not ask any questions. He had worked on this unit before. He could not take the blood-sugar levels of the diabetic patients because he did not have a code number to use the glucose-scan machine. But the nurses could do that themselves.

When I was hanging a bag of IV fluid in a patient's room, I noticed that the amount of fluid given had not been cleared since about 3 PM. The PCAs usually record the amount of fluid given each eight hours and clear the pump to zero. I told the other nurses our PCA probably did not know how to clear an IV pump. The charge-nurse showed him how to do it, but I told him I would clear my own pumps and record the amount given in the charts. I did not want any mistakes.

I thought everything was alright until I checked one of my patients' charts at about 7 AM. The vital signs, fluid intake and urine output were not recorded. I told the PCA he needed to put them in the chart. I assumed he had done everything but had just not written it in the chart yet. He did not answer me when I spoke to him but when I checked the chart a few minutes later the numbers were written where they should be. I picked up another one of my patients' charts and it was the same way, with the spaces blank where the vital signs, intake, and output for my shift should be. I told him again to put the information in the chart and he did. Then he left.

I checked the rest of my charts and the information he should have written in them was missing. I could record the numbers myself, but he did not leave a worksheet or anything with the information on it that I needed. I told the charge nurse what happened and asked her to help me find his worksheet. She found it but it did not have any of my patients' information on it. I started to panic. I knew Sam could fire me for my charts missing that information. The nurses are responsible for everything the PCA does. It is our responsibility to make sure the charts are correct.

I called the nursing office and told the supervisor what happened. She said she would call the staffing agency and try to get the PCA back. He showed up a few minutes later. It was almost 8 AM and the day shift had already gotten report. I was going to be late for my annual review.

He stood at the front desk of the nurses' station and said he did not have anything. He said he must have put it in the box that has papers to be shredded. He said I should try to call someone for the key to open it. No one at the hospital has that key. It can only be opened by the shredder company.

I was so frustrated. I told him I had to have the information to write it on my charts and pointed to the blank spots where the vital signs, input and output should have been. He just stood there, and then said he had to go to his other job. I said: "I don't care! I am not leaving until my charts are done! You have to give me my patients' vital signs, intake and output!" He said: "Do you know how old I am? I am not afraid of you! What are you going to do about it?!"

By this time the day shift staff including the manager were standing around us. One of the nurses told me to take this to the break room. I started to, but the PCA was standing between me and the break room, and he was not moving. I knew I was talking too loudly, and I tried to control my voice. I said: "I'll report you to your agency!" I grabbed a piece of paper and said: "What's your name?" He refused to tell me what his name was, and he already had his name badge off.

I knew I was getting myself into trouble by causing a scene. I just turned my back on him and went to where I had my charts on the desk. I sat down and looked at where the missing information should be, and I had to fight hard to hold back the tears.

I called Jerald's office and left a message saying I was staying late on MS3, and to call me when he was ready for my review. I went over my charts for the next 30 minutes. I had what I needed for the patient I had admitted and the two charts I had asked the PCA to finish before he left.

I went back to my other patients' rooms and asked them how much they drank or urinated during the shift. I had two patients with AIDS, and they both said the PCA had not been in their room at all. There was urine in a bed side commode and a urinal that I emptied and recorded the amounts. I took vital signs to record even though they were not taken at the right time.

I went for my review and Jerald asked me how my shift had gone. I told him: "This morning was the closest I've come to breaking down and crying since I've worked at this hospital." He told me he had already been called about: "the incident." I told him what happened and said I was more upset with myself for causing a scene than anything. I told him it would never happen again and from now on I am going to get a copy of my patients' vital signs before the end of shift. And I will never trust that something has been done without checking it.

Jerald said he agreed with what I said to the PCA, but I should have said it in private. He said it was not going to affect my review, just to make sure it never happened again. My pay raise for this year is 35 cents, the lowest I have gotten since I have been a nurse.

August 4, 2006

It is 9:45 PM on Friday night and I am getting ready to go to sleep soon. The patient census is low at the hospital. It usually is at this time of the year. But the hospital still fills up on the weekends. The hospital is using agency PCAs and nurses on every unit. I called to see if I could get a shift on Thursday but was told I called too late, and they had already scheduled agency nurses.

This morning Jerald called me and said they really needed an RN to work 7 AM to 7:30 PM Saturday and Sunday on Rehab. I agreed to do it, so I must go to sleep early tonight.

I was working on Telemetry about a week ago and saw Marian, the young nurse from India who had the abusive husband that called the unit all the time. She is working for an agency and takes shifts at our hospital sometimes. She is still married to her angry jealous husband, but he and their daughters are living in India. Marian said she wants her girls to live there because they will get a better education. She said she visits them every summer and she hopes they will come here to live when they are ready to start high school. She seems happy and I am glad she is not living with him anymore.

When Marian was working with us on Oncology, she told me about when was raised in India. All the children in her family were sent away to a Catholic boarding school. They only went home once or twice a year. She said the nuns at the school were very strict. They did not have hot water and the students had to get up before dawn every day and wash. They had a busy schedule with little time for play.

I guess that is the way her daughters are being raised. They will probably have arranged marriages like she did. But at least they will avoid the troubles many American kids have. I doubt there is any drug abuse or teen pregnancy at the Catholic boarding schools in India.

April 19, 2007

Work at the hospital has not changed much. We are still using agency PCAs and nurses a lot. I have started working the weekend DAY shift. The two nurses I work with are good at what they do and care about the patients. They are younger than me and work weekends so they can be home with their kids during the week. Sarah is charge-nurse. The other nurse is Julie.

The patients at the hospital seem to be getting sicker. I guess it is because insurance companies limit the time spent in the hospital to the very least possible. Also, we have more AIDS patients and more patients with MRSA.

Patients with MRSA are supposed to be on isolation, and staff must wear gowns and gloves when we go in their rooms. But we cannot make patients stay in their rooms. They go walking around the halls and even down to the cafeteria with no isolation masks or gloves on.

Last week when I was working an extra shift on Telemetry there was a black female patient in her forties who was on isolation. She kept walking out of her room, putting her elbows on the counter at the nurses' station and leaning over to talk to staff. It was funny, because she has a full figure and was wearing only a hospital gown that was untied except at the neck. She would lean forward on the counter and her entire backside was exposed. She was told several times to go back to her room, but she kept coming out again. The secretary cleaned the counter with disinfectant each time after the patient leaned on it.

One of the cleaning ladies walked by and said: "You need to cover her." I said: "She's supposed to say in her room." The lady said: "Someone needs to cover her!" We just laughed.

Patients on isolation have family and friends who visit them. Sometimes they wear the gowns and gloves and sometimes they do not. One young man on isolation precautions had his girlfriend in bed with him and she spent the night.

When I was on Telemetry the manager said that so many patients there were getting VRE (Vancomycin resistant enterococcus, a strain of bacteria that causes infection in the urinary tract, blood or a wound. It is spread from person to person and often occurs in hospitals), that they were thinking about doing a rectal swab of all the patients to check for it. He said they might even swab the staff. We laughed when he said they might swab the staff; we knew that would never happen.

April 23, 2007

It is 1:00 PM on Monday afternoon and my body aches. I have pain in both shoulders and a stiff neck. The weekend day shifts are not much better than the night shifts. Saturday and Sunday we had three nurses and two PCAs. On Saturday we were full at the start of the shift, and we were supposed to have four nurses, but the supervisor said she could not find another nurse. On Sunday our secretary went home at 3 PM and her replacement never showed-up. Both shifts I was on my feet the entire time doing patient care and was not able to do any charting until after the night shift came in. On Sunday night I still had to do admission paperwork on a patient that I admitted at noon.

Saturday night about 6:30 PM I started getting sharp pains in my left leg every time I took a step. It was hard to walk but I moved slow and made it through the shift. When the night shift took over, I sat down at the computer for about two hours and did my charting. When I got up it felt better. I told Sarah I did not know if I would be able to work on Sunday. I have not called in sick this year or last year so I could have taken off.

Sunday morning, I felt okay so I went to work. But I was on my feet all day again and by 6 PM the pain in my left leg came back. This time I took Advil before I sat down to do my charting. After sitting at the computer for two hours it felt better, but I was stiff walking to the car after work. When I got home, I ate supper and went to bed. I did not sleep well because my muscles ached, and I could not get comfortable.

The patient who was the most work for me over the weekend was a young man with AIDS and cancer. He is down to about one-hundred pounds and has had chemotherapy recently. Last week he had a port put into the top of his head that will be used for chemo. Only a doctor can use this kind of port. He also has a large IV line in each arm. The one in his right arm is used for TPN. He has the IV nutrition because he cannot eat anymore. He is too nauseous and if he tries to eat, he vomits. The one in his left arm is used for IV fluid and has a pain pump with hydromorphone infusing continuously. He can push a button to get extra doses. Even with the pain pump he still calls for morphine and nausea medication. He has a Foley catheter because he is too weak to hold a urinal. He is also losing his vision. He can only see shapes close-up. He cannot watch TV anymore.

Sunday at about 1 PM he was nauseous, and he called. When I went in, he said he had vomited, and he was afraid it came out "both ends." His sister was in the room with him. She had already cleaned-up the vomit, but he needed to be washed and have a linen change.

I called my PCA, but he was busy. I was tied up with my admission and another patient who needed me more. I told the young man we would get him cleaned as soon as possible, but it would be a few minutes. I told my PCA to try to do it as soon as he could, but he never did it. Later in the afternoon when I finally got back to the patient, he said his sister had cleaned him, and it took her about an hour to do it by herself. I felt bad but there was nothing I could have done.

At the time the young man needed to be cleaned, the patient in the next room was in pain and I had to take care of her. She is an overweight older woman with pale skin and gray hair. She has throat cancer and had been treated with radiation two weeks earlier. She came to our unit with severe radiation burns. The skin on her neck was red, peeling off and bleeding. She could not speak or eat. She was on IV nutrition, IV fluids and a pain pump.

She had a feeding tube placed in her stomach a week ago. Since then, she has lost weight, and the skin on her abdomen was loose. It was also dry from the radiation. Now the skin around the tube seems to have shrunk-up. The tube looked like it could fall out at any time. Stomach acid dripped out around the tube constantly and burned the skin on her abdomen. The area around the tube was red and starting to bleed. I cleaned the area and put ointment and a dressing on her. But she was still in pain and the acidic fluid started dripping again within a few minutes.

Her sister was in the room and the patient tried to tell me something, but she could not speak. Her voice was gone due to the radiation. The sister and I tried to figure out what the woman wanted but we could not understand what she was trying to tell us. The patient got so frustrated that she started crying and pulling her hair. I did not know what to do. I told her to push the button on her pain pump. That did not help, so I asked her if she was nauseous. I was not sure, but I thought I saw her nod her head as if to say yes, so I gave some nausea medication. Then I cleaned her stomach again, the second time in fifteen minutes. When I took the dressing off, green fluid dripped down her abdomen and I knew it was burning. All I could do was clean it again, put ointment on it and another dressing. I told her to hold a towel over the dressing and left.

I had orders to give platelets to her and blood to the patient with AIDS. I also had a new admit coming. I had not eaten lunch yet and I was feeling weak and overwhelmed. Doctors had been in and there were pages of orders written on my patients. We had no secretary to put the orders in, and my patients were calling constantly. I needed to get consent for the blood to be given and draw a lab sample for the type and cross. Lab called and said the platelets were ready for me to pick up.

At 4:30 PM I decided I had to stop and eat something because I felt like I was going to pass out if I did not. I went to the break room and heated a bowl of chili I brought from home. But I only got a few bites before I had to answer a call from a doctor and another from the pharmacist. I went to the desk to answer the calls and while I was on the phone a patient called for pain medicine and another patient called for nausea medication. I went back to my chili and ate it as quick as I could at about 5:30.

I did not care that I couldn't take a break, but I was upset because I was falling farther behind. New medications had been ordered to be given NOW several hours ago, and still had not been given. I also had a female patient with dementia and diarrhea, and I could not make time to check on her. I had cleaned her earlier with the PCA we had from 7 AM to 3 PM, but he was a young male nursing student, and he was not comfortable checking a female patient's bottom unless a female staff member was in the room with him. She did not get checked often enough and when we did check her she was very messy with stool.

At 3 PM he went home, and his replacement was the lazy PCA from India. I knew I would have to tell her to turn and clean the patient every time it needed to be done. I asked her to check the patient and she said the patient's daughter was in the room. I told her to check the patient as soon as her daughter left because she was having diarrhea.

I knew that cleaning the patient was a two-person job, so I asked the other PCA if she would help. But she said her shift was over at 7 PM and she was busy with her own patients. Julie must have heard what we said, because she got the lazy PCA, and they cleaned the patient. I felt bad, like I was not doing my job. I did not want staff to think I was refusing to clean a messy patient. But I had orders I was far behind on. As I tried to go faster and get everything done, I just started to feel hopeless. I wanted to tell Sarah that I needed help, but she was already one step ahead of me. She was checking my new orders and asked if she could help with them.

Sarah gave some of my medications and I was almost caught up by shift change. I never found time to change a dressing on an admit who came about noon. His left foot had an open wound that was draining a lot of fluid. The dressing was put on in the ER that morning and it was soaked by 7 PM. I wanted to change it, but I just could not find the time. I had to leave it to the next shift.

While I was putting my admission information in the computer, Sarah was charting on the computer next to me. The only footrest on our unit was under the computer she was using. I asked her if I could use it for my feet because my leg was hurting again. She gave it to me, and said her back was hurting, and she was wondering if she should report it.

On Saturday she had found a large female patient unconscious in the bathroom. The patient was face-down, and Sarah did not know if she was breathing. She called a "Code Blue" and got the patient back to bed. She hurt her back doing it. The patient was okay. She was sent to PCU where she could be monitored more closely. She came back to our unit on Sunday.

Marlene, who is charge-nurse on the night shift now, said her back is hurting too. The young Indian nurse we call Annie is still having back problems caused by lifting patients. I think it is sad that nurses spend so much time and money getting educated and trained, and then they must suffer and sometimes have their nursing career cut short because of injuries that could be prevented with better staffing.

May 10, 2007

It is Thursday 12:30 PM. This week work was not as bad as last week. I had the AIDS and cancer patients again Saturday and Sunday. The AIDS patient's pain pump was discontinued before the weekend. Saturday and Sunday he called for pain medicine (4 mg of morphine IV) about every hour. He also had two kinds of nausea medications ordered and I alternated them.

The doctor who put the chemotherapy port in his head came in Sunday and put the first dose of chemo in the port. I assisted and it was interesting to watch. The port is implanted under the skin on top of the head towards the front. The doctor drew about ten ml of fluid out of the head by sticking a needle into the port and drawing back the fluid into a syringe. The fluid was clear. He discarded it and told the patient that he would feel better, and it would relieve some of the pressure to his head. Next, he took a small vial of a white powder and mixed it with sterile saline. The needle he used to withdraw fluid had been left in the port. He injected some of the saline-chemo mixture in, then drew out more clear fluid and mixed it with the remaining saline-chemo in the syringe before injecting it all back into the port. The port itself was not visible. The top of the patient's head has a round dome-shaped area covered by skin. It is about two inches in diameter and has sutures all around it. The port was placed about a month ago.

Saturday night I left work about ninety minutes late but Sunday night I got off on time. Sarah, Julie and I all walked out together. It was still light outside, and it felt good to be going home before dark.

Tuesday, I worked a 3 PM to 11:30 PM shift on Rehab. Staffing was three nurses and one PCA. Nurses each had five patients plus an admission. My admit was an eighty-six-year-old woman who had fallen at home a few days earlier. She fractured her pelvis and ribs on her left side. She also had a long list of chronic medical problems. However, at the time her biggest problem was constipation.

She had been in bed and taking pain pills for a few days. That usually slows down the digestive system and causes constipation. She tried using a bedpan with no results. I had not looked at her orders yet when she told the PCA she needed to sit on a bedside commode for a while to try to have a bowel movement. She had a Foley catheter to drain her urine. I told the PCA I did not know if she could be out of bed yet and Physical Therapy should assess her first. The PCA said: "This is rehab, she is going to get out of bed." I said she had fractures and I needed to make sure it was okay for her to get up before we got her out of bed.

I had to run down to the cafeteria to get something to eat. Supper is only served for two hours and then the cafeteria is closed until morning, and I had not brought lunch. When I got back the patient was up on the bedside commode. The rehab doctor was there and told me the patient needed an enema. I said: "Okay, I'll do it now." I put my food down in the breakroom, got the enema and gave it to her while she was still up. I told the PCA to watch her so she would not fall.

One of my patients was a retired doctor. He was alert and sitting up in a chair in his room. He was scheduled to go home the next day. He had aphasia (neurologic condition in which language function is defective or absent because of an injury to certain areas of the brain) due to a stroke. He could only say short words.

He liked coffee and he asked for it three times during the shift. However, he could not say the word "coffee." The first time he called, when I went in the room, he tried to say something, but the word would not come out. Then he said: "sugar" and I could understand him. I said: "You want sugar?" He did not answer, and I saw there were sugar packets on his table, so I said: "Here's some sugar." He said: "No." He picked up a sugar packet and pointed to his empty coffee cup. I said: "Oh, you want some coffee to put your sugar in?" He said: "Yes." I got him a cup of coffee.

The next time he called, when I went in the room, he had a coffee creamer packet in his hand. He held it up to me and on the back of the packet in small letters was a list of uses for the creamer. He pointed to the word "coffee." I said: "You want more coffee?" He said: "Yes." I told him he would not be able to sleep if he drank too much coffee. I asked if he would like some decaffeinated coffee and he said: "No." I said: "You're drinking a lot of coffee." He said: "It helps me." So, I said: "Okay," and made him a fresh pot.

November 15, 2007

It is Friday evening. My mother is here visiting. My brother Jim has been driving her from South Dakota to our house every year in November. Then he drives her to south Texas in January, back to our house to stay for a few days in May, and back to South Dakota. She brings tomatoes, potatoes, and carrots from her garden in South Dakota. She also brings boxes of apples from her trees and makes pies. I really enjoy having her here.

Work is still about the same except they keep adding more stuff to the list of things we must do. At the start of each shift, we must walk around with the nurse coming on duty and introduce our replacement to each patient. We ask the patient if they need anything, if they have any pain, if they need to go to the bathroom or if they need to be re-positioned. We must ask each patient what their name and date of birth is and then check their armband. During the shift we are supposed to ask each patient about the three Ps (pain, potty, position) every hour and initial a paper on the door to show we did it. We also must ask the patient their name and date of birth and check their armband before giving each medication.

About once a week a manager from another unit will follow each nurse around while medications are being given. The manager takes notes on how the nurse is following procedures.

Recently I slipped at work. The floor in front of the medication machines had just been mopped and it was soaking wet. The cleaning staff had just started using a new mopping system. They were supposed to use a wet mop and then go over the area with a dry mop. It was Sunday morning and the Hispanic woman mopping had not been trained on the new system. She used the wet mop only and left the floor with a lot of water on it. My left leg went back behind me and a little to the side. My right leg went forward, and I came down almost to the floor. I managed to catch myself before I fell over, but my pant legs got wet, and my hips hurt. Sarah was standing a few feet away from me and she said: "Are you okay?" I said: "I think so." I finished getting the medication I needed and then took some Ibuprofen. Sarah said I should report it just- in-case I hurt myself. I reported it before I went home.

December 10, 2007

The last few weekends on Oncology have been busier than normal. I am usually on my feet the whole shift and then must stay late to do charting. I have had back and hip pain since I slipped in water. Our hospital has a work injury program, and we can only see the hospital's physician for any on-the-job injury. I had a visit with him, and he asked about my injury, but he did not examine me. He does not think there is anything wrong with me.

Last weekend while I was at work, I called the on-call person for the hospital's work injury program. I was worried because my back and hips were hurting more, and I thought I might have a herniated disk. I must do heavy lifting at work, and I was afraid it would make my back and hip problem worse. I said I wanted X-rays done and light duty, or to use some of my vacation time to rest.

The on-call person said there was nothing she could do, but I could go to the ER if I needed to. My shift had already started, and my patients needed morning medications. I asked Sharon, who was weekend supervisor, if I could go home early, but she said she did not have anyone to replace me. I could not leave my patients and it would be very hard for Sarah and Julie to take care of them with the heavy load they already had. I just took some ibuprofen and stayed.

Today I saw the doctor again. He did not seem happy to see me. He ordered physical therapy, modified duty (I do not have to do heavy lifting) and an MRI. The visit took about five minutes, and he did not even look at my back or hips.

December 27, 2007

I still have not gotten the modified duty the rehab doctor ordered. The first weekend Sam did not put it on our staffing schedule. The second weekend Sharon did not know she was supposed to put it on the weekend schedule. The pain has not gotten any better. When I got home from work last Sunday night, I hurt so bad I could not even sit up to eat. My mother brought a plate of food to me and put it on a TV tray next to the couch. I ate a few bites while lying down. Then I had to go to bed. I took a pain pill and muscle relaxer pill the doctor ordered.

January 18, 2008

Yesterday was one of the worst days of my life. Monday and Tuesday I had tests to evaluate if I was able to work. I passed the tests, and the work injury physician told me today that I was off modified duty and back on regular duty. He said my back was alright.

I did not know what to say. I never got the back specialist consult he ordered. The hospital denied it. I was also told I could not see another doctor about my injury, or I would lose any medical coverage I might have been qualified for. My back and hips still hurt, but I had to go back to regular duty after having modified duty for about two weeks.

I tried to tell the doctor I could not make it through a twelve-hour shift. He said I could go to the ER or go home sick if I had to. I told him I could not just leave my patients in the middle of a shift, especially on a weekend. There was no extra staff for someone to take my place. I told him that being on my feet for twelve hours and doing patient lifting made my back and hips hurt. He said to take the pain medicine he ordered. I said: "You want me to take pain medicine while doing patient care? You think that's okay?" He said: "Yes, you can take it."

I did not know what to do. I started to go home. Then I thought I should tell Jerald what was going-on. I needed to tell him to put me on the schedule with regular duty, but I did not think I would be able to make it through a hard shift. And lately all the shifts had been hard ones. I did not want to leave the unit short-staffed if I had to go home.

Jerald was in his office, and I told him what the rehab doctor said. I told him I did not think I could make it through a twelve-hour shift, and I did not think I should be taking prescription pain medicine and muscle relaxers while doing patient care. I asked if he could schedule me for some eight-hour shifts until my back felt better. Or if I could use some of my vacation time. I had enough vacation time built up to last over two months.

Jerald told me to wait in the waiting room for a few minutes while he talked to someone about it. About fifteen minutes later he called me back into his office, and said he was not going to put me on the schedule. I said: "What do you mean, you're not going to put me on the schedule?" He said: "You already told me you are not going to finish a shift. When you are put back on the schedule you will be terminated, and then you will not be able to get a job as a nurse anywhere. You really need to resign now." I was stunned. I said: "I need to think about it. Can I let you know tomorrow?" He said: "I really need to know now because there are nurses who want to work, and I need to fill your shift."

He had the resignation form in his hand. I took it and signed it. I started crying and asked if he would give me a good reference. He said he just would not answer any questions about me. I was crying as I cleaned out my locker. I felt like a failure as a nurse.

THREE

PSYCHIATRIC HOSPITAL

February 16, 2008

I have had a new job for the last two weeks. I put in a few applications, and I thought about the psychiatric hospital where I did some clinical training when I was going to nursing school. I had thought about applying there when I graduated, but Allen told me there was not enough money in that area of nursing. He was right, because the psych hospital closed, but it has recently been purchased by a large group and re-opened. I applied there and was hired immediately.

I am the only RN on the unit for my shift. I work in a unit for children and adolescents. I have a MHT (mental health tech) working with me. My shift is 3 PM to 11 PM Monday through Friday. My tech is Vanessa, a tall black woman about my age who takes care of the kids. They range from six to seventeen years old. She is strict with them. They have rules that must be followed, and she makes no exceptions. If the kids talk back to her inappropriately or argue with each other, they will be sent to their rooms. She does most of the work involved with meals and care, so this job seems perfect for my lower back and hip problem.

The paperwork involved with new orders, admissions, discharges, charting on each child and giving medications keeps me busy at the desk. The kids are usually admitted for violent behavior, taking drugs or running away. Some of them are in foster care.

One of the girls I admitted last week told me she was angry at her mother because she would not believe her about something. The mother said the daughter did something, but the girl said she did not do it. The girl took 16 diet pills and 2 antibiotics. She was only on our unit four days and went home.

Another patient, who was admitted on last night's shift, is a tall athletic black boy. He plays high school football and hopes to get a scholarship to play in college. He has an older brother and sister who have sports scholarships.

He talks constantly, mostly about what God has told him, and what God wants him to do. All the kids are given notebooks and encouraged to write. He writes about passages in the bible. He has a bible he reads and often asks Vanessa or me what a word means. He sounds like a church pastor when talking about God to the other kids.

I spoke with his mother on the phone, and she told me he had followed her around the house talking about God and what God wanted him to do. She said he got louder and talked faster until she became afraid. She left the house, and when she came back things were thrown around and broken. She called the police, and they took him away.

After being heavily sedated, he slept through the day until the start of my shift. A doctor was on our unit and wanted to talk to him. He sent me to wake-up the boy. I had to call his name a few times before he opened his eyes. The first words he said were: "I am a God." Then he said something about "my people." He was just waking up and I asked him if he was okay. He sat up and the doctor went in to talk to him.

About an hour later, he started talking constantly and pacing the unit. He was on one-to-one observation, which meant an RN or LVN must always be with him. An LVN was with him and wrote some of the things he said. He talked about killing his mother, saying he did not want to, but he would do it if God wants him to. He talked about "my people" and what he needed to do for them. He went on for hours. He asked the LVN, a black woman in her sixties, if she wanted to give him her phone number, so he could call her and talk to her more about God. He finally fell asleep after I medicated him at bedtime.

The next day he seemed a little better. The one-to-one observation was discontinued. He usually stayed in the central area of the unit where there is a big-screen TV, a sofa, chairs and a table. He would start to talk to the other kids about God, and Vanessa had to tell him several times to stop unless someone asked him a question. She told him that we were having "quiet time." When he started talking, he got excited and his words were too loud.

He stayed like that for a few days until he called his mother. He started yelling at her. He said what she is doing is bad, and she will not listen to him. He said he does not have to live under her roof anymore, and if she will come and get him, he can go live with one of his friends. He named three friends that he said he could stay with.

He became agitated and too loud. I said to him: "Tyrell, you only have a few more minutes." The kids must take turns during phone time. He yelled to his mother: "Now the nurse is going to make me get off the phone because of the way she thinks I'm talking! I've been holding everything inside since I've been here, and I'm getting ready to let it all out!"

It scared me a little. I was afraid he might do something crazy. Vanessa told him to get off the phone and go to his room because it was bedtime. I asked him if he wanted something to help him sleep, and he said: "Give me everything I can have. I need to get some sleep." I gave him his regular bed-time medication and some Benadryl. He went to bed and slept.

The next day I came in at 3 PM and was getting report from the day shift RN, when we heard Tyrell yelling at Kevin, who is a large black male MHT. He is good with the kids, and I think they listen to him because of his size. Tyrell was yelling about how he had to get out of here. He said his mother would not listen to him, and if God told him to kill her, he would. He said he had to get out and he was not going to stay with his mother.

The day shift RN called a "code purple," and about ten people came to the unit. The RN showed me where the medication for this kind of situation was, and I prepared a shot. The only syringes were of the largest size. I got an alcohol wipe and took the shot into the room where Tyrell was being held down by three men. I went past the crowd at the door watching and held the syringe down so Tyrell would not see it. The director of nursing said: "Do you have the shot?" I said: "right here" and showed it to her.

I moved quickly over to Tyrell and one of the men pulled his pants down enough to expose a buttock. I wiped the spot with an alcohol pad and gave the shot. Then I left the room to dispose of the syringe. There were enough people in the room, so I did not need to stay. I felt good about doing what needed to be done. The day shift nurse showed me how to complete paperwork that goes with a "code purple." Tyrell slept until supper time and then was okay.

February 24, 2008

It is Sunday and I am off work. I discharged Tyrell on Friday night. He was still talking about God too much, but the medication he was started on helps a lot. He was no problem over the last week. His mother and a brother came to pick him up. I went over his medications and follow-up treatment with her, and I could tell that she was worried about her son. Tyrell said the medication makes him sleepy, and he will not take it during football season.

Another of the patients admitted last week was a cute little girl eight years old. She is chubby with blue eyes, bright red hair and freckles. She was admitted by her stepmother. Her father is a truck driver and is out of town 50% of the time.

The stepmother said she was kicked and choked by the child. CPS got involved and had a problem with the stepmother. The girl has temper tantrums and says she sees things that are not there. She pulls her hair out when she is angry.

The first night I had her, she was fine until bedtime. Then she said she could not sleep and got angry when I said she had to stay in her room. I had already given her the sleeping pill and anti-seizure medication ordered to be given at bedtime. She stood in the doorway of her room and pulled out hair. She shouted: "I'm pulling out my hair! See!" She would hold up a hand-full of hair. I just told her: "Throw it away."

This behavior continued until she had pulled out a few handfuls of hair and she yelled: "You don't care, do you?! "I said: "No, I don't. You're the one who is going to be bald, not me." I did not want to seem mean, but I was afraid if I gave her what she wanted I would never be able to control her. Then she started hitting the door and yelling. I gave her a pill for anxiety, and she finally went to sleep.

Now every night at bedtime she has asked for the "sleeping pill." I usually tell her to try to sleep after taking her scheduled medications, which have been increased in dosage, but she always stays awake, and sometimes says she is seeing things. She will not go to sleep until after I give her the extra pill for anxiety.

She complained to the therapist that her head was itching. The RN on the day shift checked her head for lice but did not find any. I checked her when I came in that evening and could see the lice eggs. They are hard to see if you if you do not know what you are looking for. They look like tiny grains of sand glued on to the hair, usually about an inch from the scalp. We treated her with head lice shampoo, but no one had time to comb the lice eggs out with the little comb that comes with it, so I am sure she is not cured of the problem.

One night after I had been working at the hospital about a week, we had nine kids on the unit and only me and Vanessa for staff. One of the patients is an eight-year-old boy named Joey. He is thin with pale skin, big brown eyes, and curly dark hair. He is here because he said he was going to kill himself.

He is a very picky eater and usually does not like what is served. He threw his supper plate in the trash and demanded another meal. He was told he could have a sandwich, chips and a cookie. He refused, saying he wanted a "real meal." Vanessa sent him to his room, and he began yelling, throwing things around and tried to break the glass divider on the side of the unit close to his room. I tried to talk to him, but it did not do any good. Then it was visiting hour and Joey's mother was waiting in the visiting room. But Vanessa said Joey could not visit because of how he was acting. She said he had to stay in his room as a punishment.

That just made things worse. The secretary called from the office and said Joey's mother was waiting. I talked to the mother and explained what was going on. She told me when Joey had gotten like that before, he became suicidal. She said she would give consent for any kind of medication or a shot if needed.

While I was talking to her, I heard breaking glass in a room close to the nurses' station. Ray, a hyperactive twelve-year-old black boy had been sent to his room by Vanessa for arguing with another boy. He was yelling and crying and pounded on his window that faces outside until it broke. Then he tore-up his heater/air conditioning unit.

Joey was still trying to break the glass divider. He was trying to hit it with a wooden chair, but he was not strong enough to pick up the chair. One of the boys in the day area was watching TV and he yelled at Joey to stop making so much noise. Joey would not stop, and the two boys started fighting.

I called the nursing supervisor and told her what was going on. She said to ask one of the nurses on the unit next to ours (an adult unit) to help. I told her I was calling doctors for orders. I called the hospital's main doctor, but he would only give orders for sedative pills. I told him the pharmacy was closed and all I had available was the shots. He reluctantly gave me orders for shots, but he said he would have to talk to me the next day about being so quick to give shots. He was not Joey's doctor, so I had to call another doctor for his order.

I was going to give Ray a shot and called the supervisor to ask her to send a male MHT to help hold him down. She said she did not want us to "lay hands on the kids." At that point I did not know what to do.

Ray was tearing his room apart. I went in and asked him why he was so mad. He was crying and told me Vanessa sent him to his room. I asked him why, and he said he was picking out a movie and Robert (another hyperactive black boy) pushed him.

I told Vanessa what Ray said and she said Ray and Robert were fighting over who would pick out a movie and she sent them both to their rooms. Ray heard Vanessa telling me about what happened, and he cried that he did not do anything, and Robert pushed him.

He ran by us to Robert's room to fight him. But Ray has asthma and had just come back after being sent out to a hospital for pneumonia. He started gasping for air and vomited all over the floor in front of Robert's room.

Vanessa said everyone had to go to their room. The kids all became angry and started to destroy the day room. They threw the potted plants so dirt went everywhere, and they threw books or anything they could grab. One of the nurses from the adult unit said: "Do you want me to call a code purple?" I said: "Yes, go ahead."

The supervisor came with Kevin. He picked up Joey and took him to his room. He told him to stay there. It took a few minutes, but all the kids went to their rooms. The unit looked like a tornado had gone through it. I was disgusted, not at the kids, but at the response from the doctors and the supervisor. The kids had been yelling obscenities at Vanessa and me, but we were powerless because the supervisor said she did not want us to put our hands on the kids. And the doctors were not much help either. Joey's doctor never did call back.

The next morning the director of nursing called me and asked what she could do to help. She heard about what happened and I think she was afraid I would quit. I told her I needed an LVN and a MHT with me when I had that many kids. She said she would work on it.

Paula started working with us after that. She is a tall black woman with long white hair worn in braids. She is older than me and Vanessa, and good with the kids. She is an LVN, so she can help me with the charting and passing medications. Next week we are supposed to move to the old children's unit, which is being remodeled. It is in a separate building, away from most of the adults. It is a larger unit than the one we are in now. It will hold twenty-two kids, so I hope we get more staff.

One of the boys I admitted the first week I was here, Ricky, is a fifteen-year-old white boy. He is large for his age and is at least fifty pounds overweight. He was in foster care, but the family who had him did not want him anymore.

The night I admitted him, he talked loudly and acted like an angry gang member. He refused to remove his shoelaces or his belt, and he said we could not go through his things. He demanded a meal. The cafeteria was closed but we got a sack lunch for him.

The way he talked and acted, I thought I was going to have a problem with him. A male MHT had to check his skin for any cuts or bruises, which is standard procedure for male admissions. The MHT told Vanessa the boy's clothes were soiled with stool.

Vanessa told Ricky to take a shower and put clean clothes on, but she found all his clothes had stool on them. She gave him a hospital gown to put on and told him to follow her to the laundry room where they could wash his clothes.

Ricky was still talking in a loud angry voice, and I did not know if it was a good idea for Vanessa to go alone with him to the laundry room. But she was more experienced here than I was, so I thought she knew what she was doing.

I do not know what she said to him while they were gone, but when they got back, he apologized to me for the way he acted. He sat at the table and ate his sandwich. Then he went quietly to bed.

The next day I had to work on one of the adult units so I would be oriented in case they needed me to work a shift there sometime. While working there, I overheard a MHT talking about a boy, and I knew it was Ricky. She said that he had to wear a diaper because he could not control his stool. She said he had been molested as a child, and his rectum was damaged. She also said that when she had put him in the shower, he told her he had a small penis. She noticed he was right. She described his penis as the size of a bellybutton. He also had breasts that were larger than normal for a boy. She said she had to give him a shower three times in one shift because of the frequent stools.

Ricky has been on our unit two weeks now and he is a model patient except for the loose stool problem. The smell was terrible for the first three days. Then I decided he might be lactose intolerant. I told him not to drink any milk, and the smell is not as bad. He eats everything he can get and hides food in his room. When he walks by, we can usually smell that he needs a diaper change, but he can do it himself.

Another of our patients who came from foster care is a large 16-year- old black boy. He is not chubby like Ricky. He is strong, has facial hair and looks more like a man. He is heavily medicated and sometimes sees things and hears voices. Vanessa told me that when he was here before, he broke a male MHT's clavicle bone and kicked a pregnant nurse, causing her to have a miscarriage.

The boy has been no problem since he has been here. He always has a smile on his face. When the other kids are too loud, he asks for medication to calm himself (he has it ordered to be given as needed) and goes to his room.

One night he came to the desk and said he was having chest pain. I listened to his lungs, took his blood pressure and temperature. I thought he might have a little pneumonia. He had a dry cough and it hurt when he coughed or took a deep breath. At about 8:30 PM I called the hospital's primary physician, a doctor from India who is the attending physician for most of the kids.

He was upset that I called. He said he saw the patient at 5 PM, and he was fine. He said: "What do you want?" I said I just needed to tell him the boy was having some chest pain on the right side. He said: "This is an emergency?" I said: "No, I did not say it was an emergency. It's not cardiac." He said: "How do I know that?" I said: "Because I told you his pain is in the right upper lobe. That is his lung. The heart is on the left." He became angry and said to have the nursing supervisor assess the patient and call him back. When she called back, he ordered Robitussin.

When I saw the doctor on our unit two days later, an EKG and chest X-ray had been ordered. He said to me in a very sarcastic tone: "Thank you for telling me which side of the body the heart is on. Maybe I need to go back to medical school. Or would it be better if I went to nursing school?" I just smiled and said: "You're welcome."

After a minute he said: "I don't want to say anything that I will regret." I said nothing. Then he said: "This is not going to work out long-term. We will have to come up with a way to deal with this kind of situation." I smiled and said: "Just let me know."

He was obviously angry. I realized he thought I had insulted him, but I had not meant to. I said: "If I had more time to think of an answer, I might have said something different, but you asked me. And I had to call you."

After a few minutes he said: "Well, I was on my cell phone. Maybe I had a bad connection and did not hear you right." I said: "I could not hear you good either, and the kids were yelling." That is all that was said. I made sure I did not call him again at night.

March 3, 2008

It is Monday morning. Allen and I met our friends Bill and Teresa at a karaoke bar last night. Sunday night is "new song night." If you sing a song that you have sung less than four times before, after singing you can pick a poker chip out of a covered bucket. Some of the chips have prizes written on them. You can win a hat, T-shirt, prize bag, a drink or the money-pot. The money-pot starts at fifty dollars and goes up by fifty dollars every week until it is won. Then it starts at fifty dollars again.

Larry and I sang a duet we had never sang before, "Jacksonville." It is a fun song. Bill and Teresa each sang, and Bill won a T-shirt.

After I sang for the second time I picked the money-pot chip out of the bucket. I won one-hundred dollars. That made me happy, and we had a good time.

March 16, 2008

Work wore me out this past week. I had to stay late every night. My shift should be over at 11:15 PM, but I did not leave until 1 AM to 2 AM every night. Our unit is back where it was before the remodeling started. We have twenty-two beds and a large area. The nurses' station has glass walls around three sides of it and is long enough so that most of the unit can be seen from inside. It has a door on each end that can be locked to keep the kids out. We have a boys' side and a girls' side with a door between them that is often locked at night, especially if we have teenage boys and girls.

There is a day area with a TV, tables and chairs on each side of the unit. Sometimes during the day, we put the little kids on the girls' side and keep the older kids on the boys' side. The younger kids are hyperactive, and they bother the older kids. We also have a fenced yard and a covered patio. The kids can play outside and eat meals on the patio when the weather is nice.

Two of the boys I discharged last week were back. One of them, Billy, is a six-year-old boy who has a twin brother. He is a small boy with pale skin and blue eyes. He and his brother are foster children. They were in the same foster home, but they have been separated. Billy was sexually abused, causing him to be incontinent of stool. Like Ricky, he must wear a diaper.

When I re-admitted Billy, I asked him why he was back. He said he ran away. I asked him why he ran away, and he said he wanted a mother. I asked him if he meant he wanted his mother, and he said his mother and father were in jail. I said: "You know you can't live there with them in jail." He said: "I know, but they have been in there a long time. Maybe they got out by now."

It made me sad to think that all this little boy wanted was a parent, but it was not possible. He has had a few foster mothers, but the ones available to him only take foster children as a job. They usually have several foster children, and probably do not want one his age in diapers.

Billy must stay in a room by himself because he is on sex precautions. His foster mother reported to CPS that he tried to kiss his twin brother. I am sure Billy does not know what sex is, and he was probably just doing something he saw being done before.

There are four beds in the room we use for the little boys. Billy cried when I told him he could not stay in there. He saw there was an empty bed and asked why he could not have that bed. I did not know what to say to him. I could not tell him he was on sex precautions. Our therapist would be the one to talk to him about that. I just told him he had to stay in another room by himself.

One of the girls on our unit is named Cathy. She is eleven years old and large for her age. She is almost as tall as me and about 130 pounds. She is also a foster child, and her parents are in jail. She has pale skin, blue eyes and long brown hair. She has a grandmother who calls her but cannot have her at her home because she is taking care of Cathy's older brother. The older brother abused Cathy and there is a court order that he cannot see or speak to her.

Cathy is heavily medicated but is usually a sweet girl. She told me she wants to be a nurse, and whenever I take the kids blood-pressure and temperature she wants to help me.

Last week a few of the kids were watching a movie and Cathy started kicking the back of a chair that another kid was sitting in. Vanessa sent her to her room for a time-out, and she refused to go. Vanessa called our other MHT, Cedric. He is a young black man who transferred here from the same kind of facility in New Orleans. He is overtly gay and does not have much patience with the kids. He spends most of the time on his cell phone talking with friends.

Cedric was pushing Cathy down the hall, trying to get her to her room. Cathy became angry and hit him. The doctor and the kids' therapist were on the unit. Cathy was out of control and the doctor ordered a shot to calm her down. A code purple was called, and I gave the shot. The director of nursing came to the unit and was standing next to the doctor outside Cathy's door. She commented to him that I was fast giving the shots. We thought Cathy would be asleep in five or ten minutes. Everyone left except for me and Vanessa. I thought Vanessa would stay with Cathy until she fell asleep, so I went back to the desk in the nurses' station.

The next thing I knew the director of nursing was calling another code purple. I ran to Cathy's room and saw her crouching on top of her closet, which is about six feet high, with about four feet of space to the ceiling. She was high enough so that if she fell, she could be seriously injured. We could not pull her off because she was too heavy to catch. I said we should move the furniture and put her bed next to the closet, in-case she fell. We did that and then tried to coax her down for the next twenty minutes.

The shot was starting to take effect and Cathy looked a little sleepy. I knew she liked Coke, and I had brought one to work to have with lunch. I said: "Are you thirsty? I got a Coke in the fridge. I'll give it to you if you come down." She said: "No!" I said: "Are you sure? It's ice-cold." She said: "No!" again.

The director of nursing told me to get the Coke. She told Cathy she could have it and money for the candy machine if she would come down. Cathy came down, got the soda and candy, and was allowed to stay in the day room to watch the movie. She did not fall asleep until after she had her scheduled medications at bedtime. She has a high tolerance for medication.

Cathy was discharged last Friday. The night before she was discharged her grandmother called and told her that someone had dropped off her Christmas presents. On Friday when I discharged her to a foster mother, she asked about her presents. I called the front desk, but the secretary said she had not seen them. Cathy got upset and started crying. I felt bad and said I would look for them. I found them in a room where patients' possessions are locked-up (no one told me about the room, but my key opened the door). There was a big bag full of packages with Christmas wrapping and bows. She asked if she could open them, but I told her it would be better to wait, so nothing got lost. It is the middle of March, so she has been waiting for these presents a long time.

March 29, 2008

Most of the kids admitted last week were older. One is a large white boy fourteen years old. He is heavily medicated. The staff knew him from a previous admission. He is a bit of a celebrity. A year or two ago, he tried to kill a neighbor with a pickax. The story was on the local news. He chased the neighbor down the street while holding a pickax and yelling that he was going to kill him. The neighbor got away.

The boy is being raised by his grandparents. They are a nice older couple. The grandmother has been teaching him to crochet and he likes to do it. The therapist said it is good for him and a relaxing hobby. She said it is okay for him to have the crochet needles. It made me a little nervous. As a rule, the kids are not allowed to have sharp objects. They are given pencils to write in their journals, but they are not supposed to take them to their rooms, and the pencils are supposed to be collected when they finish writing. The boy was only here for one week and went home on Friday. He was a sweet boy, but a little sad. Sometimes he would ask for a hug. I think he missed his grandmother.

One of the medications he is on is also given to several of our kids. It is usually prescribed to prevent seizures, but these kids take it even though they do not have any history of seizures. It keeps them calm, but there are side-effects. They want to eat all the time and become over-weight. Ricky, Cathy and a new admit, Kaley, are all on it. I have noticed the boys on it have no signs of facial hair, and their breasts are larger than normal for a boy.

Kaley is a seventeen-year-old white girl who is diabetic and very over-weight. She gets large doses of insulin and has a lot of medications. She is on a diabetic diet and not supposed to have any sugar, but she gets the little kids to give her their snacks. Some of the little kids are on drugs that contain amphetamine to control hyperactivity. The drugs reduce their appetite, so they eat little of their meals. I have seen Kaley sit with them at mealtime and eat food they do not want.

I have had problems lately with Vanessa and Cedric. We do not have enough staff for the number of kids we have, and the shifts have become stressful. The kids often fight and need to be separated. Paula usually works with me unless they need her to go to one of the adult units. She is great to work with and the kids listen to her. But Vanessa and Cedric are not happy with the way things are going, and neither am I.

I usually have one discharge and one admission every shift. Some nights we have two discharges or admissions. As the only RN on the unit, I must do most of the paperwork with admissions. The doctor comes in every evening and writes orders on most of the kids' charts. We have no secretary, and I must make sure all the orders are carried out.

I have no time to help with the kids. I give medications, but most of my time is spent doing paperwork. Paula understands the amount of paperwork that must be done each shift, and she helps me with much of it. There is no computer system to do charting on. Everything is done on paper.

Vanessa and Cedric seem to think I am just sitting in the nurses' station relaxing when I am working on the patient's charts. Cedric stays on his phone most of the time and acts annoyed when I ask him to help with the kids. Vanessa used to take the kids blood pressure and temperature sometimes, but she will not do it anymore. The amount of work that needs to be done by an RN is more than I can do in an eight-hour shift, especially if the kids are not behaving well. On the nights I do not have any admissions it is usually okay, but that is not often. I rarely go home before 1 or 2 AM. Even then I know things are left undone. The late-night shift has started complaining about things that are not done by our shift. I have told Vanessa and Cedric things like picking up dirty linen and cleaning need to be done, but they do not listen to me.

The late-night RN and the nursing supervisor reported them to the director of nursing. Vanessa and Cedric thought I reported them and became angry with me. The next day at the start of shift, and in front of the day shift staff and therapist, Vanessa said we needed "better communication between staff on our shift." I said: "I tried to communicate with you when I asked you to pick up the dirty linen at the end of the shift two nights ago." She said: "There was no dirty linen." I said: "But there was dirty linen." She said I should have told her what room it was in. I had told her, but we were getting loud, and I knew the situation would escalate, so I stopped talking. I had to get shift report anyway.

The RN who has been coming in for the late-night shift is from an agency. She is a traveling nurse contracted here for six weeks at a time. Her name is Peggy. She is a white woman my age and has worked in mental health hospitals for many years. She is a good nurse and serious about her work. She is not afraid to tell staff working under her what to do.

Vanessa and Cedric do not consider themselves as working under an RN. When I ask them to do something, they usually roll their eyes and walk away, or tell me to do it myself. Cedric still spends most of the shift talking on his cell phone, and leaves Vanessa to get the kids ready for bed. He often argues with the kids and causes problems.

I have been late giving the kids their bedtime medications, usually because of admissions or fights between the kids. All the kids are medicated, and it takes time to get all the meds ready. Some of the kids become more agitated when their medication is late.

Each shift one staff member must take the kids who have visitors to the visiting room, which is in another building. That person must stay with them until the visitors leave or visiting time is over. Paula usually does that. When she is gone, Vanessa and Cedric often have a hard time controlling the kids.

We have a few hyperactive kids who are five to seven years old. They must be kept away from the older kids most of the time, because they make the older kids agitated. Vanessa watches them on the girls' side of the unit. Cedric is left to watch the older kids, but he is only twenty years old himself, and the kids do not listen to him. I must answer the phone, take care of admissions or discharges, put in new orders, get bedtime medications ready, take blood pressure and temperatures, and break-up fights.

Billy, the six-year-old boy who was on sex precautions, was discharged home again. While he was on the unit, he would ask me to dial his foster mother's phone number every night at phone time, but she never answered.

One of the little kids is a six-year-old black girl, Jackie. She wears her hair in long braids and Vanessa does her hair. She is the most hyperactive child I have ever seen. She is the leader of the little kids and makes them do what she wants. She is tall for her age and slim, but strong. She is on a lot of medication. She is given a medication that contains amphetamine twice a day and the medication for seizures three times a day (she does not have a history of seizures). She is so used to taking pills that she does not even need water with them. She can throw several pills in her mouth and just swallow them. Her parents are both in prison and she is in foster care. She must be kept away from the older kids because she will run up and grab something they are using and run away with it.

One day she instructed the little kids to push all the chairs together in the day room on the girls' side. She said they were "making a fort." Vanessa was watching them while reading a book. She probably thought moving the chairs would keep them busy and give them some exercise. Then she caught Jackie kissing Billy under the chairs. She sent her to her room.

Another little girl is Ashley. She is also six years old. She is frail with very pale, almost transparent skin. She had a black eye when she was admitted. She told the doctor that her brother hit her. But she told me she hits herself when she is angry, and she did it herself. Her chart said she hits herself and she is anemic. While she was on the unit blood tests were done, and she was found to have a thyroid problem.

Her parents are both in prison and she is in foster care. She told the therapist her mother and father took "naked pictures" of her and her brother. She is attention seeking, and always trying to touch people or hold their hand. The therapist has been teaching her and the other little kids about "boundaries," and I had to remind Ashley a few times.

Our youngest patient, Timmy, is a 5-year-old white boy with a bad temper. He is cute and often asks the older kids for a hug. It is hard to imagine that he was sent to our facility because his mother is afraid of him. She said he hits and kicks her and his siblings. The other kids in the family are also afraid of him. She will not come for a visit, but she talks to him at phone time. Every time she calls, he yells into the phone: "Pick me up! Pick me up!" Then he slams down the phone and starts crying. One of the older girls will usually go over to him and ask if he wants to play a game or draw a picture.

Nine days ago, on a Thursday night when Peggy came in to start her shift, there were two new admissions. I had done all the assessment, orders and given medications. She could see I was working as fast as I could. The only thing left to do on the admissions was put the papers in order in the charts and put patient name stickers on them.

Vanessa and Cedric were sitting at the desk at the other end of the nursing station doing nothing (except Cedric was on his cell phone). Peggy picked up one of the charts that needed stickers, walked over to where they were sitting and dropped it on the table. She said: "Sticker this." Vanessa and Cedric jumped up out of their chairs, yelling about how rude Peggy was, and how she was not respecting them. They said putting charts together was not their job. Peggy said they were not respecting me, by sitting there doing nothing while I was working hard.

Vanessa called the nursing supervisor, who was a tall black woman. She came to the unit, and Vanessa and Cedric continued to yell about how rude and disrespectful Peggy was. I tried to remain neutral. There was enough shouting going on, and I knew if I joined in, it would just make things worse. Peggy was not saying anything either. The kids were sleeping, and she is too much of a professional to be arguing at work. She knew she was right, and so did I. We tried to ignore them. The supervisor said we should talk to the director of nursing about it. On the way home, I thought it might be time to look for another job.

The next day a therapist was sent to talk to Vanessa, Cedric and me at the start of shift. We were told to make a list of who is supposed to do what on our shift. We were also supposed to make a schedule for our break times. The shift was too busy, and the list was never made.

I got two late admits. I obtained the consents needed and put the charts together, but I had not put the name stickers on them. It was 10:30 PM, and Vanessa and Cedric were sitting at the desk again. I did not want any more trouble, so I nicely asked Vanessa if they were taking their lunch break. She said they were, because they did not get to eat. I knew they had not left the unit, so they were entitled to the break time.

Their shift is supposed to end at 11:15 PM. I asked Vanessa if she was staying until 11:15, and she said she always leaves at 11:00 because she must go to her other job. She comes in fifteen minutes early to make up for it. I said: "okay" and asked Cedric if he was leaving early too. He said he was. Cedric is always at least fifteen minutes late, so he was not entitled to leave early, but I did not feel like arguing about it.

When Peggy came in, I told her I had not started on the assessment for my second admit. Even the skin check, which is something a MHT could do, had not been done. She looked over at Vanessa and Cedric, just sitting there. I said: "They're on their lunch break." She just shook her head.

April 1, 2008

Last night I had Paula working with me. The MHTs were Kevin from the day shift and Vanessa. Kevin had stayed to work a double shift. Cedric called in sick.

The boy I admitted Friday night, a sixteen-year-old, broke a hole in his window over the weekend. He broke his hairbrush and used the sharp end to punch a hole in the window. He said he did it because he found a cricket in his room, and he wanted to let it go. Staff had told him to flush it down the toilet.

At the beginning of the shift the therapist told me a patient's mother had made a complaint about me, saying I was rude to her when she came to the unit on Friday night to have her daughter admitted. Her daughter, Dana is a sixteen-year-old white girl. She is tall, thin and pretty. She is also gay. She was admitted after cutting her wrist.

I could not think of anything I might have said to upset the girl's mother. I am never rude to people, and I would certainly be sympathetic to a mother who had just brought her daughter in from the ER with a cut wrist.

After visitation Dana's mother talked to me on the phone, and said she wanted to take her daughter home. While talking to her, I realized that Vanessa was the "nurse" she was complaining about, not me. I told her Vanessa tries to keep the kids in line, but she is not mean to them. I talked her into letting Dana stay. She said she needed to know her daughter would be safe. I assured her that she would be. She asked me to call her back later.

I talked to Vanessa and told her to stay away from Dana. I was not accusing her of anything. I just told her Dana's mother wanted to take her home, but I talked her into letting her stay. I told her to only talk to Dana when she absolutely had to, and to be nice to her.

At about 9 PM I was starting to get the bedtime medications ready when I heard yelling. Jayden, a twelve-year-old black boy and Miranda, a twelve-year-old black girl were arguing. Kevin told Jayden to go to his room and he exploded. He yelled that he did not do anything. Miranda was trying to fight him, and it took both MHTs to keep them apart.

Vanessa told me later that Jayden and Miranda had been talking in whispers all day. Just before the fight started, Jayden told one of the other kids that Miranda wanted to have sex with him. Miranda got angry and said he was lying.

I let Kevin and Vanessa handle the kids and I started passing the medications. Jayden was yelling, throwing things and hitting his door. All the kids were sent to their rooms. Then I saw Dana coming down the hall, crying and holding her hand. She had punched the wall and the knuckles on her right hand were badly bruised. I asked what happened, and she said there was: "just too much drama" for her. I thought she was talking about Jayden and Miranda. I put ice on her hand and called her doctor. Then Dana's mother called and asked why I had not called her back. I told her I was just going to call her.

She could hear all the noise. Jayden was still yelling and kicking his door, which echoed throughout the unit. I told her about Dana's hand, and said I had paged the doctor, and we would probably get X-rays. I let Dana talk to her mother. She was crying, and said: "I did not say anything, and now I'm in trouble!"

I suspect Vanessa confronted Dana about what her mother said, and that is why Dana punched the wall. Vanessa had taken the kids to visitation, and when she came back, she made comments about Dana's mother. She said the woman was wearing fish-net stockings and a mini-skirt.

Dana's mother told me she is going to report us. She also threatened that she works in a lawyer's office. I am disappointed in myself because I did not keep Dana safe like I said I would. I am angry with Vanessa for upsetting Dana because she had a problem with the girl's mother.

April 2, 2008

At the start of shift the nurse told me in report that Kaley had complained of chest pain. An EKG was ordered but had not been done yet. There is no respiratory department at this hospital (they do the EKGs at most hospitals), so an RN had to do it. I had never done an EKG before, but there was an instruction booklet on the EKG machine. I did the EKG myself and it was simple to do. A stat chest X-ray was also ordered, and I had to send her by ambulance to the local hospital for that.

April 3, 2008

Today Kaley was in the day room with most of the other kids when her roommate brought a needle to me. It came from a little disposable thing used when checking blood-sugar on diabetics. She told me Kaley had been cutting herself with it. Apparently, the night shift nurse left it in the room after she checked Kaley's blood sugar. I asked Kaley about it, but she denied cutting herself. I asked her to show me her legs and she lifted her pant-legs up. I did not see anything. She refused to pull her pants down, so I could not see the top of her legs. I called the doctor, and he ordered a complete check of the room. Nothing was found.

Kaley's foster mother visited. Kaley had been in foster care for years, but her foster mother could not handle her anymore. Kaley is almost eighteen years old, and at that age she will no longer be qualified to be in the foster care system. Her birthday is soon, and she is scheduled to go to a facility for teenagers tomorrow. She will be kept there until her birthday, when she will be released. I do not think she wants to go.

Kaley did not eat supper, which is very unusual for her. Her blood sugar dropped from 358 to 152. Usually that would be good (for her). But I noticed she took only one bite of her bedtime snack. I thought she was trying to make it look like she was eating. She had 120 units of Lantus insulin (a long-acting insulin) scheduled to be given at bedtime, and she was asking for it. I refused to give it to her. She is very aware of how much insulin she should take and when to take it. She knows that if she gets her insulin and does not eat, her blood sugar will drop too low, and she could go into a diabetic coma. Then she would be sent by ambulance to the local hospital.

I called the doctor who was consulted for diabetic care and told him I thought Kaley was trying to make her blood sugar go too low, because she did not want to be transferred out in the morning. He told me to hold the insulin until she was eating. Kaley's case worker called, and I told her what Kaley was doing. The case worker talked to Kaley and told her to eat. I gave her a sandwich, but I saw she only ate the meat in it and threw the rest away. Then she asked for her insulin again. I told her she had not eaten enough to get insulin. She got mad and went to her room. Her blood sugar will be monitored closely tonight.

Jayden and Carter, a ten-year-old black boy, started fighting. Jayden grabbed a heavy water pitcher that was half full and was trying to hit Carter in the head with it. I grabbed Jayden by the back of his shirt just in time to keep the heavy water pitcher from hitting Carter.

April 7, 2008

It is Sunday and I am home. Friday's shift started out okay. Staffing was me, Paula, Cedric, and Kevin from the day shift, who stayed over 4 hours extra. Vanessa took a vacation day.

About 4 PM Carter started throwing a temper tantrum. Kevin sent him to his room. He started throwing, ripping, and breaking anything that he could get his hands on. He tried to cut himself with a broken piece of plastic, but only managed to get a scratch.

Timmy had been discharged home. His brother Jimmy, who is seven years old, was admitted last Tuesday. When I was doing his admission paperwork, one of the questions I must ask is: "Do you drink alcohol or take drugs?" He said: "No, but my daddy does."

Jimmy came up to the desk to show me he was bleeding. He has sores and scabs all over, and he picks at them constantly. He will show them to the nurse when he is bleeding, and we will clean it and put a band aid on it. I said: "I'm going to call you band aid boy." That made him smile.

He will not eat anything except cereal with milk. He is small for his age, and his skin is pale. He cries all day: "I miss my family!" He says it with a lisp because he has sores on his lips.

I was told an admit was coming, a fifteen-year-old girl named

Sandra. She had taken an overdose at school in the morning and was sent by ambulance to a hospital. They thought she was stable, and her mother was bringing her to us.

She arrived at 7 PM. Her mother and two counselors from her school came with her. She had passed out at school, and they found a note saying she had taken seven of her ADD pills, which contain amphetamine. In the note, she said that she was writing: "…so you will know how I die." A copy of the note was included with her paperwork.

I thought it would be a normal admission. Paula was gone with the kids who had visitors and I was trying to eat lunch. I put my food away and got the admission consents signed. I asked them a few questions and showed them the room the girl would share with another girl her age. The patient wanted to lie down, so I told her I would come back to the room in a few minutes to check her vital signs.

Her mother and the counselors said good-by, and I was just going to ask Cedric or Kevin to walk them out (several locked doors had to be passed through) when the girl came up to the desk and said: "I don't feel good." I told her to sit down. She looked like she was going to pass out. I tried to get her blood pressure, but the machine would not give me a reading. I tried it again and it still did not work. I thought there was something wrong with the machine, so I got my stethoscope and tried to get her blood pressure manually. I could not hear a pulse on her. I felt her wrist and I could feel a weak pulse.

I told her mother: "I can't get a blood pressure. I don't think she will be able to stay. She is probably going to need IV fluid, and we don't do that here." I called the supervisor and she said: "Call 911 now. I'm on my way." I called 911 and we took her back to her room to lie down.

The supervisor was able to get a blood pressure reading with the girl laying down. It was low, and she started shaking like she was going to have a seizure. The supervisor told me to go out and direct the EMTs to our unit. They arrived within ten minutes of the call and took her to the hospital. She got IV fluid and was sent back the next day.

One of our sixteen-year-old girls tried to cut her arm with a plastic

Easter-egg, the kind that holds candy. She broke it so there was a sharp edge. She was not able to draw blood, but she left a long scratch on her arm. Paula wrote an occurrence report and the girl's mother was called.

The mother wanted to come and talk to her daughter. Our therapist said it was okay. While the girl waited for her mother, she crawled under the desk at the nurses' station and cried. The therapist told her to go to the conference room and wait for her mother.

The building that holds our unit also has an adult unit. It is for adults who have admitted themselves, usually for drug or alcohol addiction. They have more freedom than patients in the other adult units. They usually have only one nurse on the unit for staff. The patients are sometimes taken out in a bus to go shopping or to a movie.

There are three locked doors between the two units. One on each end of our unit and one in the middle, behind the nurses' station. The door on the side of our unit where the girls' bedrooms are, is a double door with two small glass windows.

Cedric said he suspects two twelve-year-old black girls have been talking to someone on the other side of the doors and passing notes under them. He said the girls have been acting strange after bedtime, and he has heard music playing.

The girls seem to be taking showers often, late at night. When I went by their room one night their door was open, and the girls were both wearing only a towel. I think they have been showing themselves to someone who is looking through the little windows in the doors separating the units.

On Friday night when I went to the twelve-year-old girls' room to give one of them a medication, she asked me about the patients on the other side of the door. Then her roommate said something about "her boyfriend over there." I decided to knock on the door and see if anyone came to the window. No one came, but one girl was mad at the other for saying something to me about it. We told the night shift staff to watch them. I also put paper over the glass windows.

April 19, 2008

It is Saturday afternoon and I am home. Last Monday, Sandra, the girl who took the overdose, and her roommate Tiffani, both fifteen-year-old black girls started yelling. They were mad because the therapist let them make bead bracelets, but they were not allowed to wear them. The therapist said the bracelets would have to be kept in the locked room with patients' possessions.

It was 4 PM and the doctor from India was on the unit. Vanessa told Tiffani to go to her room and Tiffani started arguing with her. Vanessa said she was going to put her "on red." (her name is written on the board with a red marker, and she cannot leave the unit for meals or visitation). The kids who are not on red can go to the cafeteria for meals and walk by the candy and soda machines, where they can buy something if they have money.

Sandra said if Tiffani was going to be punished, they would have to punish her too. There was loud arguing between the girls and the MHTs. The doctor got involved and told the girls to go to their room. They refused and he became angry. He ordered that they both be medicated with an oral sedative.

Tiffani took her medication, a pill that dissolves quickly in the mouth, but Sandra refused. She put her bracelet in her mouth and said she was going to swallow it and choke herself. A code purple was called, and the supervisor came. Sandra ran to her room, with the supervisor and Vanessa after her. They bent her head over the sink and the supervisor got the bracelet out. She put the sedative pill in Sandra's mouth, but the girl would not swallow. The pill is made to absorb through the skin in the mouth, but when they let go of her, she ran to the curtains in her room and rubbed her tongue on them.

The doctor said to give her a shot and I did. The shot had no effect on her. He said to put her in seclusion, a small room off the unit. She just laughed and let her body go limp. She said: "I'm dead." The supervisor and Vanessa had to drag her over the floor to the seclusion room. I went ahead of them and opened the locked doors. A male MHT and the doctor followed us to the seclusion room. The doctor said to restrain her. She was put on a foam bed. We were told to use a "papoose board," which covers the patient and keeps her from hitting and kicking staff. We tried to put it on her, but no one had used it before, and we did not know how to tie it down. All the time we were trying to tie it over her, Sandra was fighting us, spitting and trying to bite. The doctor got the most spit on him. I thought that was funny.

We put a towel over her face to block the spit and tried for twenty minutes to get her restrained. We tried two other kinds of restraints, the wrist/leg and the net restraint, but nothing fit right. Everything we had was adult size. We finally gave up and just let her loose in the seclusion room. Vanessa stayed with her. The doctor said we all had to take a class on how to use restraints. An adolescent size papoose board was ordered.

Sandra and Tiffani were separated and not allowed to be roommates anymore. Sandra had to stay in her room for twenty-four hours after she was let out of seclusion. We did not have any trouble with the girls for the rest of the week.

Billy, the little boy who was on sex precautions and wanted a mother, was back again. He likes it here, but they only allowed him to stay three days this time. He has a new foster mother, and like the one he had before, this one also has several foster kids.

I had to work Wednesday on one of the adult units because they had an RN call in sick. The staffing person called me at home and asked if I would work the shift there and I said no. She said she really needed me there, and I asked her what staffing would be. She said it would be me and two MHTs with twelve patients. I said I would do it, but I did not want any admits. She said I could not have any admits because the unit was full.

When I got to work, I only had one MHT and then I got an admit. I guess the patient had already been assigned to the room and the staffing person did not realize the patient was not there yet. I called the supervisor and told her I needed another MHT. She talked Kevin from the day shift into staying four more hours, but nobody told me he was going home at 7 PM.

Two of the female patients started arguing over a bottle of Dr. Pepper. They were roommates, and they both claimed the soda was their own. One of the women accused the other of going through her things and stealing the soda. The supervisor was called, and the women were separated. A MHT stayed with one of them in the patients' room and the other patient stayed in the dayroom. The supervisor brought another bottle of soda, so they each had one.

When it was time to start passing out medications, I noticed that only a few of the patients' consents were signed. Medications should not be given without a signed consent form on the chart. I couldn't believe the nurses on that unit had been giving medications without it. I had to check all the charts and have several of the patients sign consent forms. I was on my feet most of the shift. I do not think I will agree to work on an adult unit again.

Friday evening at about 4:30 PM, one of the little boys on our unit told Vanessa that one of his roommates had his penis out of his pants, kissed him and said he wanted to have sex with him. Vanessa told Paula and she reported it to the nursing supervisor and the nursing director. I asked Paula if she could handle the situation and she said she would. She had to call the foster mothers of the boys, their case managers and report it to Child Protective Services. She was on hold for an hour trying to give the CPS report.

I was busy with discharges at the time. I had three kids going home and one being sent to another hospital by ambulance. The kid going out by ambulance was not sick. He was being sent out because his family did not have health insurance. Our hospital legally must admit any patient, twenty-four hours a day, if the patient is at risk of hurting himself or others and we have a bed available. But if the patient has no health insurance, we can then send him or her to another facility that accepts the patient.

The shift was busy and then an admission came at 10:30 PM. I asked

Vanessa to take the new girl's vital signs and do her skin assessment, which is just checking for bruises, cuts, or wounds. I did not have the shift report ready. I got a snack for the new girl and asked her to sit in the dayroom and watch TV until the night shift nurse could talk to her. I had her consents signed but that was all I had time to do.

April 25, 2008

Yesterday was my last shift at the psychiatric hospital. Melony, a fourteen-year-old black girl who has been on our unit before, came back on Wednesday. She is trouble and knows how to manipulate people to get what she wants. She talks about her sixteen-year-old boyfriend, and says he is going to rent an apartment for them.

Two of our female patients were thin white girls, thirteen and fourteen years old. One is bulimic and they are both runaways who were involved in gangs and drugs. I think Melony wanted them gone because she was jealous of them. Melony is overweight.

The shift was going well. Staffing was me, Paula, and Cedric. There were three kids who had visitors, and Cedric took them at 6:30 PM. Paula had all the kids in the dayroom while I worked on the doctors' orders, charting and getting the bed-time medications ready.

Melony asked me if she, the two skinny white girls and a black girl who is developmentally delayed, could go to the girls' side of the unit. She said they wanted to get away from the boys and noise of the little kids. There was no one to watch them but I thought they would be okay. I could see most of the area from the nurses' station.

They were acting a little strange, but I did not think anything about it at the time. The girl with bulimia had a one-hour restriction from going to the bathroom after meals, unless a staff member was with her. She said she really had to go, and she only had ten minutes left before her hour was up, so I told her to go by herself. But she told me I had to go with her so she would not throw up. I waited outside her room and told her to leave the bathroom door open so I could hear her.

While I was standing there, Melony and one of the white girls came up to me and started talking. They were asking me questions about the picture on my badge, about my hair and how old I was. I did not realize it, but while they were talking, one of them, I think Melony, took my keys, which were on a long rope keychain. The end of the keychain would usually hang out of one of the big pockets in my uniform top. It had a key that opened any door. Most of my uniform tops had a place to attach the keychain, but the one I was wearing did not, and I forgot to bring a safety-pin to attach it to my uniform.

After the bulimic girl came out of the bathroom, Melony started yelling about something in the girls' bedroom that I had to see. She said: "Come quick!" I ran to the room to check it, but there was nothing there.

While I was looking to see what Melony was yelling about, the two white girls escaped out the back door. There was a door on the girls' side of the unit that opened directly into a back parking lot. The door was rarely used, but the key opened it.

The developmentally delayed girl told me the two white girls had ran away. I panicked and ran through the unit to see if the girls were just hiding. That took about a minute. Then I wanted to run out the back door and try to catch them, but I did not have a key to open it. I called a code purple, and several staff came. A male MHT ran out the back door to look for the girls, and several of the staff drove around the area in their cars. The police were called, and the parents had to be called. I was a nervous wreck the rest of the shift. I knew I would be fired, and I was worried about the girls. But they had ran away before, and I knew they would do it again whenever they had the chance.

The girls were found, one of them at 2 AM and the other at 4 AM. The director of nursing called me and said to come in at 10 AM. I turned in my badge and called Allen on the way home to tell him I was unemployed again.

FOUR

LONG TERM ACUTE CARE

July 17, 2008

The last two months have been busy. I was hired at a hospital close to where I live. This hospital is a long-term acute care hospital. It is also known as a transitional hospital, because patients who need acute care come from a regular hospital and stay until they are ready to go to a nursing home, rehab, or home. We do not have an ER, so no one can be admitted unless a doctor has written orders for the patient to be sent here and the patient's insurance has approved the stay. The average length of stay for our patients is twenty-five days, but some stay for months.

The hospital is small, but it is part of a nation-wide company. They have several other hospitals like ours in this area. I was offered a five-thousand-dollar sign-on bonus, to be paid over eighteen months. I was started in a class that allowed me to test for ACLS (acute cardiac life support) certification. I have been in class one day and working two twelve-hour shifts each week. I will be working three twelve-hour shifts per week soon.

I am really enjoying the class. Our instructor has a PHD in nursing, and we frequently have guest speakers. Today we tested for ACLS certification, and everyone passed. We were all given cards which must be renewed every two years. Now I am qualified to work in a telemetry or step-down unit (level of care less than ICU but higher than acute care).

So far, I have been working my shifts on the third floor which has general medical-surgical patients (acute care). The second floor has the ICU, Step-Down, and Telemetry patients. If beds are available, acute care patients are also put on that floor. Work is busy and I usually must stay late to get my charting done.

There is only one medication dispensing machine on each floor and all the nurses try to get their morning medications out at the start of shift. After waiting in line for over thirty minutes one morning, I decided to come early the next day. But another nurse already does that, so I had to wait for her to finish. Then the night shift nurse who was supposed to give me report got upset because she could not find me.

The nurses' aides are called PCTs (patient care tech). I have already had problems with some of them. The hospital policy is that two people should work together when pulling a patient up in bed or doing turning and cleaning. Some of the PCTs will not come to the room when I call for help. I push the patient's call button, tell the secretary I need help, and I can hear it called over the intercom: "Lift help to room …" But rarely does anyone come to help me. I have waited over twenty minutes, calling several times, then give up and try to find another nurse who is not too busy to help me.

I am looking forward to going to the Step-down unit. The nursing director said I would be working there after I finish the classes. The patients there need to be monitored more closely than patients on the third floor. The nurses must take vital signs themselves every four hours, but the patient to nurse ratio is lower. On the third floor the nurses have six or seven patients each. On the Step-down unit I should only have four or five patients.

August 6, 2008

Work has been getting harder. I am out of orientation, and I have a full load of patients. Sunday, I had six and Monday I had seven. Sunday was okay and I got off on time. Monday was terrible and I got off about three hours late.

One of my patients was a large man in his eighties who came from a nursing home. Two of his toes are necrotic and will have to be amputated. But his biggest problem is a decubitus ulcer, also known as a bedsore. It started at his coccyx and now it includes much of both buttocks. It is a round hole about ten inches in diameter and it goes all the way through to the bone.

Bedsores are caused from not being turned enough, and the blood flow is cut off from the area that has pressure on it. It is a good thing that the nerve cells in the necrotic area are usually destroyed, so the patient does not feel pain there. I watched the wound-care nurse pack the patient's wound with gauze. She said she will try to get a wound-vac on it soon.

We learned about wound-vacs in class last week. I think they are great. The wound is packed with a piece of foam and attached by a hose to a suction machine. It has a low continuous suction which draws out excess fluid and bacteria. It also encourages the growth of new tissue. It is covered with a clear dressing. The foam and dressing are changed about once a week. The excess fluid goes through the tubing to a storage canister which can be changed when full.

Later in the shift I wanted to turn the patient, but I could not do it myself. The unit was short of PCTs, so all the nurses were doing their own vital signs and more of their patients' care. They were too busy to help me.

I was busy all day and was not able to chart anything until after I turned my patients over to the night shift. The last hour before shift change my back and hips hurt and I could barely walk. I was late for shift report and had missed some STAT orders that were written in the afternoon. I was trying to get an IV medication started when the patient said she was going to have to go to the bathroom soon. I told her to push her call button when she had to go. She knew no one would come, so she said she should go now. She asked if she should push her call button, and I said: "Yes, push it now." I told her we already had shift change and the night shift nurse was waiting for me to give report. I felt bad, but I was already twenty minutes late.

The next day my body hurt all over. I took Ibuprofen and stayed in bed until supper time. Allen took me out to eat because I hurt too much to cook. I had some Tequila and the pain felt better. We went to our favorite karaoke club and even danced a little.

September 1, 2008

Today is Labor Day. We have not gone anywhere or had friends over for Labor Day since we have been married. Being a nurse, it is easy to forget about holidays because hospitals never close. Someday, probably after I retire, I hope to have time for friends and entertaining. Now I am too tired. On my days off I just want to relax and rest.

My new job is not working out well. The area I hope to work in with the step-down patients is having rooms remodeled. So, for now I am usually on the third floor. Some days I am sent to the second floor, but I only have the regular medical-surgical patients. Last week I had to stay late on Wednesday and Thursday to do charting. I was busy doing patient care all shift on both days and hardly got a chance to sit down until after shift change. I had to take ibuprofen each night after I got home from work. Friday, I stayed in bed all day just getting up to eat and go to the bathroom.

I like the patients, and what I do is not complicated. Work would not be difficult if we had enough staff. But almost every shift we are told staff is short for some reason. We always must take extra patients, do part of the PCT duties or both.

I will not pull up or turn patients by myself. The hospital's policy is that two staff members are supposed to work together to do lifting and turning, and I do not want to risk injuring my back. Each PCT is assigned to certain patients, and I have learned to check at the start of shift to see which PCT has my patients. They rarely answer the call lights on the third floor, but staff on the second floor is better. I can usually get help if I am on the second floor.

Two of the PCTs on the third floor will not help me at all, even if they are assigned to my patients. When I call for assist, they will take twenty or thirty minutes to come to the room and then they come together. The PCT who considers herself the boss of all the other PCTs on the 3rd floor is Barbara. She is a black woman from Louisiana. The PCT who follows her around is a young black woman named Faith. I am not sure where she is from, but she has a foreign accent.

When I call for assist, if they come at all, they will stand by the door and say: "We have it." Then they will not enter the room until I leave. That makes it hard to do my assessments, because I cannot check the patients' skin on their posterior side if they are hard to turn.

On Wednesday I had a patient who was an anxious frail white woman. She was wearing a halo, which is metal brace with a round circle over the head. It is attached to the head with screws and is used to keep the head from moving. It is used for patients who have a neck fracture. It must stay on until the fracture is healed.

This patient had a Foley catheter and if she needed to have a BM, she had to do it on the bed pad and then be cleaned. She had a morphine pump, but I had to give her extra pain medicine five times during the shift. I also gave her anxiety medication.

At about 3 PM I was trying to start my charting when she called the desk to be pulled up in bed. Barbara was sitting next to me chatting with a friend on the phone. She was assigned to the patient with the halo. I waited to see if she would go to the room. I really needed to do some charting and I could not pull the patient up by myself anyway.

She kept talking on the phone for about ten minutes and then got up and headed down the hall towards the room. About fifteen minutes later, the patient called again. This time I went. There was someone from Physical Therapy, a white woman a little older than me, who had just finished cleaning the patient and needed help pulling her up in bed. She said she had been in the room when the patient first called for assist.

She said a PCT had come to the room, looked in and said to the patient: "You're trouble." Then she just walked away. The lady from physical therapy told me she cleaned the patient herself and then saw the PCT in the hall and asked why she would not help her. The PCT gave her a rude response. She asked the PCT her name because her badge was turned backwards, but the PCT refused to answer. The therapist was from a staffing agency and did not know the nursing staff.

I told the woman, who was almost in tears, that I had trouble with that PCT too. She said she wanted to report her, and I agreed. We went to the shift supervisor's office together and were told to write what had happened and give it to the manager the next day.

The rest of the shift Barbara and Faith taunted the lady from Physical Therapy every time she walked by the desk. They would yell: "What's your name?! What's your name?!"

The next morning, we were short of PCTs, so I had to take the vital signs on my patients. At about 8 AM, I was with the lady who had the halo and she wanted to be pulled up in bed so she could eat breakfast. I saw Barbara, who was assigned to this patient again, standing in the hall and asked if she would help me pull the patient up. She just looked at me and then turned around and walked away. I called after her: "Can you help me pull her up so she can eat breakfast?!" She turned around and said: "You don't tell me what to do!"

I went back in the room and wondered what to do next. In a few minutes she came back with a male staff member. I asked him what department he was from, and he said "Respiratory." I asked why he was pulling up patients, and he said he was asked to help. Barbara looked at me and said: "You got a bad back." She did not say it in a nice way, like she was helping me by getting someone else. This frail little patient did not weigh more than one-hundred pounds, so I could easily have pulled her up with a little help. I could lift her weight myself but pulling her on one side would make her crooked in bed. Also, she needed to be handled carefully because of her neck fracture.

I had told some of the PCTs that I needed help to clean or pull up patients because of a back injury. I had also told the director of nursing who hired me. She said it should be okay because two people were supposed to do patient lifting together.

Barbera said I had a bad back like it was something I was making up to get out of lifting. But I have never tried to get out of lifting a patient, I just wanted help. I think she wants to always be in charge and cannot stand to work with an RN. I was angry, but I did not say anything. I just walked out. I wrote up what happened both days and gave it to the manager.

Yesterday I was on the second floor and things were a lot better. I only had four patients. I had to do my own vital signs and blood sugar tests, but I did not mind. It was nice to be away from Barbera.

September 15, 2008

It is Monday afternoon, and I am at Nikki's house watching her husband John while she and Allen go bowling. They are on a senior league. Allen has been bowling on the team with his mother for the last few years. They have practice on Wednesdays, and the four of us used to practice every week for a few years. Sometimes I could not go because of work, but I liked to go when I could. But now John does not leave the house except to go to the doctor, and I cannot bowl because it hurts my back and hips.

I worked on the second floor yesterday and had a good shift. I only had five patients with no admission. We were short of PCTs, but I did not mind. I got to spend more time with each patient.

One patient was a woman who had already fallen twice at the hospital and had a bed alarm on for safety. I helped her get up to the bedside commode and noticed the alarm did not ring. I checked It, and the piece that plugs into the wall was missing.

In the afternoon she wanted to sit up in a chair and read her newspaper. I got her up and she asked if her sheets could be changed while she was up. I was taking vital signs, and I tried to find her PCT to change the linen but could not find her. So, I did it myself.

Another patient was an old man with an amputated leg and a wound vac on his sacrum. While I was taking his blood pressure, I spilled a cup of water on his tray, so I had to change his sheets and blankets.

In the next room I had a total care patient. She is a little old black woman who had a stroke and cannot get out of bed at all. She has a PEG tube with a continuous feeding. She also has IV fluid and a Foley catheter.

It was time for her medications, so I crushed and mixed them with water. I tried to put them in through the feeding tube, but it was clogged. I worked trying to unclog the tube for about fifteen minutes. When water did not work, I tried warm Coke. That usually works.

The patient spoke to me while I was working on the tube. She said: "I don't know what happened to my house, or my car." I talked to her, just trying to make conversation. I said: "You don't know where your car is?" She said: "No. And Willie is dead. I really miss him." I asked her: "Who was Willie? Was he your husband, or your son?" She said Willie was her son, and he died. She said: "Have you seen Tony?" I said: "No, I don't know Tony." She said: "We worked together at Harris Hospital." It made me think about how sad it was, for a person to be old and alone. I hope I die before my children.

I thought I should turn her over to see if she needed to be cleaned, but I could not do it myself. I called for assist and one of the other nurses came to help me. We washed her with soap and water, changed the linen and turned her. I told the supervisor about the clogged tube, and she brought a wire with a small brush on the end of it. I used it to unclog the tube.

September 19, 2008

I worked Wednesday and Thursday on the second floor. I had five patients both shifts. One of my patients was a white man about forty years old who had taken an overdose of drugs a few months earlier. He was in a coma for about two weeks. He told me that when he came out of the coma, he had a seizure and then a stroke. Now he has a contracted right arm and cannot use his right hand. His left arm and both legs are weak. He has a Foley catheter and a rectal tube that drains stool into a bag.

He can eat regular food, but he will not even try to feed himself. He insists that someone feed him. He will not try to pick up a cup, so someone must hold a cup with a straw up to his mouth when he wants a drink.

He is a very needy patient, always asking for something. He wanted to make phone calls in the morning and afternoon. I had to dial and then hold the phone next to his ear while he talked. He cannot move his legs yet, but he says they are getting stronger, and he can move his feet a little. He is taken to Physical Therapy every day.

Wednesday, he left his shorts in PT because they were dirty. He told me to go look for them and wash them. I told him nursing does not do laundry. He was upset because it was his only pair of shorts, and he needed them for PT. The patient called a friend, and he brought a new pair of shorts.

Thursday morning, he said he thought the rectal tube was leaking. He was anxious about it because he did not want to be messy when he went to Physical Therapy. I tried to check him and clean him if needed, but I could not turn him myself. I said he would have to wait until I had someone to help me.

The PCT assigned to him was late for work and had not yet arrived when two women from PT came to get him. They cleaned him, put on a diaper and the new pair of shorts. They got him out of bed with a mechanical lift and put him in a wheelchair.

When he returned from PT, he instructed me to take the shorts off, fold them and put them in his drawer. It was not easy for me to take them off him. He still had the rectal tube and the Foley catheter. I was able to do it myself, but it was not easy. He asked me if they had gotten dirty, so I checked and assured him the shorts were clean. I folded them and put them away.

I spent most of the first hour of the shift getting my medications ready and then did the short patient assessments for staffing requirements.

I was on the computer checking the lab results and new orders for my patients when I noticed the morning vital signs had not been entered. I thought the PCT had taken the vital signs but just not entered them into the computer yet. No one had bothered to tell me the PCT for my patients was going to be late.

I asked her what the blood pressure was for one of my patients. She said: "I just got here." I could tell she thought I had taken the vital signs. I said: "Just let me know when you have it." She said: "It's going to be awhile, I'm busy now." I said: "That's okay." I had to start passing medications, but I just went to the patients who did not have blood pressure meds first. One of my patients was calling for pain medication, so I took that for her. Then I checked the blood sugar levels on my diabetic patients and gave insulin.

The lady who wanted pain medication is a white woman about my age, but about eighty pounds heavier than I am. She has a wound vac attached to a wound in the middle of her back. I asked her what happened to cause the wound. She told me she had a large tumor removed from her spine and then it became infected. Now she has a wound that is deep, painful and slow to heal. New tissue will have to grow and fill in the wound from the inside. If the wound were closed, the infection would continue to grow inside.

The lady seems depressed, crying at times. She is obviously in pain and asks for pain med as often as she can have it. She also has Xanax ordered for anxiety. Her husband stays with her during the day and brings her food. She is diabetic, but I did not say anything about the fried chicken and french-fries they were eating for lunch.

Another of my patients on Thursday was a large German woman who I had as a patient the week before. She has snow-white hair, rosy cheeks and a German accent. She reminds me of my grandmother, who was born in South Dakota, the daughter of German immigrant farmers. When my grandmother's sisters visited, they would sit at the kitchen table drinking coffee and gossiping. Their conversations consisted of English and German words all mixed-together.

Wednesday the patient had a feeding tube placed in her stomach. She also had a PICC line placed in her left arm. Thursday, she had three different IV fluids running continuously. She had normal saline, amino acids with electrolytes and lipids. At about 11 AM she asked me to help her up to the bathroom. She had a Foley catheter, but she said she needed to "shit." I asked her if a bedpan would be alright, and she said it would be, if that is what we had to do. I tried to roll her over to put the bedpan under her, but it hurt too much, and she yelled out in pain. I was not sure what was causing the pain when I tried to turn her. I told her to just go on the bed pad and I would come back with someone to help clean her. I was being paged to another room, so I had to leave.

In the afternoon, when I went to replace some of the IV fluids, the patient talked to me. She remembered me from the week before, and she said I was her "buddy." She wanted me to stay and talk to her, but I was in a hurry. I was being paged again and told her I had to go.

At about 4 PM I sat down at the desk to try to do some charting. The phone rang and the secretary asked me if I could take report. I said: "I guess so. What kind of report?" She said it was for an admission and she handed me the form for report. The regular secretary had gone home and there was a young Hispanic woman taking her place. She was wearing a mask because she was sick. She did not say anything about what she was sick with. I discovered later that she had strep-throat and was coughing up blood. Our work area is small, and I was a little upset that I was working close to her, and she did not say anything about it.

After taking report, I got busy with my patients and was not able to do my charting. When I did have a few minutes, there was not a computer available to chart on. One of the computers was broken, and another was in a small room with the door locked. It had been decided that the nursing supervisor would use the room as her office. That left only three computers for all the staff on the unit to share.

At 5:30 PM I was paged and told the new patient was here. I asked another nurse about who was getting the admit and she said she didn't know. I asked the secretary and she said she thought I was. I told her I just took report. Then she asked me how many patients I had and asked the other nurses how many patients they had. I said: "You're going to decide who gets the admission?" She did not answer, but the supervisor was on her way to the desk anyway.

I had five patients and the other two nurses had five and four patients. The supervisor said I would have the admission. The other nurses said they would help me. The nurse with four patients did most of the work. She called the doctor to get admission orders and wrote the patient's medications on the order form. While we were doing the admission, I realized I was the only RN on the unit, except for the supervisor, so the admission had to be mine.

The patient was a DNR and came by ambulance from another hospital. There was no family with her, and she could not talk. She was too weak to move her arms or legs. She had a Foley catheter and a diaper on that was full of black liquid stool. One of the nurses helped me wash her. She had a terrible red rash and shingles.

At shift change I gave report about her and said I would finish the assessment paperwork. Then I went to the lab room to use the computer there. The lab person goes home at 5 PM, so I thought I would have the room and computer to myself. But one of the PCTs was there doing her charting. I waited for a few minutes until she was done, and then I sat down and charted for two hours.

On the way home I was thinking maybe I am too slow at what I do. I feel like I am going as fast as I can all day, but it's not enough. I thought about looking for another job, but I would probably face the same kind of pressure and stress at any hospital. And I like working with patients I get to know a little instead of having new patients all the time.

September 22, 2008

I am waiting for Susie to complete her cosmetology exam. She used me as a model to do a manicure and a facial. I missed a turn on the freeway on the way here, and we made it with only twenty minutes before the test started. Then we were told she had to wear a white lab coat. We frantically went looking for one nearby. Susie saw a nail salon across the street, and they sold one to us.

We made it back to the testing center just in time, and Susie signed the form to take the test. I also had to sign a form as her model, and I had to have a picture ID. I could not find my driver's license. I had left it in another purse at home. I begged the woman doing the sign-ups to let me use one of my credit cards as a form of ID, but she said it had to have my picture on it. I had my Sam's Club card with a small picture of me on the back, and she accepted it.

The people doing the testing are very strict. We could not even talk in the room where the testing is done. Susie was so nervous that her hands started shaking while she was doing my manicure. The lady doing the grading picked up Susie's bag of nail tools. She said the label written on it was misspelled. It was supposed to say "sanitized implements" but Susie spelled it wrong. The woman had a clipboard and was writing notes on everyone.

The models were instructed to leave when their part of the test was complete. The rest of the testing will take about three hours, so I drove to the shopping center where the nail salon is and bought a notebook. I came back to the testing center, and I am sitting in the atrium area, writing.

Yesterday I worked on the third floor. Barbara was off and I was glad. At the start of the shift, I heard one of the nurses was a no-show. The weekend supervisor, a Vietnamese woman a little older than me, said that she could give us each seven patients, but instead she would take four of them and give us each six. We appreciated that. The supervisor who works weekdays is a woman about my age from a Middle-East country. She never takes patients, no matter how busy we are.

In report I was told one of my patients, a Hispanic woman, had gotten the news that her son was shot and killed a few hours earlier. She was sobbing uncontrollably. The doctor had been paged because she said she had to go home. Family members started arriving. I asked what had happened, and one of them said the young man, the woman's only son, had gone to a wedding with his sister. Suddenly a shot was heard, and he fell over, dead from a shot in the head.

After taking an IV antibiotic to the woman, I had to start passing medications to my other patients. I saw the doctor go in her room as I started down the hall. By the time I got back to check on her, she had gone home.

When the night shift came in, one of the nurses asked what happened to the patient's son. I told her about how he was shot at a wedding. The nurse who had the patient the night before said it was not true. She said the young man had been shot outside a bar at 2 AM. I said I didn't know. It does not matter anyway. If the wedding story makes the mother feel better, people should just let her think that is what happened.

My PCT was a large black man from Nigeria. I know he is at least forty years old because he has some gray hair. He takes a lot of breaks, but I did not want to say anything about it, because when I worked with him a few weeks ago I said something, and he got upset.

One of my patients is a large black woman with a trach and a continuous tube feeding going into her stomach. I knew I would not be able to roll her over by myself to do turning and cleaning. At about 2 PM I heard the male PCT talking to one of the other PCTs. He said he could not check or clean a female patient by himself because he needed a female staff member present. I had not even thought about that. The nurse who had the other patient in the same room told me she and the PCT had already cleaned the patient twice, and she had been very messy.

I did not want to offend the male PCT, but I had to find a way to get him to work with me. The other PCTs on the floor had not wanted to work with me, so I usually left them to do most of the turning and cleaning. Now I was embarrassed that another nurse had been cleaning my patient all shift.

I talked to the male PCT. I told him we needed to turn and clean the patient more often. He said: "Turning is not the problem." I said: "I know you must have a female staff member with you, so just let me know when you turn her, and I will help you." He said: "She's already been cleaned twice today." I said: "I know, but we need to do it a little more often." He said: "okay."

About two hours later, I was taking an IV antibiotic into her room when he said: "Do you want to turn her now?" I said: "Yes, I was just on my way in there with an antibiotic." I smiled, and so did he. I think we can work together alright now. I have recently discovered that if you say something with a smile, it is a normal reaction for the person you are talking to, to smile back. It makes it easier to get along with people.

At the end of the shift, while I was charting, I heard one of the nurses who is an LVN talking about how one of the new LVNs was having a hard time with his charting because he was being trained by an RN. She said: "I think an LVN should be trained by an LVN." She asked me: "What do you think?" I said: "What difference does it make? We all do the same charting." She said: "No, the LVNs' charting is completely different. We don't chart anywhere near as much as you do."

I had no idea they charted less. I have recently become aware that there are very few RNs on the third floor. Maybe the fact that the LVNs have less charting and cannot do admissions, makes it easier for them to leave work on time.

September 26, 2008

Wednesday and Thursday I worked on the third floor. Wednesday was okay. Barbara was there but she did not have any of my patients. At the start of shift, I was arranging my patient information in a binder I use for work. There was a cup of coffee in front of me on the table. I heard someone say: "Where's my coffee?" I did not pay attention because I was busy getting my papers in order. Another voice said: "It's right there." Then the first voice said: "I hope no one put something in it. I know someone despises me, and the feeling is mutual."

I was the only person in the room except for the two voices, and I realized they were talking about me and the cup of coffee sitting in front of me. As a hand reached for the cup, I looked up and saw it was Barbara. The second voice was Faith. I started to get angry, because the inference was that I would poison her coffee. But it was the start of shift, and if I did not get right into the medication room, I would be last in line to get meds out of the dispensing machine. I just ignored them and walked out.

At about 10 AM Barbara was helping Faith, who was the PCT for my patients, to clean the large black woman who had needed cleaning often on Sunday. After they were finished, Barbara asked me why the patient did not have a Foley catheter. She said the woman's skin was going to get sores from being wet. I told her the doctor had not written an order for it. She said I needed to call him and get an order. I said I would call.

About an hour after I got the order, she said: "Did you get that order?" I said: "Yes, I did. I'll put the Foley in as soon as I get caught up. I'm too busy right now."

When I went in to place the catheter, I told the patient what I was going to do. She knew what it was because she has been unable to get out of bed for a long time. But she did not want it. She yelled: "No! I don't ever want a Foley catheter!" I just said: "Okay, never mind then." I could tell by how emphatic she was that she would not change her mind.

I thought maybe Barbara and I were getting along better, because at least she was speaking to me. I told her I tried to put the Foley in, but the patient refused it.

The shift went well, and I was able to get most of my charting done by 6 PM. I was expecting an admission. It was a returning patient, a 400-pound woman with chronic MRSA that caused puss-filled blisters all over her body. The lady had been sent to a nursing home after her last admission.

A nurse called report from the hospital the patient was at. She had been sent to the ER there and inpatient treatment had been started a few days ago. The nurse said there was so much infection in the patient's abdomen that drains were placed, and puss had been draining out into collection bags. She said the patient had at least eleven dressings, all over her body. She told me that every time the dressings were changed, they found new sores.

I got report at about 4 PM and was told it would be a while before the patient could be sent over. The nurse said they were very busy and medical transport had to be arranged. She sounded apologetic that it was going to take so long. I said: "Don't worry about it, take your time. We'll be having shift change here soon, so the next shift will probably admit her." I was glad she was not coming right over.

The secretary said something about the room not being ready yet because a patient had just been discharged. I told her the admission would probably not be here until after shift-change. I should not have said anything, because at about 6 PM another admission came to our floor. He was being admitted with a foot wound and amputated toe. He had been sent to the second floor, but he said his roommate was a "crazy man," and he would not stay in the same room with him. The supervisor decided he needed a private room, and we had the only one available.

The secretary said he was going to be my admission. I said: "But I'm already getting an admit." She said: "You're admit is not coming until next shift, so you are getting this one." The supervisor was standing at the desk. She said: "Just take his vital signs and do an assessment."

I spent the rest of the shift on the admission. He had a wound vac dressing, but I needed the wound vac machine. I asked the supervisor for it, and she brought one to the room, but she brought the wrong size drainage canister, so I was not able to get it started before the end of shift.

I asked the patient if he was hungry. It was already past supper time, and I knew the kitchen would be closing for the night in a few minutes. I got his diet ordered just in time for him to get a supper tray. His TV remote control was gone. I found another one for him, but it did not work. I told him the next shift would have to see about getting him a remote. At least the TV worked, someone just had to push the buttons on the front of the it.

Thursday was not a good day. At the start of shift, one of my diabetic patients had a low blood sugar. Normal is 70 to 110. At 6 AM her blood sugar had only been 20, which could cause diabetic coma and death. The night shift nurse had given IV dextrose (sugar). The patient was taking morphine for a necrotic wound where her right toe had been amputated. It looked like the whole foot will have to be amputated, because it is obviously gangrene. The night shift nurse had given the patient 4 mg of morphine at 5:30 AM, and now she was unresponsive. I took her vital signs myself and her temp was only 93. Her skin was cold to the touch. I was worried.

Just then a young black doctor came rushing in. He had been notified of the patient's low blood sugar by the night shift nurse. He called the patient's name and tried to get her to open her eyes, but she was not responding. I told him her vital signs and went to get the blood sugar monitor to check her blood sugar again. It was up to 40. I told him I was going to give another dose of IV dextrose. He said to also start her on IV fluid with dextrose in it. I gave the dextrose immediately, but we do not have IV fluid mixed with dextrose in stock, so I ordered it from the pharmacy. The pharmacist brought it to the desk, but I was busy with other patients by then. I had to take my other patients' vital signs because there was only one PCA. The doctor got upset that I did not start the IV fluid right away and told me he talked to the supervisor about it. I told him I would start it immediately. I checked her blood sugar again and it was up to a normal 110.

I finished taking my patients' vital signs and giving morning medications at about 10 AM. Then I had a quick cup of coffee and half of a Danish roll. The patient with the low blood sugar was still sleeping, but she would open her eyes when I spoke to her. A dialysis nurse came to her room with the portable dialysis machine at 10:30 AM. The patient wanted to get up and go to the bathroom before she started dialysis, but her bathroom was blocked by the dialysis equipment which drains fluid into the sink.

The patient stood up and almost fell over. She is a large woman and was very weak. I pushed the call light and told the secretary I needed a bedside commode. The secretary said my PCT was in another room giving a bath. I told the patient to sit on the bed and stay there until I came back.

I was going to get a bedside commode, but I was being paged to another patient's room. He was a little old man with one eye. He said he had been on the bedpan for a long time and needed to get off it. I told him that he would have to wait a few more minutes.

When I went towards the storage room on the other end of the unit, I saw Barbara sitting at the nurses' station charting on a computer. I knew she had heard the call for the bedside commode and ignored it. I said: "I need a bedside commode in room 306." She said: "They are in the storage room at the end of the hall." I said: "I know-can you get one for 306?" She said: "You can just get it yourself."

I was angry. I looked for the supervisor and found her in the ICU (it was on the way to the storage room). The young black doctor had already talked to her about not getting the IV fluid with the dextrose in it up right away. He had told the supervisor I needed to pay more attention to that patient. But Barbara was sitting at the desk and would not help me at all. I told the supervisor about it, and my voice was too loud, because the nurses in the ICU were looking at me. The supervisor did not want to get involved. She told me to tell the director of nursing.

I had to get back to my patients, so I went to get the commode. It was heavy and I dragged it down the hall. When I got back to the patient's room she was gone. I left the commode there and went to the little old man's room. I took him off the bed pan and cleaned him myself. I put cream on his butt. There was a red ring from sitting on the bed pan for so long.

The PCT assigned to him was a nice young black woman. She came in just after I finished cleaning him. I asked her if she put him on the bed pan and left him. She said she had checked on him twice, but he said he was not done yet. I told her: "I don't like having to do patient care by myself. You might like to clean patients yourself, but I don't. I'm 50 years old!" She said: "No, I don't like working by myself, but he turns himself good."

I realized that I was yelling at the wrong person. I was angry at Barbara, but I was taking it out on this girl. I said: "That's alright, I'm just upset. I asked Barbara to get a bedside commode for 306 and she told me I could just get it myself. It's okay." I wanted to apologize, but I just ran out to see what was going on with the lady who had the low blood sugar.

She was back in her room. She told me she went to the bathroom in the room next to hers. Then she came back and sat on the bedside commode I had left in her room and tried to urinate. The doctor ordered a urine culture, so I told her not to throw tissue in the commode until after I got the sample. But she could not urinate. She had her dialysis treatment in her room and then ate lunch.

I went to talk to the director of nursing, but she was in a meeting. Later in the afternoon I talked to her about Barbara. I told her the patient was unsteady on her feet, and I was worried she might fall if I left her alone while I went looking for a bedside commode. She agreed that a call for patient care took priority over charting. She said she was "working with Barbara."

At about 6:30 PM a PCT from the night shift came in. Barbara was sitting at the computer next to mine. The night shift PCT asked her how many PCTs were on the day shift. She said: "There was only two." The night shift PCT said: "Oh, that's hard. How many nurses were there?" Barbara said: "Four nurses." The secretary looked at the board and said: "Five nurses." Then Barbara said: "No, we only had four nurses."

I thought about what she said, and I looked at the board. There were the names of five nurses on it. She was implying that I did not count. I just kept on with my charting and ignored what she said. I was already about two hours behind, and I needed to keep focused on what I was doing.

But in my mind, I saw myself turning towards Barbara, who was sitting next to me, and punching her in the face, knocking her off her chair. I could almost feel her cheek against my knuckles. I knew that doing it would mean the end of my nursing career. So, I just imagined it, and it was a sweet daydream.

September 29, 2008

Yesterday was Sunday and I worked on the third floor again. Barbara was not there. I had the older male PCT that I worked with the Sunday before. I had seven patients and four of them were male. I let him handle most of the cleaning and turning for the male patients, but I put ointment on the ones who needed it.

One of my patients was a large white man, about six-hundred pounds, with congestive heart failure. He is only fifty-one years old, and he used to be a police officer. He has a dry sense of humor. He says mean-sounding things to staff and then he will watch to see what your reaction is. I realized that he acts the way he does for his own amusement. He is obviously bored with staying in bed all day. I think he has been bed-bound for a few years. He has gotten too big to get out of bed at all. He eats a lot, even though he is not supposed to. Whenever he has visitors, he asks for food and acts like he is starving.

He almost got a reaction from me the first time I brought his medications in. He asked me what the pills were for, and what they did. I did not know what two of his pills were for, and he said: "Are you an RN?" I said: "Yes," and he said: "And you don't know what you're giving me?" I said I would have to look them up. He said: "I want to know!" So, I went out and found a drug book. I took it to his room and read to him what it said about his pills.

The respiratory therapist came in to give him a treatment and he told her he did not want it then. She knew how he acted, and she said:

"You're going to get your treatment right now!" The PCT and I were both in the room, and the patient yelled: "Will somebody throw this woman out of my room?!" The therapist knew he was not serious, and she just laughed.

He is the largest patient I have ever seen. He cannot even roll over without three or four people to help. He does not have a Foley catheter. He told me to look under his belly to see if a towel was there. I lifted his lower abdomen and told him there was no towel. He told me to send the male PCT back in, because he knew what to do. I finished giving his medication and told the PCT the patient wanted to see him.

I had to go back to his room with Tylenol he had asked for, and he was yelling at the PCT for not leaving a towel under his belly. The patient told me to watch and see how it was supposed to be done. The PCT folded a towel, lifted the man's lower abdomen, and placed the towel under it. The patient said: "You might want to look the other way." I did not look away because I wanted to see what he was doing, and I needed to inspect the patient's skin for my assessment.

In the area where I expected to see a penis, there was only a hole. I realized the man's abdomen had grown around and over his scrotal area. He told the PCT to come back in a few minutes and remove the towel. The PCT said he was going to lunch. The patient said: "It will only take me a few minutes!" The PCT said: "I'll think about it." The way the patient urinates is that a large bath towel is folded and pushed in the area under his abdominal fat. He urinates into the towel and then it is removed.

Even with seven patients, I got off work by 8 PM. But I do not think I did as much patient care as I should have. One of my patients was an elderly man with a huge bed-sore on his coccyx area. The wound care nurse changed his wound vac dressing. I did not really do much for him except give his medications. I crushed them and mixed it with chocolate pudding. He likes pudding, so I fed him a whole container of it. I do not think he was turned every two hours like he should have been.

After work I picked up hamburgers on the way home, and then Allen and I went out to karaoke. We met our friends Bill and Teresa at the bar where Sunday is "New Song Night." Bill had a large button on that read: "Officially Retired." He had worked for the railroad for many years and decided to retire at age sixty. His wife, Teresa, is about two years younger than me. She is cutting her work hours back to part-time so they can enjoy Bill's retirement. I must admit that I am a little jealous of them, being able to retire now, but I am happy for them.

They are taking their boat and motorhome to a nearby lake soon, and I have scheduled a week vacation time so we can meet them there. Nikki and John own a cabin at the same lake, and we are going to stay there for a few days. I am really looking forward to some time off.

October 13, 2008

Last week we spent four days at the lake. The cabin is small, old and has not been lived in for twelve years. John's brother, who lost a leg in World War II, lived there for many years until he died. His military uniform is still in the closet, and there are still old cans of coffee and canned vegetables in the kitchen. John has always paid the utility and phone bills for the cabin, and the electricity and phone were left on after his brother died.

The roof leaks a little and needs to be replaced, but Allen's brother put a tarp over it, so it's dry. The cabin still has furniture in it, and the TV, air-conditioner and kitchen appliances all work. Allen's brother is going to inherit the cabin someday, so it has been left up to him to see about putting a new roof on it.

We only used the cabin for a place to sleep and shower. We met Bill and Teresa for breakfast every day at the local café, and we cooked outside every night at the park where Bill and Teresa had their motorhome parked.

The weather was nice, and I went swimming in the lake a few times. We went fishing but did not catch enough for a meal, so we just let the fish go. Every night we made a fire by the lake in a pit we made with big rocks. We had a good time.

Yesterday was Sunday and I was on the third floor. I had seven patients to start and discharged one at about noon. The hospital census was low, so a few nurses were canceled. I did not complain about having seven patients. The supervisor told us the hospital must make a profit, and when the patient census is low, everyone must work harder to keep the profit margin up.

One of my patients is a large white man who is in wrist restraints. He is only fifty-five years old. He was sent to our hospital from another hospital after being unconscious and not breathing for a few minutes. His brain was injured from a loss of oxygen. Now he can move his arms and legs, but he is confused and weak. He has a feeding tube with a continuous feeding. He has the worst sleep apnea I have ever seen.

He fell asleep at about 1 PM, and he would stop breathing. He had a monitor on, and an alarm would ring whenever his oxygen saturation got too low. I would have to go in and yell at him to wake up and breathe. A few times I had to shake him before he would wake up and take some breaths. Then he would fall into a deep sleep again. I could not stay in the room with him, so I called the respiratory therapist and asked her to put his C-PAP on him. It is a machine that forces oxygen into his lungs when he stops breathing.

But the therapist would not put it on him. She said it was only ordered for at night. She said he was a DNR anyway, and it would probably be the best thing for him if he just stopped breathing. The patient was always tied down, and when he was awake, he was yelling to get out of bed. I told her she was probably right, but I was too busy to deal with all the paperwork that goes with a patient death. I said I just wanted him to make it through my shift. He slept the rest of the afternoon, and every time I went by his room, I would look in to see if he was still alive.

Another patient was a young black man with HIV. He has a Foley catheter because he is too weak to use a urinal and he cannot get out of bed. He has a rash on one leg, and I put ointment on it. He has a bump and a small open area on his neck where a trach was removed. He asked me about it and said there was a little clear fluid coming out of it. He would dab at it with a tissue. He seemed like a very neat person and asked me to clean his bed-side table before I left. I had gotten a little ointment on his bedrail when I put it on his leg, and he pointed to it, so I cleaned it off.

The wound-care nurse who worked on the weekends found a better job working for the VA. Sunday was her last shift at this hospital. Some of the nurses started crying when she started to leave. She said she would stop in to have lunch sometime and she rushed out. I think she was going to start crying too. She had been at this hospital a long time and she is a good nurse. But she is only an LVN, and the VA is going to send her to classes to get her RN license. They are even going to pay her for the time she spends in class. She has a daughter to support, and this is a good opportunity for her.

One of the doctors who saw patients at this hospital committed suicide last week. I heard some of the nurses talking about it, but they did not say anything specific about what he did. One of them said she heard he was going through a divorce.

October 17, 2008

I worked Wednesday and Thursday on the second floor. I had to stay two hours late on Wednesday and three hours late on Thursday. I do not know how much longer I can do this job. I feel competent in what I am doing, but the physical part of it is wearing me down. Both shifts my feet, hips and back hurt during the last few hours before shift change. I was struggling to walk up and down the hall between my patients' rooms, the medication room and the nurses' station.

I had the German lady again on Thursday. She was not doing well. She was in restraints with mittens over her hands. She had a continuous tube feeding going to her stomach. She was not allowed to eat or drink anything. Her mouth was dry, and the skin was peeling off her lips. The respiratory therapist came in and did mouth care for her. I cleaned around the tube where it went into her stomach and put a fresh dressing on it, but I did not have time to do much more.

The German lady had said I was her "buddy" and had spoken to me clearly before. But this shift, she did not recognize me. She yelled: "Take it out!" repeatedly. I asked her where she hurt, but all she would say was "Take it out!" I did not know if she was talking about her Foley catheter, her feeding tube or her PICC line. Later I noticed her arm was swollen where her PICC line was.

The second time I went in to give medication, she started calling: "Mama! Mama!" I wanted to give her something to help her relax, but she did not have anything ordered. She had Darvocet ordered for pain, so I crushed one and put it in through her feeding tube. She slept for the rest of the shift.

Another patient with a tube-feeding was an elderly Hispanic dialysis patient. He had gone to Mexico to have a dialysis shunt placed in his arm and it got badly infected. Now he is dying. He was sent to this unit from the ICU after having a tracheostomy done. The trach has oxygen going to it from a ventilator. He also has cardiac monitoring. He is my first vent patient.

He was made a DNR, and his family wants comfort care including frequent morphine. One of his daughters was in the room just before shift change, and asked me: "How long do you think it will be before he can rest?" The patient was already asleep and had not been awake all shift, so I knew she was asking about when he would pass away. I told her it would be soon, but I could not tell exactly when. I said it could be any time now or a few days. His vital signs were still good.

I think it is a mistake to have a tube-feeding running on a patient who has no hope of recovery. It just extends the death process. It does not make the patient feel any better, especially when he is non-responsive. When a tube-feeding is running continuously, the patient will usually have frequent loose stools. It is a lot of work for staff to keep the patient clean, and the turning and cleaning is uncomfortable and sometimes painful for the patient. Family members are usually asked to leave the room during cleaning, and they do not realize how much the patient is suffering from it. We often must wake patients from a sound sleep and listen to their screams of pain while we clean them. Patients' bottoms become red and excoriated. Those who live long enough get ulcers that can go through to the bone. In theory this should not happen. But it does happen, and much too often.

October 27, 2008

This past week I was on the second floor Wednesday, Thursday and Sunday. The first two days I had a busy group. All my patients were on IV antibiotics and two of them asked for pain medicine every three hours.

At about 7:30 AM on Thursday, a patient who was legally blind and had a wound vac asked me to make him a pot of coffee. His family had brought him a coffee-pot and bottled water from home. I told him I was too busy, and there would be coffee with his breakfast in a few minutes. I had to give insulin to the diabetic patients and one of my dialysis patients must have medication before breakfast.

The patient refused to drink our water or coffee made with it. He said he did not want the coffee that came with breakfast. He got angry and called administration. He told them I refused to make him coffee. The director of nursing and the supervisor came to the unit about noon and had a talk with me about it.

Wednesday, I stayed two hours late and Thursday I stayed almost three hours late. Both days I started with six patients, and Thursday I got an admit. I was seriously thinking about transferring to the night shift. I was tired all day Thursday because I had to stay so late the night before and I did not get enough sleep. By the end of the shift, I was so exhausted and aching that I felt sick.

Sunday, I got a different group of patients. I had a good day and got off on time. At about 4 PM the secretary from the third floor came down to get away from her desk for a while and take a break. She was talking to our secretary and one of the nurses at the desk. She said one of the patients on her floor had been calling 911 repeatedly on Friday night, and the calls had been recorded. The patient had a trach and his nurse, a male LVN, put the Passy Mir valve on it without deflating the cuff. The Passy Mir valve allows the patient to talk and eat, but the cuff must be deflated first, or the patient will not get enough air.

The nurse is lucky the patient did not die. The patient's family is planning to use the 911 recordings to sue the hospital. I do not know what they are going to sue for, because the patient is okay, and is still at the hospital.

October 29, 2008

It is Thursday morning, and I was supposed be at work, but I called in sick. I had to work on the third floor yesterday and I had Barbara for all my patients. In the morning I had to take the blood pressures on my patients who had blood pressure medications due. I did not know if Barbara had taken the vital signs or not, but there was nothing entered in the computer. I was not going to ask her because I knew she would not give the vital signs to me, and she would say something rude that would upset me. Work is hard enough already, and I do not have time to waste arguing with someone who is just looking for a fight. I will not let myself get into a yelling situation at work again.

I had five total care patients and a patient with an autoimmune disorder and a low hemoglobin level. She had blood ordered but refused it. I spent more time with her than any of the other patients. She is allergic to almost everything. She has TPN (IV nutrition) running to a PICC line because she is afraid to eat most foods.

She is in her forties and is thin and pale. She had questions about everything, including her treatment options. I had to tell her I could not recommend any treatment or medications because I am only a nurse. She would have to talk to her doctor about those things.

She said she wanted to talk to a doctor about her risk of having a reaction to the blood that was ordered. She was also afraid of the heparin that was ordered for her. She said her blood was already too thin. I called her doctor, but he said he did not care if she got the blood or not. He didn't care if she got the heparin either.

I did not have any lift help with my five total care patients all shift. When one of them was brought back from physical therapy, they left him in a special chair next to his bed. He wanted to get back in bed, but I did not know how to do it myself. I noticed he had a plastic sheet with nylon loops on the sides and thought it was for the mechanical lift. I brought the lift into his room and tried to figure-out how to use it.

The physical therapy tech was bringing his roommate back and asked if I would like some help. I said yes, and she showed me that the plastic sheet was not for the lift, but for sliding the patient onto the bed. The special chair could be positioned flat, placed next to the bed, and the patient could be pulled onto the bed using the nylon handles on the sides of the plastic sheet.

The patient is a very large man, and he had an extra-large bed. The PT tech expected me to reach across the bed and pull him over. I could not reach the nylon handles without laying over, on the bed and reaching across. In that position I would not be able to pull him over. Anyway, I am not willing to risk injuring my back. I told her we would have to get more help.

There was a young black female PCT in the hall delivering lunch trays, and I asked her to help us just for a minute. At first, she said that she couldn't because she had to pass out all the lunch trays. I told her I just needed help pulling the patient over. I also said: "Why are you passing out all the lunch trays?" She said: "Well, someone has to do it. I couldn't just leave them sitting there." She was obviously frustrated that she had to do more than her share of the PCT work. Barbara must have intimidated her like she does all the other PCTs. When she brought the lunch trays in for my patients, she stopped and helped us get the large man onto his bed.

Just after lunch I went to the office of the lady who does the staff scheduling. I told her I would like to transfer to the night shift. I said I had worked most of my nursing career on the night shift and I wanted to try it again. She said she would talk to the nursing director about it.

The shift was busy. I had a lot of IV antibiotics, tube feedings and patients with problems. I got the consent form for blood signed by the patient who is allergic to everything and drew her blood for a type and cross. While I was busy doing that, one of my patients was having trouble and could have died. She was a DNR, but she still deserved more care than I gave her.

I had paged the doctor for the DNR patient at least five times during the shift, but he never called back. When he finally came to the hospital at about 5 PM, she had a blood sugar level of 34. Then he got all excited about it and started giving orders. The patient did not have blood sugar checks ordered, and now he was acting like her condition was my fault. I gave IV dextrose, and her blood sugar came up to a normal level within twenty minutes. Then he ordered IV fluid with dextrose in it to run continuously. That was a mistake, because the woman had a feeding tube that could be used instead. She already had edema and her lungs sounded wet. I think her heart was weak, and not able to handle all the fluid going in. Even the IV antibiotics I had given her earlier made her swell up more. She was foaming at the mouth before the next doctor came in. He is a young doctor, and I do not think he really knows what he is doing yet, because he did not order any Lasix to help get rid of the excess fluid.

It was close to the end of shift, and I was behind on giving antibiotics for other patients. I had too much that needed to be done right away. The director of nursing had told me I should ask the nursing supervisor for help if I needed it. I went to the supervisor from the Middle East and told her I needed help. She said: "Why are you always so busy? You always say that you have too much to do." She said it in a very critical way, so I just said: "Never mind."

I tried to catch up with my other patients and I did not do the blood sugar check that the doctor had ordered to be done on the patient with the low blood sugar. He ordered it to be checked every fifteen minutes. The doctor was at the desk and paged me to ask what it was. I was in another patient's room and did not answer right away. It was a patient who had complained of chest pain earlier in the afternoon. I went to the desk as quickly as I could, and I told him I had not checked the blood sugar yet. I went to check it, but the blood sugar monitor was gone. There is only one for the unit, and I looked for it but could not find it. The doctor told the supervisor to have someone else do it. He treated me like I was incompetent.

Then the blood bank called and said the blood samples I had sent for the type and cross did not have the paperwork with them. I had labeled the tubes correctly and filled out the paperwork properly, but I did not know the forms were supposed to be sent to the lab with the blood tubes. Now I had to start all over and draw new blood samples.

By the time I had the blood draw finished it was time for the next fifteen-minute blood sugar test. The doctor had already left and wanted to be called with a report on the patient's condition. It was already after shift-change time, so I told the night shift nurse to call him. I was trying to get started on my charting when she told me the doctor had ordered a 500 ml bolus of normal saline. She was worried about it because the patient was already very swollen-up.

As I charted, I realized there were still a few things I had not done. One patient had a colostomy bag that needed to be emptied (the PCTs at this hospital refuse to empty colostomy bags) and another had a 6 PM medication I had missed. I also had a patient who needed a dose of protein powder that was scheduled at 6 PM.

I finished doing the things I had missed and then went back to charting. There were workers waxing the floor, and when they started doing the nursing station I had to move. I went to the second floor to continue charting in the lab. The lab tech was gone, so the room was available for me to use.

I was working on my last patient's charting when the supervisor came in and looked at the phone number on the phone. Then the phone rang, but I did not think it was for me, so I didn't answer it. She opened the door and looked at me. I said: "Was that for me?" She said it was, and she would send it through again.

It was a woman I did not know, and she was asking what I was doing. I told her I was just finishing-up my charting. She said: "You work a twelve-hour shift. You need to give report at 7 PM, clock-out and go home." I told her I was almost done, and she said: "You need to clock- out right now and go home." So, I did.

On the way out I went by the supervisor's office and told her that I did not feel good, and I would be sick in the morning. She just said: "okay." This is the first day I have called in sick in long time. Allen was worried I might get fired, so I set the alarm for 4:20 AM and made the phone call to make sure it was noted that I called in sick.

November 14, 2008

I started on the night shift Monday. For the first two nights I only worked 7 PM to midnight, because there is an RN who comes in at that time. She is a young married woman from India, and her husband gets off work at 11:30 PM. She puts her two small children in the car and goes to pick him up from work. Then he drops her off at the hospital and takes the kids home. She does not like waking the kids up at night and is looking for a day shift job.

On Wednesday I worked the entire shift. I liked it better than the day shift. It was busy until midnight, but then I had time to start my charting. The first two nights, I worked on the second floor and was too busy to get to know the staff. The third night I was on the third floor. Staffing was me and a young black male RN who is American, two LVNs and three PCTs. The LVNs were a white female nurse, about my age, and a young black male nurse from Nigeria. The PCTs were black women from African countries.

During the first few hours of the shift, when I was busy and could have used some help, my PCT seemed more interested in eating than working. One of my patients needed urine and stool samples collected, and I had to do that myself. I started to get a little frustrated with the PCT, but I made up my mind that I was not going to create problems between myself, and the night shift staff.

At 10 PM I needed to give my diabetic patients their bed-time snacks and there was nothing to give them. I had already given them insulin, and it was important they had a snack, so their blood sugar levels would not drop too low before morning. I checked both floors, but only found jello, pudding, milk, and one pack of gram crackers. There were a few packs of saltine crackers, but they were old and crumbled. I complained to the nursing supervisor about it. I had two diabetic patients in one room, so I gave them each a gram cracker out of the pack which contained two crackers. Then I gave all the diabetic patients jello and milk.

After midnight the patients were quiet, and all the staff were at the nursing station. I was charting on one of the computers and listened to the conversation, which was louder than it should have been. The staff were talking about prejudice between black and white people, between black Africans and black Americans, and between blacks of darker and lighter shades of skin.

Everyone was in a good mood, and there was a lot of laughing. The women teased the young Nigerian nurse because he was not married. He said he was not ready to commit yet, but when he did, he would want a woman from his country. He talked about how many wives his father had, and the African PCTs agreed that it was okay for a man to have as many wives as he could afford to support. They talked about some of the wealthy men in their countries who have many wives. They said some men continue to marry young girls and have children, even into their 80s. One PCT said she knew of a man who had so many children, he could not remember all their names. The PCT working with me made coffee for everyone and offered me some. It tasted like cappuccino and was good.

One of my patients was the lady who is allergic to everything. When she was admitted she weighed only about eighty pounds. She has gained a little weight. She has TPN running continuously and is eating fruits and vegetables. She sleeps all day and stays up all night. She wanted someone to help her take a shower at 3 AM.

She is upset because she is going to be discharged soon, and she is afraid to go home. She is forty-eight years old, but she does not drive and will not shop for food or prepare her own meals. Her mother lives a two-hour drive away from her. She prepares fresh fruits and vegetables in jars and takes them to her.

Another of my patients was a large white woman in her fifties. She cannot move her legs, so she stays in bed all the time. She has a Foley catheter to drain urine, but she is incontinent of stool. She has a wound vac attached to several deep wounds on her buttocks.

She has a suppository ordered to be given every night and she asked for it. When I turned her to give it, I saw she already had a small BM. I said I would give the suppository later. I asked the PCT to help me clean her, but the PCT said she would do it after she ate lunch, because it would ruin her appetite. I just said: "Okay" but it was hard not to say more.

I finally got the PCT to help me clean her at about 3 AM, and then her wound vac dressing was loose and covered with stool. I had to take the dressing off and pack the wounds with wet-to-dry dressings. I could have put fresh wound vac dressings on, but they are locked in the wound care nurse's cart, and she is not here at night.

I finished all my charting, and the morning blood draws by 6 AM. I just had to give a few morning medications and I was ready to go home at shift change. I know it will not be this easy every night, especially if I have an admission, but I am optimistic that I will do okay.

November 19, 2008

It is 4 AM on Wednesday morning and I am on the third floor. I am the only RN with three LVNs and three PCAs. I have seven patients and they are all asleep. I have finished my charting, except for the 6 AM meds. I am working 7 PM to 7 AM on Monday, Tuesday and Wednesday nights. Monday night was busy, and I left about thirty minutes late, but I think that was good, considering I had six patients plus an admission.

I think the night shift will work out okay for me. I do not really get sleepy, and I drink coffee when I start to get tired. The hospital keeps a large coffee machine in the cafeteria full of coffee all night.

The lady who is allergic to everything went home tonight. Her mother came to pick her up. We were all glad to see her go.

Tonight, I helped the young black male LVN to re-attach the wound-vac dressings to the large woman with the deep wounds on her buttocks. She was not my patient, but I was sitting at the desk when her PCT called for help to clean her. The LVN was busy in another room and the other two PCTs were sitting at the desk. No one would get up to answer the call for help, so I got up and said we should all go. The patient is large, and it takes four women to pull her up.

While we were turning her to clean her bottom, there was a loud noise that made us all jump. I thought the air mattress popped or something. But it was just the patient, passing gas and stool.

By the time we finished cleaning her the LVN came in. The wound vac dressings were loose, and I told him they would have to be fixed or removed and replaced with wet-to-dry dressings. I said I would help him, and I found some of the wound-vac dressing that had been left in the room by the wound care nurse. He held the patient on her side, and I was able to replace the clear dressings that cover the wound-vac foam. He asked if I would give the nightly suppository and I did. If it works like it should, she will need to be cleaned again.

November 20, 2008

I got off fifteen minutes early yesterday morning. Tonight, I had seven patients plus I did the admission assessment and got the admission orders for a new admit that came to the unit just before the start of shift. I have completed most of my charting and my lab draws. I am the only RN on the third floor again. I am sitting in the doctors' room behind the nursing station. There are no doctors here at this time of night, except the house doctor. The house doctor is usually a young intern who sleeps in a room at the end of the hall. We can wake him if we need orders or a doctor for a code blue.

January 13, 2010

It has been over a year since I have written anything. My mother visited like she does every year, from November to January. My brother drove her to south Texas, and they left last Monday. I miss her already.

Susie is working as a hair stylist. She drives about 45 minutes each way to work and back. She does not make much money, but she thinks the experience is good because she is working at a well-known salon.

Work is okay some nights and bad others. I never know what kind of shift it will be until I get there. Sometimes I work on the second floor and sometimes on the third floor.

Last week two nurses called-in sick just before the start of a shift. One nurse said she had a headache and the other said she could not get away from her day job. The nursing supervisor could not find anyone to replace them. Everyone was in a bad mood because of the extra workload. I was on my feet about ten hours out of the shift and my legs started to feel weak. I had taken some ibuprofen earlier, so they did not hurt. They felt the way a person's arms do when you have lifted weights as many times as you possibly can, and then you just cannot lift anymore. I have been careful on how I turn and pull up patients, but I still get pains in my hips and lower back.

I know I cannot continue here for much longer unless the

nurse-to- patient ratio changes. We have a lot of total care patients. They are supposed to be turned every two hours and cleaned as needed. It is not getting done. I see a lot of skin problems due to patients being wet and not turned for long periods of time.

March 4, 2010

This week I worked my regular Monday, Tuesday and Wednesday night shifts and was on the second floor. One of my patients all week was the German lady who reminds me of my grandmother. She has been back at the hospital for the last few weeks. Her feeding tube is gone, and she can be fed soft foods. She is alert at times and can answer simple questions. She has a dry sense of humor and is sometimes sarcastic. She makes me and some of the other American nurses laugh, but the foreign nurses do not understand that she is joking. They think she is confused.

She has been having a heart rhythm called A-fib, and I was worried about her on Monday and Tuesday night. Her heart rate was fast, and her blood pressure was either too high or too low. She had a lot of edema, so the doctor ordered Lasix. It helped and she had less edema on Wednesday night. I think her heart is getting weaker and cannot circulate her blood like it should.

She was started on a new heart medication and her heart rate was much better on Wednesday night. At the start of shift, she was sitting up and trying to read something when I went in to check her vital signs. After a few minutes she said: "You know, I can't read anymore. I think I need new glasses." I was happy she was doing so well.

I asked the PCT to help me turn and clean her twice during the shift. She has a Foley catheter, so she does not get wet too often, but she is having watery yellow stools. She has an ulcer on her coccyx, with a dressing that the wound care nurse changes. I cannot get any of the dressings that are used on it. So, when the dressing gets dirty, I must change it using a cloth dressing with tape.

It is getting harder to get supplies for the patients, especially at night. We cannot get the moisture barrier ointment that used-to be kept in stock. Now we can only get ointment if a doctor writes an order for it, and it must come from the pharmacy. The day shift usually uses all the ointment and leaves an empty tube, and the pharmacy is closed at night.

On Monday night one of my patients was a large white man, only fifty-seven years old. He did not even have gray hair yet. But he had edema all over, and yellow fluid was leaking out of his arms and legs. His arms were red, purple and black with multiple skin tears. There was so much fluid leaking out of his arms that we could not use dressings. We just put disposable pads under each arm and changed them when we turned him.

His wife was with him and asked a lot of questions about his condition and treatment. His lungs sounded wet at the start of shift and the respiratory therapist started him on oxygen. He is a dialysis patient, and he does not produce urine. He had dialysis in the afternoon and over two liters of fluid was removed. He was not getting IV fluid and was only taking small sips of water, but his lungs still seemed to be getting wet.

His wife left at about 10 PM and he was okay, just a little uncomfortable. He asked for a pain pill and a sleeping pill, and I gave them. He kept calling every few minutes and I went in several times. The PCT helped me reposition him, but he could not get comfortable. Then he said he could not breathe.

I called the respiratory therapist, and she checked his O2 saturation. It was only 86%. She put him on an oxygen mask and told me his lungs sounded very wet. I called his doctor twice but did not get a call back. I talked to the supervisor about it, and she said to try another doctor. I did, but he did not call back either. We usually have an in-house doctor sleeping in a room on the third floor, but he was not there. I was worried because the patient was not a DNR. The supervisor was not happy either. There was no doctor to assist and give orders if we had to call a code.

Luckily, the patient's oxygen level came up after the oxygen mask was put on and he made it through the night. The next morning, I was able to call a doctor and get orders. I did not get the call back until 8 AM and I was late getting off work. The patient was sent across the street to the ER later that day.

Tuesday night started out okay, and I thought it was going to be a good shift. I was worried about the German lady with the A-Fib heart rhythm, but everyone else seemed alright. Then at about 9 PM, I was passing medications and went into a room that had two male patients. Both had leg amputations of the right leg but were doing well.

The first one was a Hispanic man forty-seven years old. He could eat, but he had a tube feeding that ran at night. He was a dialysis patient and did not urinate. He had a rectal tube that drained liquid stool to a bag that hangs on the side of the bed. He did not speak much English, but he knew enough to ask me for a pain pill, which I gave him. I crushed his medications and mixed them with water, then put it in his feeding tube.

I started to crush medications for the other patient, who also had a feeding tube, when I heard the Hispanic man yell. He said "It burst! Something burst!" I went over to him and looked at his arm, where he was pointing. There was blood all over. I pulled back the fabric sleeve he had on his arm over his dialysis shunt, and blood squirted out. I ran and got a roll of dressing. I quickly wrapped it around the arm, but it did not help. Blood was still squirting out. I had gloves on, and I put one hand over the place where the blood was coming out to put pressure on it. With the other hand I grabbed his call light. I pushed it and when someone answered, I said: "Is Karen (the supervisor) there!" She said: "I think she's on the third floor." I said: "I need Karen now!" Then I looked down and saw that the blood was not slowing down at all. I yelled into the call light: "Code blue! Code blue!" She asked me which bed it was and called it over the intercom. I waited and kept pressure on the arm. The blood was dripping down the side of the bed and on the floor.

Luckily, we had an in-house doctor that night. It was a young oriental man, an intern, and it was his first night at the hospital. But that did not matter; he could give orders. He and Karen were in the room quickly, as well as several nurses and PCTs. Karen took charge of the situation and asked me what happened. I did not know, and it took a few seconds for me to tell her it was his dialysis shunt that the blood was coming out of. I had forgotten that he even had a dialysis shunt. It was like my mind went blank, and all I could think of was stopping the blood.

She yelled for someone to grab towels and hold pressure. Someone brought towels in and put them over the arm. I was going to continue holding pressure on the arm, but she yelled: "Someone else hold pressure!" Everyone looked around, wondering if they should do it. She yelled: "Anyone! Not a nurse! Just not Alice!"

One of the other nurses stepped up and held pressure. Karen said: "Alice, go get cleaned up!" I did not understand why she was telling me to leave. Thinking about it later, I realized she must have thought I was incompetent because I didn't tell her immediately that the blood was coming from the dialysis shunt.

I started to walk away, but I could not. He was my patient and I had to stay. The doctor told Karen to call an ambulance and send the patient to the ER. While Karen was gone, I put a fresh bag on the rectal tube and disconnected the tube feeding. I flushed the tube-feeding line so it would not get clogged-up. The ambulance was there within about five minutes, and they were gone about ten minutes later. The whole thing only took about twenty minutes from the time I called for a code blue.

Karen told me to call the ER and tell them about the patient. I did that, and then she said to call the family. I was glad she asked me to do it, because I needed to feel like I was doing everything his nurse should be doing.

It all happened so fast after I saw the blood, and I knew he would bleed to death if it was not stopped quickly. My shoes were covered with blood, and it had soaked through my socks. Karen said she had a pair of shoes she could lend me. I was surprised they fit because I have big feet.

I had put an extra pair of socks in my work bag because it was raining when I went to work that day. I cleaned my feet with alcohol pads and put the fresh socks and shoes on.

About two hours later, we got an admission, and the same ambulance crew delivered the patient. They said my patient had made it to the ER. His blood pressure was half of what is normal, but he was alive. They said the patient's arm had split open where the dialysis shunt was, and it was very infected and necrotic. Somehow that made me feel better. I was worried that people might think it was my fault. I kept going over it in my mind, wondering if I did something wrong. Karen said there was nothing I could have done to prevent it from happening. But from now on, I am going to check dialysis shunts better.

Karen and one of the PCTs were talking about the patient, and how his sisters and mother would visit him. When they left, his mother would always say: "You take good care of my boy!" Karen said: "We did take good care of him. He was still alive, and he made it to the ER."

March 9, 2010

Last night I had three step-down patients and two med/surg patients. One of my med/surg patients had just been made hospice. All medications except those for comfort had been discontinued and she was made a DNR. The IV fluid and tube feedings were also stopped. The patient has been in our hospital for about three months, and I have had her before. She was doing well for a while, then she just started going down-hill. At least one of her family members is always in the room.

One of her daughters came in about 9 PM and was angry because I did not bring pain medication to the room immediately when she called for it. I was passing the night-time medications to other patients, but I only made her wait about fifteen minutes. She yelled: "If you cause me to see my mother die, I am going to report you!" I said: "The morphine is not going to keep her alive." I felt bad after I said it, so I went into the room about every hour and gave her morphine frequently.

I heard from Karen that the Hispanic patient who had the ruptured dialysis shunt was doing well, and back here on the third floor. She said the shunt had been repaired and it was being used for dialysis again.

March 10, 2010

It is Wednesday morning, and I am home from work. I'm having a beer and a hot-dog while watching "Cash Cab." Last night was not too bad, but it was too busy to keep up. I did not get all my charting done. I just charted all my medications, my intakes and outputs, and some of my re-assessments. I wonder if anyone will notice. I have been late getting off work almost every morning, and I am afraid I might get fired for staying late so often.

I had two PCTs working with me. One of them had four of my patients and the other had two of them. These PCTs will not work together. Instead, they each want a nurse to work with them to do all turning and cleaning. If they worked together, they would each have twice as many patients to care for as if they split up and had nurses doing half of the care.

One of my patients was a large eighty-five-year-old white woman from a nursing home. She is still alert and oriented. She has a wound vac to her right hip. Last night was the first time that I had her. She called to be cleaned at about 10 PM and we cleaned her. She had black, tarry stool, which is a sign of a GI bleed. She said she needed a pain pill, but she only had it scheduled twice a day, and I had already given her one. She asked when she could have another one and I told her it would not be until 9 AM. She said: "Oh great! So, I have to just suffer!?"

A few minutes later she called and said she needed one of her heart pills. She said they were in her make-up bag in her bed-side dresser. I found them and they were nitro pills, the kind a person would take if they were having a heart-attack. I checked her orders again and she did not have nitro pills ordered. I told her she could not just take her own pills in the hospital. I said: "The doctor has to order all the medications you take while you are in the hospital and the nurse has to give them to you."

I took the pills out of her bag and told her they would be locked in her medication box. She started screaming at me and cried that she has had several heart attacks, and if I did not give her one of her pills, it would be my fault if she had another one. I asked where her pain was, and she pointed to her chest. I said I would call the doctor.

I called the in-house doctor and told him I did not think she was having a heart-attack, but she was going to keep yelling about it until she got a pain pill. He said she could have an extra one of her scheduled pain pills. I gave it to her, and she slept for about an hour, then she was awake and calling again. I talked to Karen about it, and she said to order an EKG. That is standard with patients who are having chest pain, but we did not think she was having heart pain. She probably had an ulcer in her esophageal area, and that is what caused the GI bleed. But just to be safe we had the EKG done. It showed her heart was fine.

The extra time I spent with dealing with her "heart attack" put me behind and I did not finish passing the bed-time medications until midnight. I had six total care patients and one of them was a step-down (recently out of ICU) patient.

The PCT who had most of my patients was the black woman from some African country who likes to make coffee for her friends at night. She spends half of her shift talking to other people from Africa, and she often goes to one of the other units so she can sit and talk, away from her assignment. She is in her 30s, single, and always wears clothes that are at least a size too small. She has a huge butt, which she seems very proud of. She sways it from side to side as she walks slowly down the hall. It is very frustrating to work with her because she will not do what I ask her to. Sometimes it seems as if the PCTs think of the hospital as more of a place to socialize than a place to work.

May 28, 2010

It is Friday night, and I am home. Our friend, Bill, died this morning. He was in the hospital for a few weeks. He was diagnosed with cancer again about three months ago. He was started on chemotherapy, but after a few treatments he started having stomach problems. He could not keep any food down and the chemo was discontinued. He quickly lost weight, became very weak and then was admitted to a hospital. Teresa stayed with him most of the time. He had pain and was started on morphine. He passed away quietly and had donated his body to science. Teresa is planning a memorial service.

This summer I need to study for my ACLS renewal, which is due in July. I also need to think about what I want to do with the rest of my nursing career. I am getting too old to keep working as a hospital nurse. I would really like to be a clinical instructor and take students to hospitals for their first nursing experiences. Or I might try to become a case manager. I have talked to a few nurses who went into that area, and said they liked it. Whatever I do, I will be thankful to God for giving me the opportunity to become a nurse. I complain a lot about the job, but I really like helping people, and every time I go to work, I have the chance to do that.

ABOUT THE AUTHOR

Alice Marlett has a Bachelor of Science in Nursing degree and is a Registered Nurse.

Printed in the United States
by Baker & Taylor Publisher Services